EVERYTHING HARDER THAN EVERYONE ELSE

Why Some of Us PUSH OURSELVES to EXTREMES

JENNY VALENTISH

APOLLO
PUBLISHERS

CONTENTS

How can I be substantial if I do not cast a shadow?
CARL JUNG

INTRODUCTION

T HIS IS A book about people willing to do the sorts of things that most others couldn't, shouldn't or wouldn't. From the get-go, I was so wired by writing it that I could barely sleep. It's the antithesis to my last book, an addiction memoir that dove so far into its own navel that I thought I must surely have emerged from the process newborn and pure. Or maybe, as it turns out, just raring to go again. This time, despite not being the subject, I will be choked unconscious, strapped to a table and thrashed, staple-gun someone's face, experiment with performance-enhancing drugs and wind up in a livestreamed fight. It's a bit like method acting, I suppose.

In a way, though, it was that last book, *Woman of Substances*, that triggered the idea for *Everything Harder Than Everyone Else*. While there are all sorts of reasons why people consume substances, I noted that there are those who treat drug-taking like an Olympic sport, exploring their capacity to really push their bodies and, frankly, wanting to be the best at it. Those people, when they quit, might turn to a similarly annihilating pursuit— such as marathon running, getting the same gory kick out of predawn starts and food rations as they did with their predawn crashes and lines of coke, not to mention the glory of going all in. It made me wonder, what other reasons are there for somebody to repeatedly push themselves to the edge of annihilation?

Extreme athletes, death-defiers and those who perform incredible stunts of endurance have been celebrated throughout history. Ancient Greek poets such as Pindar and Statius hailed the demigods of pankration—an early form of mixed martial arts, but with the referees wielding big sticks—and the violent scenes were recorded in pigment on pottery. The heroic bastards of medieval jousting tournaments verily made their way onto tapestries and canvases. Between the sixteenth and nineteenth centuries, "broadside" ballads in Britain, Ireland and North America were printed on cheap paper alongside crude woodcuts, immortalizing pugilists, hardnuts and hellraisers. In the 1927 anthology *Frontier Ballads*, edited by Charles J. Finger, the songs are described as "glorification of wickedness, and the product of men of emotional instability who advocated breaches of the moral law."

But pushing way beyond the comfort zone is also a sign of our modern times. In a world where the perfect temperature can be achieved at the push of a button, dinner can be delivered on cue and communication occurs ever more through screens and devices, the primal chemical surges designed to deliver us through situations of risk, such as hunting, fleeing predators and confronting rivals, still yearn to be released. So we engineer situations that will trigger them.

There are the destination adventures: running with the bulls in Pamplona; taking hallucinogenics to indulge in postapocalyptic, *Mad Max*-style fantasies at Burning Man; survival vacations, where guides upskill suburbanites in not dying in mountainous or desert terrains; treks up Mount Everest, which can have two-and-a-half-hour queues near the summit. Some of the most grueling adventure and ultramarathon races are now so oversubscribed that organizers have implemented lottery systems.

In every major city, fight gyms run pricey "pretender to contender" training programs, designed to give desk jockeys a taste of glory in the boxing ring. And thanks to the exaltations of Russell Brand, Liam Hemsworth and Oprah, Dutch athlete Wim Hof's three-pillared method of cold therapy (such as immersion in an ice bath), breathing and meditation has become accessible to anyone with the app. Hof recommends: "Die once a day, because it makes you so alive!"

Armchair athletes prefer to dabble in endurance tourism from the comfort of their lounge rooms, but are no less enthralled. Basically, most of us think we ought to get out of our comfort zone, but we'll just let someone else test the water first, while we think about it. Everyone's reading the wisdom of former Navy SEALs on leadership and discipline, turning to Joe Rogan's podcast for the lowdown on turbo supplements and talking about "grit." At conferences, professional adventurers are booked to give motivational talks about resilience and risk-taking to sales executives and real estate agents. Among the highest-rated television shows is the United Kingdom's brutal *SAS: Who Dares Wins* (which *The Guardian* dubbed "a sadistic PE lesson") and the Australian spinoff, *SAS Australia*, in which contestants are challenged to complete an SAS selection course, while being cursed at by former Special Forces soldiers, dragged through mud, launched backward out of helicopters into freezing lakes and shot at with blanks. *Alone*, an American concept, follows ten hardcore survivalists abandoned separately in the Patagonian wilderness, or in northern Mongolia, or in the Northwest Territories of Canada, depending on which season you watch, and they regularly lose around 30 percent of their body mass. Back in the United Kingdom, the five-part adventure series *Don't Rock the Boat* pitched celebs into freezing waters to row the length of Britain, resulting in mass vomiting and fainting.

Whether vicariously or directly, we give ourselves permission to feel these ugly, primal emotions—and the chemical rewards are bountiful. Endurance athletes experience what's colloquially called "runner's high"—a blissful cocktail of endocannabinoids, endorphins and serotonin, the flood of which can feel transcendent, even spiritual. There's a similar rush going on during high-octane thrill-seeking. When BASE jumpers are about to leap into the unknown, the amygdala senses the risk and triggers the release of a blend of chemicals: dopamine, which provides focus; adrenaline, which increases heart rate, boosting oxygen and glucose for energy; and endorphins, to protect against pain. The brain releases testosterone, for a boost of strength and confidence. In bondage, discipline, sadism and masochism (BDSM) play, the endogenous opioid system responds to the pain, releasing opioid peptides. It seems some of us are more wired than others to activate those ancient biological systems, be it through being caned in a dungeon during a lunchbreak or climbing a sheer rock wall over the weekend.

IT SHOULDN'T COME as a surprise that research into extreme behavior started in earnest in the decade of experimentation. The 1960s introduced the work of University of Massachusetts psychology professor Seymour Epstein, who studied parachutists' physiological arousal when approaching a jump and observed the immense sense of well-being derived from surviving fear. Daniel Ellis Berlyne, associate professor at Boston University, investigated levels of hedonic arousal through stimuli such as novelty, complexity, surprise and incongruity.

Marvin Zuckerman, a professor of psychology at the University of Delaware, deduced that volunteers lining up to participate in experiments on hypnosis and new drugs were—judging by their other lifestyle choices—likely to be sensation-seekers hoping to groove on a trippy experience. In 1964, Zuckerman and others developed the sensation-seeking scale, a personality test that revealed there were multiple dimensions to sensation-seeking behavior. Among its adherents were psychologist Frank Farley, who formulated the concept of the Type T (thrill-seeking) personality, theorizing that such individuals require an increased level of stimulation to maintain their energy levels. This built on Zuckerman's belief that high-sensation seekers need a lot of stimulation to reach what he calls their optimal level of arousal (and similarly, there's a theory among drug researchers that those drawn to drug-taking naturally produce low amounts of dopamine).

Farley is particularly interested in the positive aspects of thrill-seekers—among them extreme athletes, entrepreneurs and explorers—and what we can learn from them. He loves getting his own hair blown back by watching them up close and personal.

The wealth of research into endurance focuses on genetic advantage and physiological prowess. But I'm more interested in rummaging around in personal histories, to examine the psychological drive and see—a bit like Farley—what patterns and divergences it can illuminate. For some of my interviewees, a physical focus quietens an overactive mind. Others pressure-test, exposing their bodies to a small dose of stress or pain to protect against a potential larger threat in the future, in the same way that we might use a vaccine. They tend to be those who have already had reason to be fearful. And for some, physical pain might distract from emotional pain in the same way that digging the fingernails into the webbing of the thumbs seems to help when getting tattooed. Sigmund Freud labeled as "repetition compulsion" the unconscious tendency to repeat the most destructive or distressing events of our past; it's sometimes also called "traumatic reenactment." On occasions, maybe the motive isn't at all obvious to the individual, which might explain the tendency of some major athletes to equate their suffering and sacrifice to that of Jesus himself.

Woven through the tales of these outliers are themes familiar to all of us, but amplified through their heightened drives: sensation seeking and euphoria chasing; instant gratification and impulsivity; compartmentalizing and the development of double lives; humble mastery versus the need for validation; fighting as catharsis; death wishes and self-sabotage; obsession and addiction; retirement and reinvention; and that fine line between pleasure and pain.

It must, of course, be noted that it's not always the case that people who take part in a pursuit that pushes their body to extremes have a common disposition or personal history. It's more accurate to say that what the pursuit has to offer can be a particular draw for some kinds of people. Take bodybuilding, which requires unforgiving scheduling—every hour of the day is structured and regimented. It's a natural fit for those like my interviewees Karen Adigos and Kortney Olson, who grew up in chaotic households with inconsistent parenting, and who yearned for order and control in their adult lives.

Elsewhere in these pages, strongman athlete Camilla Fogagnolo uses her childhood adversity as grist for the mill and wonders if top athletes use training as a form of self-harm. Performance artist Stelarc seeks erasure of the self by turning his body into an artistic medium. Wrestler KrackerJak employs bloodletting in the ring as an outlet for his natural-born agitation, and observes the effect on his well-being when injury prevents him from indulging in this curated ultraviolence. Christine Ferea, a bare-knuckle boxer whose gnarliest opponent is herself, reveals the nexus between ego and anger, and causes me to ponder whether the death drive that Freud hypothesized in his Viennese salon is a much more tangible concept for fighters.

In the world of BDSM, Sir James, a sex worker specializing in domination, helps those who believe that being degraded sexually gives them the power to withstand anything in their daily life. Engaging in play as the dominant can give him a "top high" that verges pleasurably on mania, and for which he joneses if he doesn't experience it for more than a few weeks. Designer Anna tells me that her perception of body and mind was that they were two very separate entities, until she discovered the transcendence of flesh-hook suspension. Now she feels completely connected.

Ultrarunner Charlie Engle draws parallels between his epic adventure races and his former life smoking crack, wondering if the same need for validation powers both. Former ballet dancer Chloe Bayliss digs deep into the way her sense of self was tied to her profession, to the point that quitting was a terrifying prospect. Then there's the neuroscientist continuously violating his senses to override his disgust response. Through him and others, I discover that disgust endurance—be it through television gameshows where contestants eat what most of us consider to be repulsive, videos of horrific injuries and porn sites that specifically curate stomach-churning content—is its own genre, and that disgust has a valuable evolutionary purpose. And, in the chapter that may destroy my hitherto exemplary Goodreads rating, porn-star-turned-MMA fighter Orion Starr explains how, for her, sex and violence are two sides of the same coin, because both allow her to test her limits and stick it to the doubters in her childhood who thought she was a pipsqueak.

In delving into my interviewees' stress-testing adventures, there's a lot that can be learned about the human condition. What you choose to do with their hard-fought wisdom is between you and your conscience.

Chapter One

DON'T KNOW WHEN TO STOP
Endurance Athletes

CHARLIE ENGLE WAS eleven years old when he swung himself into a boxcar on a moving freight train, having tired of stacking pennies on the rails. He landed hard on his stomach, then rolled onto his back, his senses assaulted by the smell of urine.

After five or so minutes of trundling through the suburbs, the adrenaline rush wore off. Empty boxcars, as it turned out, were boring. Still, there would be another rush when it came time to dare to leap onto the blurry ground beyond the wheels, and then make the two-hour run home through unfamiliar terrain.

So began a life of running that no destination could ever satisfy.

Charlie, an ultrarunner two years shy of his sixtieth birthday, says something early in our conversation about validation that I wind up repeating to everyone I interview after him, to see if they nod in recognition. They generally do. We're talking about his crack-addiction years, before he pledged his life to endurance races—the six-day benders in which he'd wind up in strange motel rooms with well-appointed women from bad neighborhoods, and smoke until he came to with his wallet missing.

"Part of ultrarunning is a desire to be different," he says.

"And for the drug addict, too, there is a deep need to separate ourselves from the crowd. It sounds crazy to say this, but street people would tell me, 'You could smoke more crack than anybody I've ever seen,' and there was a weird, 'Yeah, that's *right!*' There's still a part of me that wants to be validated through doing things that other people can't."

When we speak, Charlie—a deeply affable chap—is bustling around his kitchen in Raleigh, North Carolina, reheating his coffee. It's a fair guess to say he's the sort of guy who'd have to reheat his coffee a lot. He's in planning mode for what will be an epic mission even by his standards: the 5.8 Global Adventure Series. The idea is to be the first athlete to run from the lowest land point to the highest summit on every continent, and it's so named because the lowest place on Earth, the shore of the Dead Sea, is 5.8 vertical miles from the highest peak, Mount Everest. His first stop is Africa, to trek from the depths of Lake Assal in Djibouti to the peak of Mount Kilimanjaro in Tanzania.

Charlie has already completed some of the world's most inhospitable adventure races. He's been chased by crocodiles, hung off a cliff tangled in climbing ropes and had a tarantula squat in his sleeping bag—although none of that comes close to the actual running component in terms of endurance. Matt Damon was the executive producer and narrator of a documentary about Charlie, *Running the Sahara*, and he's been profiled in countless media stories. If his biggest fear is being "average, at best," then he's moving mountains to avoid it.

It helps that he's goal-oriented in the extreme. In fact, you might call him a high achiever. Even in his drug-bingeing years, which culminated in his car being shot at by dealers, Charlie was the top salesman at the fitness club where he worked. At fifty-six, he ran twenty-seven hours straight to celebrate his twenty-seven years of sobriety.

About a decade earlier, when he did time for mortgage fraud for filing an inaccurate stated-income loan under the alleged guidance of his broker (which, as a columnist in *The New York Times* sympathized, was something millions of Americans were doing), he immersed himself in Jack London's *The Star Rover* (1915), a story of an imprisoned professor who is further punished by being made to wear a constraining jacket, and so escapes mentally by going into a trance state and walking among the stars.

Charlie's version of this was to recreate the infamous Badwater Ultramarathon, held annually in California, inside the jail. Badwater is described as the world's toughest footrace, as contestants run in the summer heat from Badwater Basin, the lowest point in North America, to the trailhead to Mount Whitney, the highest point in the continental United States. Competitors' shoes have melted while running it, and only 932 people have ever finished. To mimic this, Charlie ran 135 miles on the jailhouse exercise track, mentally picturing the landmarks of the course, such as the way station Stovepipe Wells and Mount Whitney. "You don't belong in prison," said an inmate called Butterbean, who'd watched him go around and around and around, 540 times. "You belong in a fucking insane asylum."

Perhaps belonging—or, more accurately, not belonging—is a key to Charlie's story. When he was a kid, his parents divorced. So far, so ordinary. But his parents were very different cats, whose conflicting ideas of child-rearing brought out particular traits in their son. Living with his free-spirited mother, who threw wild parties and was immersed in the local theater scene, meant having to be self-sufficient and to expect the unexpected. Moving on to live with his exacting and athletic father, in whose eyes he could never do anything right (and in any case, praise was for sissies), Charlie adopted that critical voice as his own.

When he began using drugs—before he'd even hit his teens—he temporarily found something to distract himself from his antsiness, which he likens to squirrels in the brain. It doesn't take much prompting for Charlie to draw parallels between drug use and running—in fact, the tagline of his website is "I'm an addict who runs and I'm a runner who writes." He says he's noticed a certain restlessness common to endurance athletes that comes from a fear of missing out, which might work in a similar way to chasing a high. If there's a race he doesn't take part in, he tortures himself that it was surely the best ever. He took control of this fear by starting to plan his own expeditions, which couldn't be topped.

"And hey, I freely admit there's ego involved," he says. "There's now a weird normalization of running marathons—there's always somebody's grandmother who's done it—so I remember when I started running ultras that I definitely dug telling people, 'Oh yeah, I'm getting ready to run a seven-day race across the Atacama Desert.' That can't be anything but ego. It doesn't necessarily mean bad ego; it just says, 'I don't want to be normal.'"

Even before he quit drugs and alcohol, Charlie Engle ran. He ran to prove to himself he could. He ran to shake off the day. He ran as a punishment of sorts. In fact, he says, he craved depletion. "Running was a convenient and reliable way to purge. I felt badly about my behavior, even if very often my behavior didn't technically hurt anybody else. It wasn't like I was coming into the house and doing crazy stuff. I was a disappearer, so I would just go away for a while and then come back."

Which he still does, for months at a time, but for expeditions rather than benders. "Yeah, well, that's true."

Charlie's first wife, Pam—with whom he had two children—only saw a fraction of his blowouts, but his sudden, days-long disappearances indicated the depth of his dependence. Once he got sober and started going to Alcoholics Anonymous meetings, his races interstate and overseas became more frequent, so that he was absent for even longer spells. His second wife, Astacianna, who is a wildlife biologist and an athlete, is often a crew member on his races.

A common hypothesis is that former drug users who hurl themselves into sports are simply trading one addiction for another. Maybe so—both behaviors are goal-oriented and activate the same reward pathways, and when a person gives up one dopaminergic behavior, such as taking drugs, they are likely to seek the same sense of stimulation elsewhere. In the clinical field, it's known as "cross-addiction." But plenty of people achieve both in tandem, grimly determined to prove they have their drug use under control by forcing their bodies through their paces. In fact, Charlie did his first marathon wasted.

Whether they have a history with the sport or not, marathon running—and particularly ultramarathon running, which means a distance of at least 26.2 miles—seems to be a prevalent pursuit for that incredibly driven breed of drug user. High-wire memoirs about this lifestyle swap include Charlie's *Running Man* (2016), Rich Roll's *Finding Ultra* (2012), Catra Corbett's *Reborn on the Run* (2018) and Caleb Daniloff's *Running Ransom Road*

(2012). Perhaps it's the singularity of the experience: the solitary pursuit of a goal, the intoxicating feeling of being an outlier, the meditative quality of the rhythmic movement, the adrenaline rush of triumph; and on the flip side, the self-flagellation that might last as long as a three-day bender. Running such long distances can result in macerated feet, blisters, muscle cramps, gastrointestinal upset, respiratory distress, stress fractures, hyponatremia and hypothermia, and even rhabdomyolysis—a breakdown of muscle tissue that can lead to renal failure, also associated with CrossFit training. The risks are not entirely dissimilar to those of the prolific drug user: the long-term effects can shorten the lifespan, and there have also been plenty of fatalities mid-race. It makes me wonder, where does hedonism end and endurance begin?

This sling-shotting into a new identity can be intoxicating in itself. In their memoirs, both coincidentally titled *The Long Run*, Australian journalist Catriona Menzies-Pike and American writer Mishka Shubaly describe having once scoffed at morning joggers as they themselves staggered home curly after a bender.

"Becoming a runner was so antithetical to my idea of who I was," Catriona tells me. After a decade of grief over the death of her parents in a plane crash, she gave up gin in favor of becoming "speedy gristle," and would eventually run five marathons. But in the early stages of her transition, her enthusiasm reminds me of an adage my mother would use, "somebody's eyes are bigger than their stomach." The persona was forming faster than the athletic ability, illustrated by all the sportswear newsletters she subscribed to in a heady rush. She was now officially a Runner—the marketing departments of Nike and ASICS recognized her as such.

"Trying that new person on made me feel really gleeful," she confesses. "As a way of social interaction, I found the novelty was delightful. Even now, if I run into people that I haven't seen for ten years and tell them I wrote a book about running marathons, I watch their surprise register and it gives me a real kick."

As a former anarcho-boozehound-come-musician, Mishka's lyrics include "I'm never gonna quit until the day that I die / I'll be snorting fat lines of vodka, eating a big cocaine pie." He admits that the question of whether abandoning substances for the healthy high is "selling out" is something he's devoted far too much time to in his head. "Here's the thing: selling out is real and it's shitty … but almost every single factor we use to evaluate whether we're selling out or not is an illusion," he tells me. "It's a hard life being a penniless drunk raging against the status quo; it's also a hard life being a parent in the suburbs, getting up early and trying to get a run in before the job you battle through in order to pay your mortgage to provide a home for your family."

A sometimes comedian as well as a musician, he had built his entire identity around being what he calls an alcoholic burnout. "And when I stopped drinking, I felt the person I had been was entirely erased. Or worse—only the bad shit remained, my rages and my depression and my weakness and my poor impulse control and my shitty reputation," he says. "The further along I get in my sobriety, the more I see that's not quite accurate. It's more like a cheap, dangerous, illegal apartment building was erected on top of a historical structure, and as I tore the crap away, I kept finding pillars that were still incredibly strong or just needed some shoring up, and occasionally artefacts of great value."

Mishka recognizes garden-variety runners—let's say people who log three miles four times a week—as being balanced individuals making good, healthy decisions, but ultrarunners … now, they're a different breed. "Whenever I was lining up at five in the morning with these other maniacs, I would look around and wonder, 'What secret shame is fueling this for you?'" he says. "Every once in a while, I would encounter someone who just came to ultrarunning for sheer love of running and that blows my mind, even creeps me out. It's like … we're all here because we're addicts or alcoholics or survivors of eating disorders or molestation or cancer, but if you're just out here for kicks … man, then you are *really* messed up."

THESE DAYS, CHARLIE goes to AA meetings very occasionally, but it's more for the fellowship aspect than as a white-knuckle need to stay sober. When he first quit drugs and alcohol, he felt like taking a knife and surgically removing the addict, so strong was his rejection of that part of his identity. It took three years to figure out that the "addict self" had plenty to offer: tenacity, ingenuity, problem-solving, stamina and that restless drive, forever in search of satisfaction. Perfect for the all-or-nothing world of extreme-long-distance running.

"I get a lot of questions from people who've read the book and they want running to be the answer," he says. "There is no one answer. For me, it took both. I needed the AA community and I needed the physical release of running and the burning off of extra fuel. I am that guy with a ball for every space on the roulette wheel. When I start running, all the balls are bouncing and spinning and making that chaotic clattering noise. Somewhere three or four miles into the run, they all find their slot. I always carry a recorder—either just my phone or something else—when I'm running because, for real, my best ideas float to the top."

For Charlie, part of the attraction of entering races, just as with taking drugs, is the pursuit of novelty and the chasing of firsts, even though he knows by now that the intensity of that initial high can never be replicated. That explains why he takes such pleasure in the planning of his expeditions. "The absolute best I ever felt in relation to drugs was actually the acquisition of the drug," he says. "There's nothing more powerful than having the drugs in my pocket; the idea of what it can be. Once the binge starts, it's all downhill from there. But the idea of what it can be is huge. In a way, running is the same because there's this weird idea that you're going to enter a hundred-miler and this time it's going to be different. This time it's not gonna hurt so much, and everything's going to be perfect."

It's like the old adage, often heard in AA, that the definition of insanity is doing the same thing over and over again and expecting a different outcome. Haruki Murakami, in his book *What I Talk About When I Talk About Running* (2007), explains his thought processes in the period after an epic race is run, with all the agony that entails. "I forget all the pain and misery and am already planning how I can run an even better time in the next race," he writes. "The funny thing is, no matter how much experience I have under my belt, no matter how old I get, it's all just a repeat of what came before."

My own aversion to running far outweighs any penance I might feel it necessary to pay, though I'll happily endure other forms of exercise. With weights, you exert yourself for a short period and can count down the reps till you get to stop. With combat sports, you smash through stray thoughts before they have time to take root. The problem with running is there's no escaping the monotony. You can't outrun the infernal looping of your mind. In fact, circular breathing becomes a backing track, a form of percussion for your horrible mantras, whether they are as blandly tedious as, *You could stop. You could stop. You could stop* or something more castigating. No wonder runners' bodies look like anxiety made flesh. No wonder their eyes have the jittery look of whippets.

Charlie hears the "I hate running" sentiment all the time. "I myself don't like it as much as you think I might," he says. "It's the results of running I like. It's the stopping—because that's when the endorphin release comes."

The endorphin release is more colloquially known as a "runner's high." Some researchers think there's also a boost in anandamide, an endocannabinoid that scientists Lumír Hanuš and William Devane, who discovered it in the human brain in 1992, named for the Sanskrit word *ananda*, meaning "bliss." And there's the serotonin, which might be what calms Charlie's squirrels somewhat.

Perhaps this heady cocktail evokes the kind of purifying experience more commonly described in episodes of religious transcendence. Actually, the world's longest footrace is called the Self-Transcendence 3100 Mile Race, founded by Indian spiritualist and long-distance runner Sri Chinmoy. He believed that athletic accomplishment could lead to deeper meditative consciousness and spiritual growth. Chinmoy wrote, in what the Sri Chimnoy Library claims was his 1565th book: "These long-distance races remind me of our Eternity's race. Along Eternity's Shore we are running, running, running. We are running and running with our birthless and deathless hopes. We are running and running with the ever-transcending Beyond."

Cruelly, the Self-Transcendence Race demands that participants run 5649 laps around a single New York City block. But Episcopal priest Christian Hawley wrote in *Trail Runner* magazine that connecting with nature through running is key—a revelation he had when he studied Buddhism in Nepal for a summer and witnessed Tibetan monks reading sacred texts in caves and scaling mountains to offer prayers. "We need to feel small," he wrote. "We need to recognize we are part of some-thing grander, and bridge the ever widening gap between a vague spirituality focused on the self, and Bible idolatry obsessed with a calcified point-of-view." He describes one of his own trail runs: "The creation story plays out in real time before me as the sun casts hues of burns and bruises, millions of years flashing by in the exposed faces of the mountains." As he admits, he was saturated with endorphins.

When writer Adharanand Finn traveled to Japan to meet the monks of Mount Hiei, some of whom run a thousand marathons in a thousand days as part of their quest for enlight-enment, a priest at the temple tells him that the idea behind the constant movement is to exhaust the mind and the body until nothing is left. "When you are nothing, then something, pop, comes up to fill the space," he says. This "something" is the vast consciousness that lies below the surface of our lives. A sense of oneness with the universe.

Catriona Menzies-Pike explores this link between endurance and rebirth in *The Long Run*, observing that stories of running are often tales of shape-shifting, of the desire to shed one skin and slip into another. "One running story may be a parable on persistence or denial; another a warning," she writes. "It took more than running, of course, for me to haul myself out of the quicksand of grief. But the practice helped me rewrite the script I'd been following and craft a new set of stories about enduring, flight and change."

Another commonality in endurance racing is hallucinating. This, combined with runners under stress being forced to drill down to the very essence of self, reminds me of the ego death that psychedelic pilgrims pursue, in order that the shell of our constructed identity might fall away. In the Discovery Channel's *Eco-Challenge* (1995), a series about a three hundred-mile adventure race in British Columbia, a member of the First Nation Lillooet tribe offered runners a piece of wisdom that translates as: "Push yourself until the pain comes, until you feel you cannot survive, and then go on. Here the ego will let go; here you will be purified."

Charlie Engle remembers watching and feeling as if those words were being spoken directly to him. "There's almost nothing else that you can say for sure, 'If you do this regularly, you're going to get these feelings out of it,'" he says. "It's reliable in that sense. If I don't reach that point where I'm questioning myself and I want to quit, I haven't actually achieved my goal, because the goal is to reach that edge of the cliff and find a way not to jump off."

IT'S PERHAPS UNEXPECTED that Charlie is indefatigably cheerful, given that endurance sports are all about suffering. Races have names such as Triple Brutal Extreme Triathlon and Hurt 100. One of the earliest US events, in 1928, was the Trans-American Footrace, nicknamed The Bunion Derby in the press.

In his book *The Rise of the Ultra Runners* (2019), Adharanand Finn writes about the hellscapes that appear irresistible to this breed of runner. "It seems that every ultrarace has to produce a slick, short film with dramatic, sweeping shots and lots of high drama. And always, at some point, it shows someone looking broken, close to tears," he writes. "The runners look more like survivors of some near-apocalyptic disaster than sportsmen and -women. It is telling that these are the images they choose to advertise the race. People want to experience this despair, they want to get this close to their own self-destruction."

The late ultrarunner Don Ritchie, known as the "Stubborn Scotsman," who ran races for forty-eight years, observed, "A certain type of mentality seems to be advantageous. I think you require to be a calm, determined, patient person with a high toleration for prolonged discomfort and a high capacity for delayed gratification."

That final point is particularly interesting. The most famous psychological experiment on delayed gratification, the Marshmallow Test, has entered common parlance. In this 1972 study, led by Stanford psychology professor Walter Mischel, children were offered a choice between one marshmallow to be eaten immediately, or two marshmallows if they could hold off for fifteen minutes while the researcher left the room. Mischel hypothesized that children who strategically distracted themselves from the temptation (and thus, from frustration) would be able to delay gratification for longer than those who just tried to think of something else. The kids who succeeded best in delaying gratification employed tactics such as constructing fantasies, making up songs, pounding a rhythm with their feet, praying and even attempting to sleep.

Can we still draw parallels between ultrarunning and heavy drug use if delayed gratification is a factor? It doesn't seem to fit what we assume about committed drug users—that they're impulsive, with little self-control. But consider that most drugs require a lengthy routine: earning the money to score, sourcing the drug, traveling somewhere to take it. It requires perseverance. And those in it for the long haul are certainly not ones to take the easy road.

Of course, not all ultrarunners have a history of addiction and torment. Charlie tells me there are many high achievers in business who find themselves drawn to the sport—and certainly it takes a fair bit of personal wealth to participate in a sport with expensive registration fees and the kind of preparation time that might require spells off work. (In 2018, runner Pam Smith calculated her costs for entering Badwater. The entry fee was $1,500; then there was crew travel, van rental and gas, accommodation, food, hydration, ice and other race supplies—it totaled $6,800.) Perhaps an ultramarathon might be such an individual's only conduit to feel peaks of ecstasy and agony, and is a penance for privilege. Otherwise it's all spreadsheets and expense accounts.

There *are* more budget options when it comes to experiencing endurance, such as The Sufferfest, a cycling and endurance athlete-training app that can be used with spin bikes, roller bikes and turbo trainers. It's been adopted by cyclists of all abilities in more than 110 countries, some of whom might be more interested in achieving personal bests than reducing themselves to ground zero. In fact, it's become cult-like.

Its founder, David McQuillen, is a former Swiss banker who gave it all up to develop the app and brand full-time. He moved to Hobart, the city of his wife's birth, which has the added bonus of rugged, hostile terrain. When we Skype, I can see the Tasman Sea through the large window in his stylishly monochrome living room.

Endurance cycling is ultrarunning's lycra-clad cousin, so hardcore that as far back as the 1880s and 1890s, racers were experimenting with cocaine, caffeine, nitroglycerin and strychnine for energy and pain relief. "Suffering" is part of cycling's nomenclature, as illustrated by the title of racer Jon Malnick's popular book, *Into the Suffersphere: Cycling and the Art of Pain* (2016).

As Sufferfest's Chief Suffering Officer, it's David who came up with much of the language, demonstrating a fine gallows humor. If you're new to the app, you're invited to "mistreat yourself to a paincation in Sufferlandria"—a kingdom that lies "on the shores of the great inland Lactic Acid Sea." There, you can journey the "rolling expanses of the Amber Waves of Pain; from the sparsely-populated Whine Country to the brutal beauty of the Valley of Nine Hammers." Sufferlandrians live by the motto "I will beat my ass today to kick yours tomorrow."

David grew up in Erie, Pennsylvania, on the shores of one of the Great Lakes. He wasn't a particularly active kid—until he and his brother discovered cycling races when he was seventeen. "We thought it was the coolest-looking thing we'd ever seen and decided to start doing it." Other than that, he swears he's normal. And so are the Sufferlandrians. Most of them.

"These people who dig so deep and push themselves so hard, it's not apparent just by looking at them," he says. "We've got mild-mannered house-husbands or -wives, who are taking care of kids during the day and might not have an ambitious career, but at night, they're beating the hell out of themselves because they want to beat their friends or finish at the top of a 5K or a short road race or triathlon in their neighborhood. That's their source of pride. You might not see that if you see them at the grocery store—you might not realize there's a beast within."

But that unassuming person in line at the till could be eyeing you back and thinking, *I'll have you know, I'm a knight.* Because in Sufferlandria you can indeed achieve knighthood, in a double life that lies somewhere between Fight Club and Dungeons & Dragons. It's a fictional framework for a real epic struggle.

I ask David if mental toughness—or "grit," as people who feverishly buy books and listen to podcasts on endurance prefer to call it—is innate, or whether it can be taught.

"Oh, absolutely, 100 percent it can be taught," he enthuses. "This is the one area of sports that are almost totally neglected, especially by everyday athletes, and yet will yield the greatest benefits with the least effort."

David recommends Alex Hutchinson's *Endure* (2018), on the power of self-talk. "Studies show positive self-talk is where performance is improved," he says. "Our areas with Sufferfest are around focus, positive thinking, goal-setting and reflection, but for me personally, positive self-talk has been the biggest improvement in my riding. Finding that mantra is deeply personal. For me, it's that I need to 'get the work in, get the work in, get the work in.'"

He tells me that on the sports-science side—and Sufferfest has its in-house experts—suffering is actually necessary, not just a personal persuasion. "If you want optimum physical improvement, you do have to suffer, because you have to go into zones that completely remove your body from its comfort zone. It completely destabilizes your body, and that only comes in these upper reaches of effort."

And yet, one thing David and his team realized early on is that some people would need help to understand that exercise isn't *all* about suffering. "Because when you have folks who are addicted to that and want those endorphins, getting them to back off and recover can be difficult," he says. "Your improvement only happens when you have something that challenges you and pushes you further, but then that stress has to be taken away and you have to recover. It can be difficult for the mindset of someone who wants to push themselves hard all the time to realize that actually, if you do, you're going to break down."

A challenge now lies ahead for Sufferfest. Its very extremity attracted the initial demographic, but now it's a hindrance to further growth—not every cyclist grooves on the idea of suffering, so the team has to find a way of expanding the app's appeal without diluting the Sufferlandria mythology.

"Maybe suffering has a greater purpose," David muses. "This is getting into philosophy now, isn't it? It's teaching us something about ourselves that we can apply in the rest of our lives. I know with our mental program, a lot of folks who have gone through it then talk about how they use the techniques when they're applying for a job, or confronting something at work. I know folks that have said, 'Look, if I can get through Nine Hammers, I know I can study and finish this degree.'"

That said, he does sometimes wonder about the appeal of ultrarunning. "You could almost think it's running away from something. *Why are they by themselves, for so long, in such deep pain?*" He chuckles.

I confess to having had the same thought about cyclists.

FOR AS LONG as Luke Tyburski can remember, he has wanted to win. He grew up in Bathurst, an Australian town known for the Bathurst 1000 and other motorsport races, and his family excelled at a range of sports. If they'd had a motto, Luke says it would have been the unforgiving, "Never, ever give up."

As it is, on Luke's bicep there's the tattoo *fortis*—Latin for "strength." He shows me when we meet in a London café, struggling to stretch his improbably long legs out in our booth. We're here to discuss his horrible feats of endurance, which have been immortalized in a documentary, *The Ultimate Triathlon* (2016), and his memoir, *Chasing Extreme* (2018). The former depicts a one-man Boschian nightmare of Luke's own design that took him from Morocco to Monaco in twelve days. In order to cover the 1250 miles, the average day saw him clocking up two hundred miles on the bike and running a double marathon. Luke wound up running on crutches, and was only able to mount his bike with the aid of his support team.

It was a classic hero's journey—from the call to adventure to crossing the threshold to encountering trials, facing atonement and traveling the triumphant road home, having achieved his goal.

That trip had its origins years earlier, when Luke suffered multiple inoperable injuries as a promising young soccer player. His professional ambitions thwarted, he typed "world's toughest ultramarathon in Sahara Desert" into a search engine and reassessed his options. I laugh at the audacity of this, but then, pretty much everything Luke puts his mind to eventually manifests. When he got hitched, he entered "endurance adventurer" as his occupation on his marriage certificate.

"What that meant was, *I'm going to write books about my challenges around the world and other people are going to pay for them. I'm going to speak on stages, I'm going to get paid to talk. I'm going to write magazine articles, I'm going to have documentaries made*," he says. He's largely pulled that off. When we meet, he's designing an online course, The Performance Mindset for Athletes.

Luke's race history oozes suffering. His toes are rubbed raw in Marathon des Sables sand. An intestinal parasite plagues him during the Everest Ultra. He's mistaken for a shuffling beggar in a town on *The Ultimate Triathlon*'s course, and his tongue swells to twice its size from a five-hour salty swim across the Gibraltar Strait. Luke calls it "suffering as salvation," though it does raise an interesting question: is it better to run a race *well*, or to finish it at all costs? To Luke, the prospect of permanent damage is simply not high in the hierarchy of importance. "I think if you ask people in this world [of endurance sports] about damage, they'll say, 'Yeah, that will happen,' but they don't focus on that," he says.

I've already spoken to Dr. Bernadette Fitzgibbon about this kind of thing. She's a senior research fellow at the Epworth

Centre for Innovation in Mental Health in Melbourne, and her work of late has been based around ultramarathon runners and pain tolerance.

Bernadette tells me that most studies around endurance have been conducted by sports scientists, who look at things such as the VO2 max test—a measure of a person's oxygen-carrying capacity, a big factor in how fast and far you can run—resting heart rate and recovery time. In other words, they're interested in physical anomalies that might explain someone's increased capacity for endurance. Her team is more interested in psychological factors. In 2017, they took a group of ultramarathon runners and a control group of non-ultramarathon runners and asked them to stick their hands in a bucket of ice for up to three minutes.

"Of the non-UMRs, some people lasted about a minute and a half, but they were really struggling," she says. "For almost all the UMRs, we had to ask them to withdraw their hand at three minutes."

The participants then completed psychometric questionnaires that looked at escape and avoidance behaviors toward pain: the Pain Catastrophizing Scale, the Pain Anxiety Symptoms Scale, the Pain Vigilance and Awareness Questionnaire and the Pain Resilience Scale. They rated statements such as, *I think that if my pain gets too severe, it will never decrease* and *I am very sensitive to pain* and *When faced with intense or prolonged pain I get back out there.*

The researchers concluded that ultramarathon runners have reduced pain-related anxiety compared to non-running controls; have a higher tolerance for pain due to cold; and that this elevated tolerance is partly due to reduced avoidance of pain.

Every endurance athlete has their tricks for dealing with pain, fatigue and plummeting spirits. Luke relies on two methods. The first is his "you're the best" pep talk, which he's employed since his soccer days. He'd sing the Joe Esposito power ballad (which he first heard when watching *The Karate Kid*) into the bathroom mirror, then tell his reflection that he was the *best* tackler, the *best* passer and about to be man of the match. The second is envisaging a little man inside his head whose job it is to get through extreme ordeals. He's entirely independent of Luke, detached from Luke's negative thoughts and emotions. "There were times during *The Ultimate Triathlon* where I was cracking jokes," Luke says, "but when the little man upstairs is talking, it's one of the very few times in life when I look serious. People can talk to me and I'll ignore them, because the little man upstairs has taken over, and it's like, nothing can get me out of that."

Luke says, "The thing that I've realized from stripping myself back and getting into nature is that when you're in that moment where you've been running for ten hours, you don't care about what Sally wrote about you in social media comments or what society is trying to push on everyone. It's irrelevant. When everything sucks, breathing hurts and just thinking about taking a step hurts your legs, you ask yourself, *Why am I here and who is this person?* You can really strip yourself bare, but then the cool thing is that when you strip yourself all the way back to a framework, you get to rebuild. The people I've seen come furthest in their personal journeys are the ones who build themselves up during these endurance challenges and then live their life like that every day."

The flip side is that being an endurance athlete can be a supremely selfish pursuit. It takes a toll on relationships, be it with partners who tolerate long absences—overseas or simply at the gym—or the friends and peers who wind up copping abuse and worrying themselves sick as race support crew. In an episode of *The Losers* (2019), a Netflix documentary series, runner Mauro Prosperi recalls his ordeal during the Marathon des Sables in 1994, when he became lost in a sandstorm and wound up in Algeria, eating bats for survival and drinking his own urine. When he was found, nine days later, he had lost forty pounds.

Mauro, who was married with children, remembers the disclaimer he had to sign beforehand, which asked where, in the event of death, organizers should send his corpse. He signed up over his family's protests, and even entered the race multiple times after his dramatic rescue. His wife was irritated by the press adulation when he returned safely to Italy. "They asked him, 'What did you eat?' but never, 'Did you learn your lesson?'" she points out.

As psychologist Nathan DeWall commented, "One of the challenges of coming back from the Marathon de Sables is you realize you are living in two different worlds. You're living in a world where all that you were doing was really being comfortable, whereas out there you're self-sufficient, you're in survival mode and you're constantly seeking to press your limits. And some people never really never make it back. They catch the bug and they have to go back and back and back and back, even if their lives are falling apart."

Luke can relate to that kind of comedown. Between races he

would mentally crash, finding himself in debt, struggling to pay rent and berating himself for the occasions he could have pushed himself harder. In a desperate attempt to feel a sense of purpose again, he'd compulsively sign up for more ultramarathons in quick succession. When his long-term relationship broke down, his training regime became even more extreme, and bizarre, too—midnight marathons, or long, long gym sessions designed purely to exhaust himself. It seems similar to the way that some choose to obliterate themselves with alcohol and other drugs.

"Exactly the same," he agrees. "And in both cases you feel pretty shattered the next day. As soon as you get off the couch or finish the race, reality hits. For a large portion of people, it's about testing themselves, and for a significant proportion of people it's about punishing themselves and running away from something, but they don't necessarily know what it is yet, or they're not at a place where they can face up to it. I was running away from something. My training was my form of feeling alive and expressing myself, but it was also a form of self-punishment."

Since his twenties, Luke has suffered from clinical depression and what he calls an intense fear of failure. At its most alarming, his depression would manifest in suicidal thoughts, insomnia, self-harming behavior, binge-eating and overtraining. Punishing himself physically started off as escapism and eventually grew into full-blown addiction. As he writes in *Chasing Extreme*: "Like any drug, it met my extreme emotional need while I was in the endorphin-filled euphoria of the intense physical exercise—but the crash afterward was crippling ... And each hit of self-administered punishment had to be longer, harder or more extreme for me to reach the emotional high. Eventually something had to give, and in 2015, it did. *The Ultimate Triathlon* was my overdose."

Nobody questioned Luke's eating habits between races, because his binge-eating tended to happen at night. Unable to sleep, he'd get up to find a snack and return to bed to watch videos on his laptop with tubs of ice cream, bags of nuts and twenty peanut-butter sandwiches. At around 5:00 a.m. he'd give up on sleep and go for a four-hour run. To make up for the binge, he wouldn't eat for a day or two.

The term for restricted eating and overexercising in athletes is called RED-S (relative energy deficiency in sport) and it's often an eating disorder masquerading as training. The kind of perfectionism that makes an athlete excel can become warped, even pathological, when it comes to diet. With female athletes, it can lead to menstrual dysfunction.

Amelia Boone is a world-champion obstacle racer and high-powered career woman who has practiced as an attorney and provided legal counsel to Apple. The homepage of her website shows her scrambling up a dirt ledge in shorts and a sports bra supplied by Reebok, her sponsor. Her entire body is goosefleshed and streaked in mud. In July 2019, she posted a blog titled, "The Recovery I Needed."

"I'm not dense," she wrote.

I've known for a long time that I'm the living, walking example of RED-S. I've known that probably a huge reason that my bones keep breaking is because I have a 20-year history with anorexia … When I started racing and gaining attention for my athletic accomplishments, I didn't talk about it during interviews. I didn't mention it during my rise to dominance in obstacle racing. I didn't tell interviewers who asked me about my athletic background that the reason I didn't play sports in college was because I was too sick and weak to even walk upstairs … I was racing strong, running strong, feeling strong, and, in my mind, I no longer identified with the disorder.

Amelia swapped her identity as "anorexic" for that of "athlete," all the while clinging onto disordered eating habits. Being at the top of her field and muscular, with a normal BMI for an athlete, she convinced herself that her eating patterns, and her habit of comparing her body to other women on the start line—as well as dehydrating and starving herself before cover shoots—was all part of the job. What's more, obsessing about avoiding food was a distraction from life's greater worries: fears of losing, fears of loss of relevancy, a need for connection to others. And before she publicly confessed to RED-S, she was getting away with it.

Being an athlete, but also a coach with a degree in exercise science, Luke says he can quickly gauge from a runner's behavior and body composition whether they're going through an eating disorder. "Amelia Boone has talked about how she would do everything she could to not go out with people for dinner, because then she would have to eat," he says. "You often see that of athletes in the endurance world. Normally, when you're racing, it's stuff as much food down as you can. But you see people not even trying to eat. And during training, a lot of people put videos online, and if you read into the clip they've chosen to show, they're being very restrictive in the type of food they're eating, like avoiding carbs. The bottom line is if you're doing fifteen-plus hours a week exercise, you've got to properly fuel for that."

Luke felt like a fraud, coaching others in training and nutrition while secretly binge-eating. He decided to face things head on and talk to his family about his depression. Writing his book helped him make sense of everything, as does checking in honestly with his wife. And now he plans his missions with the caveat that he thinks beforehand about what he is willing to go through to achieve it. Risk assessment, if you will.

"For an outsider looking in, it's very easy to say, 'Why would you do that to your body?'" he says. "When my documentary first went up on Amazon Prime, ten reviewers gave it about two out of five stars. The comments were hilarious. 'I don't get it— no doubt he's done long-term damage,' 'Why would you push yourself this far when it's not for money?,' 'There's no one else even in this race!'

"I read those comments from haters and I sat with them and thought, *Okay, why are they saying that? Is there any merit to it? Have I missed something?* The thing I noticed nobody wondered was, *Were you going through anything personally at the time, to want to push yourself to that limit?* Because as someone who's been through that journey, if I see someone literally dragging themselves through an event, the first thing I wonder is what's going on in their personal life."

Perhaps, but perhaps it also speaks to someone's core beliefs about themselves. I think about a transcontinental US odyssey that Charlie had planned, in which he would run eighteen hours a day for six weeks. He had to cut it short when he was besieged by one injury after another, contending with staphylococcus-related sores on his legs, aching joints, Achilles problems, bruising and blisters on the soles of his feet, and a garden-variety cold, all of which he castigated himself for soundly. At one point, as he was icing his red, swollen ankle and beating himself up for losing sensation in his toes, one member of the film crew asked him, "Do you consider yourself a compassionate person?"

Charlie looked up. "Yeah. I try to be."

"Do you feel any compassion at all for yourself?"

The answer, he knew, was no.

I asked Charlie about public perception of his feats, wondering if he gets the same kind of feedback as Luke. He describes being at a Rotary Club function one day, giving a talk about his running. "I got a question from a guy who was a little overweight," he says, "and he's going, 'I saw with the Chicago Marathon there were three people who died last week. Do you think running's dangerous? Like, the body's not meant to do this?' I said, 'Yeah, I read that article too. It was really unfortunate. I'm sorry that that happened and sure, running can absolutely uncover some flaws in a person's body. Absolutely.'

"And then, because I'm a smartass, I said, 'Oh, did you see though that last week 5,233 people died sitting on their sofas extending their arm out with a remote control? That's some dangerous shit right there and I would absolutely not just sit at home watching television by yourself because that is the definition of danger.'"

On a far less epic scale than Charlie, I found that when I threw myself into Muay Thai—Thai kickboxing—and daily gym workouts, I had more people suddenly expressing concerns for my well-being than I did when I was getting wasted. One friend texted me as the pandemic hit, to warn me that people who exercised heavily were at particular risk of succumbing to COVID-19's effects because of a weakened immune system.

"In my experience," Charlie says to this, "it's rarely based in true concern, because if they're around me enough, they're going to see how running makes me happy, you know? Misery really does love company, and a lot of times I find that people who very likely feel badly about themselves and what they've managed to accomplish tend to soft-criticize. It's an indirect, backhanded compliment of sorts."

Perhaps the psychology of ultrarunners is, at base, uncomplicated: they simply prioritize the goal above the body. The meat cage is a mule to be driven, and is viewed dispassionately as a result, whether that be for practical purposes, from lack of self-regard, or a bit of both.

Charlie supports this idea. He says that when he gives keynote talks to "high net worth" people, most have obsessive personalities and believe they ought to be seeking balance. He disagrees. He thinks "balance" is a buzzword. "Balance is overrated," he assures me. "Very few people who've actually accomplished anything big, like writing a book or running a marathon or whatever it is, have balance in their lives. If you're not obsessed with it, then why are you doing it? That's what I don't even get. I don't even understand how someone can do it just a little bit, whatever it is."

As someone who regularly tips over into obsession, I'll admit it feels validating to have Charlie's blessing.

Chapter Two

TASTING THE LIMITS

Performance Artists and Rogue Scientists

DURING THE FIRST few hours of the hunt, there's boredom. You've been in the Papua New Guinean jungle all day, focusing intently, looking for signs of disruptions in the greenery. Then you spot something. Anxiety, fear, anticipation and rage compete inside you. Riding smoothly above all those is entitlement. You've waited a long time for this, and you deserve this battle, this victory. And in any case, it has to be done if you are to eat tonight.

Dr. Jack Allocca is describing to me one of the many hunts he's been on with tribes and remote communities across the continents. The hunts relate to his hobby: challenging his notions of disgust by eating what many would consider to be inedible. So far, one hundred or so insect and animal species have passed through Jack's digestive tract, including monkey, vulture, cat, dog, Asian black bear, grizzly bear, caribou, fox, flying fox, wombat, koala, peacock, lion, tiger, whale and zebra ... and long pig.

By profession, he's a neuroscientist and a bioengineer, specializing in sleep research. One of his inventions is Somnivore, a data-mining tool for the study of consciousness, and he conducts studies at the University of Melbourne. A personal interest in psychedelic pharmacology ties in with that. "Sleep is just one of many altered states," he tells me. "The one with the least stigma attached to it."

Jack arrives in my country town for our interview in a banged-up, borrowed Honda Civic. He's bearded and dressed in black, with his hair tied back. The monocle hanging around his neck is to correct irregular astigmatism and shortsightedness in his left eye, but it doesn't hurt that it gives him the aura of an explorer from centuries past. He's a loud, gregarious talker. In the bar where we meet, people look over when he booms "Cannibalism in Australia is not regulated," gesticulating over his wine glass, and on quite a few other occasions besides.

"Then there's the pursuit," he says, turning back to the hunt. I lean in, over the wildly suburban pavlova we're sharing. "The pursuit is a mixture of wrath, coordination, cruelty. And finally there's the actual assault, where you are next to the animal and you are fighting it. You're stabbing it, or strangling it, and there's a specific functional panic response in which you just have to beat that other animal."

When the death occurs, it's emotionally destabilizing. All that rage dissipates. "Instead, you get this insane rush of opioid-like substances, in which you feel the most meaningful and the deepest form of peace," he says. "It's an altered state. You have a carcass in your hand, you're covered in blood and bruises, and you look at the animal and you experience what I think is one of the manifestations of true love. The process of pursuing an animal, killing it, butchering it, is one of the most complex psychological and neurological experiences that I can possibly recount."

Behind Jack's physical adventures there's a more specific mission: to advance his "ever-going training in cognitive liberty."

I first encounter him at a meeting of the Australian Psychedelic Society, and then at many more such gatherings. Even among these seasoned trippers and libertarians with a taste for the weird, Jack's adventures were talked about as being *out there*. That's where I heard about him eating laboratory mice with Huntington's disease that were due for culling. "Their brains were eaten fresh, battered in flour and deep-fried, and simmered with olive oil on a pan. They were tangibly delicious," he announced, seeming to enjoy the reaction to that last sentence. People keep telling me I should interview Jack, and Jack, often within earshot, is nonchalantly receptive.

Jack grew up in northern Italy. His father was a former paratrooper who owned a pizzeria and did stand-up comedy on the side ("trained to kill, make people laugh and make pizza," says Jack). His mother managed hotels. It was a fairly ordinary existence. But when he was sent to spend time with his farming grandparents in the south, things got weird.

"My mother's side of the family were some of the most grotesque individuals you could find," he says, with Roald Dahl-style relish. "My grandfather could not write or read. He would mostly speak in swear words and dialect." Jack likens his nonno to a troll doll—small and stocky, with wide, worn hands. Carlo was built for the field, but was also ginger-haired and chronically sunburned because of his time in it. Up until his eighties he was still climbing olive and almond trees and banging them with a stick for their bounty.

"Their eating habits were peculiar, to say the least. I can still picture my grandma, just going to the fridge, opening it, grabbing a steak and eating it. Sometimes, keeping eye contact with me. Like, a raw steak. Sometimes, raw sausages. Then she would butcher animals, execute them in front of me, like a rabbit. I was hysterical."

His grandmother would give him a mysterious, quite delicious drink in a glass every day. It wasn't till he was a teenager that he discovered it was cooked and seasoned horse blood. Perhaps that's why his brother became a butcher, but Jack took a different route.

"As a kid I had these loops of self-inquiry, which became deeper and deeper," he says. "I definitely had an early exposure to the semantics of flavor and what it is to really enjoy the aesthetics of food, but I also have a very intricate relationship with memory."

He asks me if I can remember the third-to-last pizza I ate. The reason I can't is because the brain is designed to forget more than it remembers. So why are there certain things the brain automatically decides to retain, like the first time we had sex or tried cocaine?

"Okay, so it's novelty. But then we go deeper into novelty. Novelty is you discovering a new part of the world, which now becomes one of your compartments within the self. Every time you introduce a new compartment, you can use it for your day-to-day prediction models about survival, about thriving. But if you can't quite remember your biographical narratives, how do we really know that we are embodying some kind of life?" he says. "Considering the overwhelming amount of psychedelics I exposed myself to, this question became compelling."

During his years of study in his twenties, Jack traveled widely. Food is often the gateway to culture, and the anthropological side of eating came to interest him. In East Timor, he saw children playing with animal guts and flicking eyeballs at each other. These kids, he realized, were at one with the jungle, and did not experience dogmatic morality around death. "That was, in many ways, very moving."

He went on to eat capuchin monkeys with locals in Puerto Maldonado, Peru ("intense"). Then the "fusion cuisine" in Laos, which he dubs Dog Squirrel Porcupine Opium Pizza, on a trip that also saw him kidnapped by police and then protected by local poachers. In the Chocó Department of Colombia, he ate vulture, cooked by an incredulous local woman who at least wasn't deterred by the folk superstitions that surround the bird. In Australia, he's eaten roadkill—wombat, fox and koala—but he baulked for ages at Vegemite. "It was one of the most obnoxious things I'd ever tasted; like some waterproofing material for boats or something. I violated my brain with Vegemite until there was a switch, and now I love it."

Over time, he realized it was easiest to have a mission to present to locals when visiting a new place. "Otherwise, you go there and say, 'Show me what you are about,' or you take photos of people and then make an inspirational post on Instagram, no different from taking a photo in the zoo next to a panda bear."

Testing his mental gag reflex became a manic pursuit. "Once I removed the layer of squeamishness, it didn't matter whether it was a rat or a raccoon—they were all so interesting," he says. "I developed the fitness of a wine connoisseur; all the different layers of musk, versus earthy, versus what most of the world uses one word for—gamy. Once you gain that fitness, your hedonic spectrum widens."

Sometimes Jack pays guides to take him on his missions; other times, locals are intrigued enough to guide him on his venture for free. He's good at finding that one person in the main settlements who speaks some English, and who then becomes his emissary into the remote communities. Very often, people would also approach him because he was a lone white person— particularly true in Papua New Guinea.

"They would approach me with a level of amusement and fear: 'Why are you here? You're here for our resources,'" he says. "But they could understand easily enough, over time, that I do not have any dark agenda. When you do these deep, true, intrinsically interesting things, people want to help you. Money ended up being maybe 10 percent of it because sometimes I had to buy transportation, or I had to pay a woman in Peru to cook me my first cat, or I had to pay a lady to snatch me a flying fox in Vanuatu."

Jack tells me about the time he couch surfed with a young Korean man and discovered that his sofamate had never eaten dog. The pair wound up trawling the alleyways of Seoul, looking for the authentic experience. "It's part of his culture, but it's becoming more and more archaic because exposure to the West warps their moral compass," Jack says.

Does he care about the treatment of the dog in the back-alley restaurant before he comes to eat it?

"Yes and no," he says. "From a moral standpoint, this becomes quite a debate. Factory farming of domesticated animals drives the loss of biodiversity. To have a farm you must bulldoze a large area, plant massive monocultures to feed the animals and carve in the roads that lead in and out. Let's take cows. They are mistreated, they are misfed, they're injected with things. From the point of view of the individual cow, this is hell on Earth. From the point of view of cows as a species, we are doing so much work for them to thrive. We impregnate them, we give them space, we give them resources. It's actually quite spooky when you think about it. If aliens were to look at us as a planet, they'd be like, 'Oh, cows are the rulers of planet Earth.'"

Jack knows his missions are not to everyone's taste, but with a few perverse exceptions, like the lab mice—and the dog—the meat he's eaten on his missions has been hunted with traditional communities who have a respectful understanding of the process. He invokes moral relativism: the idea that morals change from border to border, culture to culture, molded by context, spirituality and practicality. "Indians eat buffaloes because cows are sacred," he says. "There's halal and kosher ... which one is right? It gets very arbitrary, and I don't really like arbitrary, so I try to get around it as much as possible. I'm also particularly fond of eating cats and dogs for all sorts of disrupting reasons."

So Jack's stance is that eating animals is conditional. If it was a threatened species but it was already dead, for instance, then he wouldn't hesitate. But in any case, he argues, if we were forced to eat wildlife like our ancestors did, we would see species dwindle and the notion of what is or isn't unsustainable would be at the forefront of our attention. "This is actually what happens with tribes—they self-correct, especially in islands where they move around," he says. "Most people are completely oblivious to these ecological checks and balances. Cows and sheep are never going to disappear, so we have this blind spot, where people just think that they can eat more and there's never going to be any repercussion. Food has lost meaning to us because we just go to a supermarket and see this pink stuff under cling film and then we eat it. It's preposterous how limited our range is. And we have bastardized the process of eating meat, so that those emotions we once felt during a hunt are not organically packaged into the experience. Instead, we seek them elsewhere. You're searching for a car park to go to work and somebody steals it: wrath. You get a pay raise: you're excited. You take heroin and you're at peace. You do calisthenics and you feel powerful."

Undeniably, there's also the shock of the new at play here for Jack, as well as mindfulness of ecobiology—and that's ongoing. In the Ica region of Peru there's a cat festival he'd like to partake in. As for other future missions, in Alaska he's already eaten rotten baby walrus—considered to be a delicacy—which, to his surprise, cured the diarrhea he'd had for two weeks from a dodgy smoothie in Texas, and he'll be returning there, to Barrow, to hunt with Inuit tribespeople. Then there's his search for traditional Sardinian casu marzu—"rotten cheese"—which contains live insect larvae. It's sometimes called "maggot cheese." It's necessary to enlist a corrupt cheese dealer to buy it on the black market, since it has been banned in the European Union.

"There will have to be an expedition just to find it," he says, with pleasure. "As my grandfather used to describe it, it was 'electrically addictive.' My grandparents were embedded in a certain culture. They weren't just crazy."

SIX MONTHS PASS before my next conversation with Jack. This time, I travel to him. He lives out in the sticks, in Bacchus Marsh, thirty miles northwest of Melbourne. That's because it's cheap. He rents a large house with an overgrown garden that overlooks a valley the map doesn't bother to name. As I swing my truck into his street, young men in tracksuit pants standing on the porch of the corner house crane at me like lemurs.

I warned Jack in advance that I have a cold, but he confidently claims to have a bulletproof immune system from eating so many oddities, which expose him to different bacteria, soil and micronutrients. For my purposes, he prescribes starvation, to kick my system into gear. It's okay, though—I'd picked up some Soothers from the service station.

Seated at the kitchen bench, I start to talk to Jack about how our need for novelty can lead to a corruption of taste—hence the popularity of porn sites such as eFukt that curate "disgusting" content.

"I used to *love* eFukt when I was a teenager," he interrupts. "I would spend hours on it, with a deep sense of wonder at what could be done, beyond the realms of somatic and moral athleticism. Someone might shove an entire school of fish inside them—and not just do it but really enjoy it. It made me realize the sky's the limit."

It shouldn't be a surprise it's Japanese porn that has ventured most steadfastly in the direction of disgust endurance, since Japan's mainstream culture has explored the same avenues. Japanese television has long broadcast "torture" game shows that marry ordeal and humiliation in front of a live audience. One of the best-known was the 1980s series *Za Gaman*, which translates as "Endurance." It pitted male university students against one other for *batsu gēmu* (punishment games) and *gaman taikai* (endurance contests). In similar shows since, contestants might be encased in a plexiglass cube and attacked by a grizzly bear, or given blowjobs by gay men behind a modesty box with the goal of humiliatingly bringing them to orgasm, or be urged to eat things widely considered to be disgusting.

It strikes me there's not a huge difference between the Japanese porn fetish of *gokkun*—drinking copious amounts of semen from a receptacle—and the endurance-eating challenges of primetime television show *I'm a Celebrity … Get Me Out of Here*, in which contestants must drink pig-brain smoothies or chow down on marsupial testicles during the Bushtucker Trials. This component of the show is so popular that there's an official board game that comes with real insects, and *The Daily Mail* was moved to publish the helpful guide "How to Recreate *I'm A Celebrity…* Bushtucker Trials at Home."

In his book *The Anatomy of Disgust*, law professor William Ian Miller posits: "Disgust allows us to play at violating norms in certain restrictive settings … [it] can be indulged playfully fully for rather low stakes. And this is true not only for comic transgression but also for the entertainment derived from genres that truck in violence and horror."

Jack thinks our fascination for disgust is related to our fascination with getting hurt. I think of relatively benign examples, such as *Jackass* and *Funniest Home Videos*, chili-eating competitions and the Russian Slapping Championships, in which two men stand face-to-face and take turns slapping each other, but also the kinds of closed Facebook groups in which members share videos of gruesome injuries that have befallen unfortunate strangers.

"Anything that is high intensity has the potential of disrupting survival, so it's really worth your attention," Jack explains. It allows our brains a mental rehearsal. "You can try to imagine someone eating a venomous fish, but it will be a low-quality simulation and may not be very accurate. But what if somebody eats a blowfish and dies, and this has been televised? That's the most precious information you can come across, and the areas of the brain tune in because they want to soak in every single detail possible to apply to your survival if you come across a similar situation.

"You're basically delegating risk-taking to this other person out there. With the near-misses, there's this added layer of hilariousness to protect the witness from getting traumatized. If you see people getting stabbed in the face every other day, you will develop PTSD. Instead, you see people tripping and hurting themselves but being okay. You can't empathize with them all the time because you'd end up neurotic, so that stuff gets labeled as funny for you to still tune in your attention."

Jack has also challenged his disgust response in sexual situations. In his late twenties and early thirties he worked as an escort, largely for the novelty, and catered to men as well as women, despite being straight. "I was even semi-homophobic, coming from Italian traditions," he says. "I had to break that down within myself, and I did it methodically through the sex industry. I never had the mildest of attraction toward men, but now I can do it. In the right context, I can do it."

It sounds a bit like exposure therapy, I observe. "If it has a name, I guess," he says. He prefers not to reduce an experience to a label. "As a writer, you kind of have to," he concedes kindly.

In the same vein of testing his mental mettle, Jack estimates he's taken eighty psychoactive compounds—mainly research chemicals (the term given to ever-evolving drug analogues and derivatives, sometimes designed to evade legislative controls), but some natural, such as *salvia divinorum*, known as "sage of the diviners" in its native region of Oxana, Mexico. Unlike hallucinogens that give the user a sense of shared consciousness with the world, salvia tends to embed the idea that you are inanimate and might not even exist. "Like having your soul torn apart; an existential disemboweling," is how Jack describes the experience.

In Papua New Guinea, Jack bemused the young men who had agreed to take him hunting in the Highlands by drinking brugmansia tea, made from vivid orange bellflowers that can provoke terrifying delirium. The hunters only use it to kill prey—and their enemies—but Jack was hoping that he would get the men on his side with his sense of daring. Or at least make them laugh.

"They didn't drink it themselves," he says. "It would be like me coming up to you and saying, 'Jenny, shall we find some arsenic?'"

Most of the youths had never seen a white person before. They spoke pidgin English, barely enough to communicate. "But that didn't matter because with brugmansia you're not you anymore anyway," Jack says. "You're a person without social conditioning."

Brugmansia, sometimes known as angel trumpet, is a reliably bad trip. The plant affects the muscarinic receptors of your body. It disrupts the moisture in your skin, your eyes, your tongue.

Your vision begins crisp but becomes interrupted. All of a sudden you lose lucidity, and so forget you have consumed anything. You lose your bearings. You only retain a sense of self as in a dream. It's like you're sleepwalking, in fact. Your eyes are open, but there's a hyperrealistic overlay, like an augmented reality. The delirium can last up to twenty days in some users, say toxicologists.

"I remember maybe 5 percent of it," Jack says. "You are propelled, nine hours later, miles from your last memory. Confused, exhausted, you've lost all your possessions. Maybe there's a missing finger. Or there's someone dead next to you. You're shocked."

You could hardly have put yourself in a more dangerous situation, I say, shocked myself.

"I did that on purpose," he says. "It was the ultimate stress test. I've seen so much gnarly stuff in my life, I thought, *I want to strip back these layers and know the most radically primal version of me. Can I really be trusted with my own core?*"

I've always been fascinated by human guinea pigs, committing themselves to fantastical and fearsome missions, but Jack pushes safety to its limits. He's what humanist psychologist Frank Farley would call a "Type T," a thrill-seeker; someone who thrives on novelty and uncertainty. Farley has said that these people have the cognitive habit of reframing as invigorating the situations that most of us would find unthinkably dangerous.

I ask Jack if he thinks he has unusually low levels of fear, and he responds that it's hard to quantify without studying his amygdala—but he gets asked it a lot. He definitely experiences fear—sometimes intensely—but it seems to relate to loss of freedom. He's never gone as deep into martial arts as he would like, for instance, because he is cautious about injuring himself in a way that would impinge on his ability to travel.

"And I wouldn't say I'm impulsive," he reflects. "There's an element of impulsivity in some of the things I do, like when I've been in places that were bordering on war zones and you need to be quite impulsive to make quick decisions, but on a day-to-day basis I wouldn't say so. I don't think I've exhibited impulsive behavior in interpersonal contexts."

It was actually for practical reasons that he had decided Papua New Guinea would be the perfect place to take brugmansia, he tells me. In the jungle he wouldn't be arrested, fall from a balcony or be run over. "My thinking was: I'll be surrounded by no-bullshit people. And they are so strong that they could crush my head with their hands," he says, demonstrating with a motion. "If a person that's weird comes out of me, I will be executed on the spot—and that's what needs to happen. I was willing to go through any of the repercussions."

Despite his propensity for high-risk activities, Jack doesn't focus on death. "Death is an outcome of making certain mistakes, or the time has just come," he says. "I focus on living the best I can, and as long as I do that, death won't feel like missing out."

IN PAPUA NEW GUINEA, Jack had hoped to find a tribe that would facilitate his sampling of human flesh. That didn't happen. Instead, he wound up turning cannibal in suburban Melbourne.

A close friend of Jack's—I'll call him Dan—had the idea of severing the tip of his finger as a body modification, and Jack asked if he could eat it. The pair discussed the implications over three months: whether Dan's mental and physical health was robust enough, his persona and how that was likely to change afterward.

"He wanted to be more masculine," says Jack. "He was a graphic designer who was raised in a working-class environment by men who would lose digits when using tools. He tried to get into accidents, but that didn't work. I said, 'If you want to lose a finger by accident, you'll end up losing half a hand.'"

On the allotted day, as Jack hovered, Dan used bolt cutters to sever the middle finger—the least useful digit—close to the first knuckle. Then the pair cooked it on a barbeque—"as Australian as it gets," says Jack. He shows me the photographs of a sautéed nub of flesh. "The nail was crispy. I sucked the marrow from the bone and removed all the bits of flesh until there was nothing else that could be extracted. The closest thing I could think of was sweet pork."

It felt taboo, even to him, but he points out that this was the most ethical meat he's ever eaten: it was provided consensually, and its production had no directly attributable impact on the environment. "It was a major paradigm upgrade within myself. Things got more meaningful. I digested a close friend of mine and bits of him would be integrated within my cells, and all those proteins would become part of me."

Dan was hospitalized for two days to have plastic surgery to seal the stump, which caused him pain. He had more surgery a year later when the nail bed, now inside his stump, started growing fingernail again.

Despite their new biological bond, Jack and Dan fell out.

"We had an agreement that I could broadcast it in some way, but the way that I did it was not what he wanted," Jack says. "I was basically telling people about it at parties: 'You know what I did last week?' It got back to Dan's family. I am very sorry for that mishandling," he says.

Most of us only encounter cannibalism in the context of ethnography or survival or psychopathy. But there's a lesser-known category, performance art, which seems to have most in common with Jack's avenues of self-enquiry.

In a 2018 work titled "Eschatology" (the theological study of the end of things, or the ultimate destination of humanity), Latvian artist Arturs Bērziņš carved a chunk out of each of the backs of two assistants, fried the meat and fed it to them. In 1988, for a work titled *A Cannibal in England*, Canadian artist Rick Gibson ate a preserved-tonsil canapé in Walthamstow Market. "I became the first cannibal in British history to legally eat human meat in public," he wrote on his website. A year later, he ate a slice of human testicle (donated) next to the Lewisham Clock Tower. "England is a marvelous country because it has no laws against cannibalism," he observed.

In 1989, Gibson introduced the public to Sniffy the Rat, who was displayed in a transparent box with a heavy weight suspended above his head. A sign around the box read: *Free art lesson soon. This rat is going to die.* Gibson said he planned to crush Sniffy, who was purchased from a pet store, between two canvases to create a diptych. Spurred on by a newspaper story, a mob of protesters—who hadn't expressed the same kind of outrage at the pet store feeding live rats to snakes, who may have accepted setting mousetraps in their own homes—chased him down the street until he sought refuge, under police protection, in a hotel.

Gibson's intention, as with most of his work, was to force the audience to consider the hypocrisies in their own moral code. Other performance artists have used their own bodies to challenge the observer. In her 1974 work "Rhythm 0," Serbian artist Marina Abramović stood still for six hours next to a table laden with items ranging from a rose to a gun, and let the audience use them on her. She concluded the piece after six hours: her clothes had been sliced off with razor blades and her skin similarly slashed in places (one person wanted to suck her blood). She had been repeatedly groped, and one participant had loaded the gun and curled Abramović's finger around the trigger. In 1973, Taiwanese artist Tehching Hsieh took a two-story jump for "Jump Piece." "It was conceived quickly—all I needed was a window and a camera—and I knew the pain would be quick, too. I wouldn't do that kind of thing anymore. I knew I'd likely get hurt, but I didn't even think about the possibility of broken legs," he told Abramović when she talked to him for *Interview* magazine. Certainly it was quicker than his series of gruelingly sustained works, such as *One Year Performance 1981–1982 (Outdoor Piece)*, for which he avoided any kind of shelter while living on the streets of New York City.

American Chris Burden somehow lived to the age of sixty-nine, despite—for various works in the 1970s—getting a friend to shoot him in the arm, cramming himself into a locker for five days, nailing himself onto a Volkswagen Beetle and trying to breathe water for five minutes. The work of another American, Ron Athey, has its origins in subversive nightclubs such as

Club Fuck! in Los Angeles and draws heavily on sadomasochism and body modification themes, as well as the writings of French philosopher George Bataille on transgression, befouling beauty, human sacrifice and self-destruction. Athey's *Torture Trilogy* (1992–1995) utilized branding, scarification and anal penetration. In 2007's *Self-Obliteration*, a glamorous blonde wig is revealed to be attached to his scalp by large needles. Günter Brus, of the avant-garde Viennese Actionists, covered himself with his own feces, drank his own urine, masturbated and sang the Austrian national anthem for the 1968 performance *Kunst und Revolution*.

For his 2005 work *Blender* with fellow artist Nina Sellars, the mononymous Stelarc took subcutaneous fat, peripheral nerve endings and blood from his body and displayed the mixture in a sealed container surrounded by four gas tanks. The vigorous liposuction the work required was performed under local anaesthetic. Plastic surgery clinics aren't keen on handing over biohazardous waste for art's sake, but Stelarc feigned a sentimental desire to keep his bodily fluids in the same way that some mothers wish to keep their umbilical cord—and that seemed to be better accepted.

Professor Stelarc is now the director of the Alternate Anatomies Lab at Perth's Curtin University. I arrange a meeting with him in Melbourne shortly before he state-hops again to set up a new work, *Reclining Stickman*, a thirty-foot robot that functions as a kind of exoskeleton, at the Adelaide Biennial of Australian Art. We meet in Readings bookstore, in the Italian district of Carlton, where he is searching for a new art magazine he's heard of. He is short and slight, in the gray trilby he told me he'd be wearing. Although he's agreed to talk about suffering for his art, he warns me politely as soon as we sit down at a nearby café, "I am the least tormented person you'll probably ever meet."

Stelarc was born in 1946 in Cyprus and raised in Sunshine, Melbourne, by a family who would be reliably perplexed by his life choices. When he was growing up, his sister worked in a department store, one brother was a banker and another was a car salesman. Initially, Stelarc was going to study architecture at the University of Melbourne, before realizing he was more interested in the architecture of the body and going to art school. Since the 1970s, he has used his body as a medium, subjecting it to surgical construction, piercing, suspension, implantation, sensory deprivation and internal probing with recording devices. His practice is not to find out what the body is capable of, but to understand its limitations.

Throughout our conversation, Stelarc refers to his body as "the body"—as in, "Above the theater in Copenhagen, the body was suspended two hundred feet. A gentle breeze of street level turned out to be a much more powerful wind, and in fact the body was shaking."

By that point, 1985, Stelarc was well-accustomed to suspension work—piercing his skin with hooks and hanging in the air. This was before the practice became popular in "modern primitive" circles—he had to consult an anatomy book to figure out how to avoid inserting hooks into muscle tissue and major nerves. When he was amid his series of twenty-five body suspensions, a fellow artist—body piercing pioneer Fakir Musafar in San Francisco—reached out. "Fakir's approach was more connected to traditional Hindu practices," Stelarc says. "There was also a very enlivened sadomasochistic practice in San Francisco among some of the clubs there, but I very naively didn't know anything about that."

Unlike those who find suspension to be a quasi-spiritual experience, Stelarc sees the body as an object among other objects, to be assembled as part of a greater structure. As such, he rejects the notion that the act has particular meaning. While he concedes that such intense physical endurance results in the release of adrenaline, serotonin and endorphins, he finds the word "transcendent"—often used by those who suspend their bodies for BDSM practices—problematic. "Our language and our social and cultural expectations define the way we construct experiences we tag as spiritual or transcendent," he says.

Nor does he get a kick out of pain. "I would scream and shout in the dentist's chair as much as anyone would," he says. "The suspension performances were not done with sadomasochistic or erotic intent. The suspended body is a sculpture, a landscape of stretched skin. But inflicting pain does collapse the Cartesian distinction between mind and brain into one throbbing body."

For one work, Stelarc sequestered himself in a gallery for a week, tethering himself to the wall by two hooks in his back. "I stitched my own lips and eyelids shut with a surgical needle and thread," he says, "and for one week I couldn't see, couldn't speak, couldn't eat, couldn't drink. It was bloody cold in the gallery."

He disagrees when I venture that this must have been the most unpleasant thing he has endured. No, that would have been *Stomach Sculpture* (1993)—which entailed inflating his stomach with air in order to insert a medical endoscope inside a framework fifteen inches into his stomach cavity by way of a control cable, where it would then perform a choreography of opening and closing, extending and retracting. Prior to extraction, it had to be relied upon to safely close so as not to rake open his flesh.

"If you've ever had an endoscopy examination you'll know it's not nice," he says. "Without anaesthetic spray it's terribly painful inserting past the epiglottis, down the esophagus. And then when it's in there you feel internally ill. Not only did I have a control cable for the sculpture, which was about eight millimeters in diameter, but then an endoscope, which was ten millimeters in diameter, filming the whole thing. It involved six insertions over two days to film about fifteen minutes and it was one of the most difficult actions to undergo."

Stelarc's idea of risk assessment is minimal, and when his works are associated with institutions, such as galleries or universities, he dodges getting ethical approval where possible—since he's unlikely to be successful. "Of course you think through all the possibilities and problems—like, if you're going to insert a sculpture inside you, you have to make it a design that is not going to fail and must be elegantly simple in its mechanism while still being able to produce an interesting choreography in the body," he says.

It strikes me that he's mastered the sort of skills that might be necessary in elite military units: switching off adrenaline and cleaving emotional meaning from a cortisol-raising situation. But he's had no such training, has no kind of meditation practice and doesn't prepare physically for his performances. "I have friends who overthink, and it generates unnecessary concerns and anxieties, because the world is a complex place and all sorts of unexpected things happen," he says. "I think it was Nietzsche who said that there's a point in time when thinking ceases and the action has to begin."

It took Stelarc ten years to find three surgeons willing to assist his notorious *Ear on Arm* (2015). He pushes his coffee aside and rolls up his sleeve, allowing me to have a feel. An ear was formed out of a porous biopolymer scaffold and inserted into his left forearm. The skin was then suctioned over this scaffold, and over a period of six months his body absorbed the structure through tissue growth and vascularization. He had originally wanted to put the ear on his head, next to his actual ear, "but, you know, no surgeon would do it."

It does look impressively earlike, having held its shape. Originally it was to have a microphone embedded in it that would transmit the noises around Stelarc to an internet portal, allowing others to eavesdrop. He might even whisper things into his forearm for them to hear. But the site became infected when wires were introduced to test the microphone, and "I almost lost an arm for an ear." He was hospitalized for a week. Every hour, his arm and ear were flushed with a sterile saline solution, and he was put on industrial-strength antibiotics for six months.

It's hard to draw Stelarc to express any sense of sentimentality toward "the body." I try, though. When I take calculated risks and injure myself, I say, I feel a sense of failed responsibility toward my body, as if I am the steward of it.

"I don't see it that way," he says pleasantly. "My performances were never meant to generate meaning; they're states of erasure, or states of sculptural experience. The more performances that

I do, the less and less I think I have a mind of my own, nor any mind at all in the traditional metaphysical sense."

Long after we meet, his phrase "states of erasure" stays with me. At first it seems chilling, as though he is trying to will his being into nonexistence. But perhaps he means merely learning to see his body as a medium without his consciousness getting in the way. After all, a canvas doesn't try to apply meaning to an artwork.

STELARC AND JACK buck the mold of many endurance athletes and performers, in that they're not tapping into any deep-seated emotional anguish as fuel for their endeavors.

"For me, it's the opposite," Jack says, the third time I speak to him. He's in Croatia now, doing something too mysterious to yet reveal. "I thrive from inspiration. I don't know if I should try to reverse engineer it at the level of some kind of childhood trauma; I'd be trying too hard. Sometimes I recognize some physiological friction in my body—the fact that I'm not really enjoying it—but I capitalize on trauma. Everything is data, good or bad. It's your job to find the meaning in it."

I try to interest a newspaper editor in a profile on Jack and we go back and forth on edits for weeks. Her creeping concern about the ethics of Jack's eating mission becomes more and more prominent in our discussions. She wants me to hold him to account. Her voice rises on the phone as she mentions the zebra and the peacock. She worries that readers will revolt against him. She suggests I get another voice in, a vegan, "for balance." We are both relieved when I suggest we just drop the piece.

Jack's not surprised when I break the news. He knows his

actions can be interpreted as irresponsible and appalling, and while he's had enough debates to be able to stand firm in his beliefs, a nine-hundred-word article isn't the ideal forum to showcase this complexity. "Totally get it," he says. "This is a very triggering and politically charged discourse."

Actually, with his derring-do and flair for entertaining language, he could easily find a large audience by filming his own Bear Grylls-style survival show, or at least cultivating a You-Tube following. If he did, he'd probably be a regular guest on the shows of Joe Rogan and Tim Ferriss; yet instead his exploits have become known through word of mouth, and he's very careful about what he posts to social media.

"I have pondered fame a lot, then realized that fostering it would be mutually exclusive with the genuine nature of what I do," he says. "This has been my demon for the past fifteen years. I have these otherworldly experiences and I don't know how to portray them, because I have to be very careful about how I choose my words depending on who I'm talking to or it's a recipe for disaster."

He gives the example of Jordan B. Peterson as a public intellectual with left-field opinions who has been widely vilified, including during his well-publicized addiction and mental health treatment. It's a warning to Jack that boundaries need to stay in place. "So my answer to that is communicating what I've learned from my experiences to my consulting clients," he says. Roughly a quarter of his time these days is committed to giving talks at global conferences for thought leaders and psychedelic researchers, but also to being a shadowy consultant to wealthy entrepreneurs who want to broaden their horizons—be it through altered states of consciousness or some other guided adventure, he doesn't reveal. "These people have become extremely supportive of what I do and want me to speak to their networks."

He's due to be flown to the United States in a few months, where he will be paid ten thousand dollars for a one-hour speaking engagement. "Everyone who's attending is signing nondisclosure agreements," he says, making me ferociously curious as to what the other speakers will be discussing. It sounds like the psychedelic equivalent of Beyoncé being flown to St. Barts to sing to Muammar Gaddafi.

In May 2020, at some point on his return journey from a trip to Johannesburg, Jack contracted COVID-19—though from a fellow traveler, not from a bat. He was ecstatic. In the computer game of his life, he'd just "leveled up."

Breaking from his usual convention, Jack posted his stats—temperature, oxygen saturation, number of squats—in a series of Facebook stories that he filmed on his phone in his hotel room, along with his philosophical take on the virus:

I am digesting it like food … I can taste it in my mouth, my mind and my emotions. This virus is actually having a conversation with me. I feel almost like I'm surfing on a wave with a Komodo dragon on the fucking board in front of me. Komodo dragons are tough motherfuckers, they'll bite your face off but if they sense you're strong they don't do that … I'm actually enjoying this virus. It's a cool experience. I feel like it's testing my entire system and it's not finding any specific vulnerable spot to attack and destroy ... Viruses don't have any benefit in killing their hosts. They want to replicate. If they kill you they fucked up and you couldn't handle a relationship with them. I am handling a relationship with COVID.

After recovering—"within four or five days I destroyed COVID and went back to my life," he tells me—he ate nothing for eleven days, bathed in cold water, walked more than six miles a day and drank gallons of his own urine. "Urine therapy is very powerful, and for me it's been borderline lifesaving. I couldn't vouch for it more," he says, adding with what sounds like it could be a hint, "but that's a whole other chapter."

Chapter Three

BRINGING ORDER TO CHAOS
Bodybuilders

THE WOMAN IN the neon yellow sports bra and rainbow cheetah shorts leaves CrossFit Las Vegas and strides across the boulevard toward a car, pulls off her headphones and says to the man inside, "Did you just catcall me?"

He reluctantly confirms that he was blowing her a kiss—because she's sexy. She says, "I'm just going to tell you right now, a lot of women get intimidated when you do that. You've got dark windows, you don't have a license plate, and women feel really vulnerable. Most women are like, 'This motherfucker's going to throw me in the back of the car,' you know what I mean?"

Without waiting for confirmation, she continues. "I dress like this because it's hot as fuck and I work out really hard. Pow! I'm strong and powerful and I'd fuck you up. But what I'm saying is, a lot of women get really intimidated by catcalling. You got me? So that's what's up. What's your name?"

"Jason."

She fist-bumps him. "Jason, I'm Kortney. It's nice to meet you. Take care."

The man in the car didn't know he'd chosen Kortney Olson

to holler at. Kortney bench-presses men like Jason. She's the bodybuilder who's smashed watermelons between her thighs on television shows such as *Jimmy Kimmel Live, Guinness Book of World Records Gone Wild* and *Stan Lee's Superhumans*. Stan, creator of Marvel Comics, dubbed her "the woman with the world's deadliest thighs." When she did the same at the Arnold Sport Festival in 2018, Schwarzenegger himself had a gawk and snapchatted: "Now, that woman is definitely fit."

She's also leader of the GRRRL Army, which is her name for the hundreds of thousands of fans who subscribe to her online workout programs to "Get thighs like Kortney" and buy apparel from her GRRRL activewear company. They follow her candid chats on social media about anything from addiction to eating disorders—it was to her Instagram channel that she uploaded the video of Jason that she'd recorded on her phone. She's a prolific speaker, ably delivering impassioned speeches on whatever's hijacked her attention that day, from her car or bathroom or mid-workout, like she's her own reality TV crew.

Over the course of writing this book, I get to know Kortney well. She splits her time between Vegas and Melbourne and we hang out more and more often. She's generous to a fault, energizing to be around and one of the most driven people I've met; being busy, I come to realize, is a defining feature of bodybuilders. Everything about Kortney is larger than life.

Born at the beginning of the 1980s, Kortney grew up in the heyday of aerobics: all high-cut leotards and super-toned, tawny limbs. She'd watch her mother's *Joanie Greggains' Super Stomachs* VHS tapes in wonder, lamenting her own stocky tomboy physique but also determined to get fitter.

Fortuna, where she was raised, is a lumber town surrounded by the redwood forests of Northern California, in what has been coined God's Country. Kortney thrived on the rough-and-tumble side of bush life—the monster trucks, the tree forts, being the only girl on the softball team. Her brother, Brian, was eight years her senior, and she was devotedly drawn to the things she saw him do. Like him, she started lifting weights in their father's garage gym, surrounded by posters of topless girls. She even endeavored to pee standing up.

Perhaps it can be put down to a lack of attention during her mother's heavy-drinking, prescription-drug years, but Kortney also garnered a reputation for never being one to turn down a dare, be it riding a sheep at a rodeo or arm-wrestling boys. The latter skill served her well: she would later become Australia's first-ever women's arm-wrestling champion when she moved to the Gold Coast with her husband.

"Always wanting to go harder was pride-based," says Kortney, on a video call from Vegas when we first speak. "It wasn't about wanting to compete with myself; it's always been, 'I can do this better than you.' And primarily that competition was with men."

Kortney was fascinated by the idea of having a six-pack from an early age—partly from idolizing her older brother, but partly from an experience that left her feeling decimated. When she was seven, she was horsing around with her best friend and the friend's older brother. The brother asked Kortney to come with him alone into the woods, where he molested her.

"It was the first time I had ever disconnected from my intuition, because my friend hadn't wanted me to go and I wasn't about to listen," Kortney says. "And then I got violated."

Many women who have experienced sexual abuse will write the tale on their bodies. Some self-harm with blades or flames. Some develop an eating disorder, becoming very underweight, or very overweight (both have the effect of disappearing from the male gaze). Kortney chose the opposite route—strength. From that point on, she visualized herself as being powerful, and braided herself into a tougher being, muscle fiber by muscle fiber.

The path was not smooth. Kortney discovered that methamphetamine made her feel more focused and productive, and aided fat loss, but it became a volatile component of her life when she added alcohol. At eighteen she was raped by her boxing coach, a man who told her she had great potential and wanted to make her his final project. After that happened, she careened her way through a few years of university, clocking up DUIs and winding up in endless brawls.

Kortney had her initials, KO, tattooed prominently on her arm. In fighting terms, it also stands for "knockout"—"as in, I will, if you don't get the fuck away from me." In the tradition of wrestlers, fighters and porn stars since time immemorial, she had created an alter ego. The single-mindedness of bodybuilding appealed to her.

"The majority of female bodybuilders I know are fucked up," Kortney says. "A lot of them are addicts or alcoholics, and a lot of them have experienced rape or domestic violence—had some kind of baggage that they were running from—and bodybuilding has replaced it and become their new point of focus."

Her competition debut was in 2010 at the National Physique Committee Contra Costa Championships. Kortney competed in the "physique" division, which means the body is judged for clear muscle separation, full muscle bellies, and muscular development that is well-balanced between the upper and lower body. She placed fourth—game on.

Women's competitive bodybuilding didn't start in earnest until 1977, with the launch of the Ohio Regional Women's Physique Championship. That's when women's categories stopped being a bikini contest add-on to male contests. The International Federation of Bodybuilding and Fitness (IFBB), a major world governing body for bodybuilding, held its first Women's World Body Building Championship in Los Angeles in 1979. Its winner was Lisa Lyon, "whose sculpted, sinewy look caused a stir among fashion photographers," as Shaun Assael puts it in his book *Steroid Nation* (2017). "When Robert Mapplethorpe photographed her nude, with her arms outstretched in a flexing pose and a long willowy sheet draped over her face, the photograph helped Lyon become a female archetype for a new generation."

The 1985 documentary—though it was scripted and staged—*Pumping Iron II: The Women* shadows female bodybuilders as they prepare to compete, examining the debate over femininity versus steroid-assisted strength in women's bodybuilding. Through the steam of a group shower, the women are visible lathering themselves up, running their hands over bulging biceps and abductors. One complains, "I think one of the things that grosses people out about bodybuilders when they flex is this: people are seeing muscles on us that they don't even know they have themselves. It should be something that's beautiful to see. It's not gross to see your abs."

Bodybuilding is an expensive pursuit. There are special diets, supplements, endless coaching sessions and competition fees. To make ends meet, Kortney worked as a personal trainer, but then discovered, at the age of twenty-seven, that she could make four hundred dollars an hour by working in muscle fetish. In five-star hotel rooms she would "scissor" men's heads between her thighs until they blacked out, or overpower them in a wrestling contest.

"You saw a strong, powerful woman back then and it was like, 'Whoa, taboo!' Like it was a fetish," she says. "This was when CrossFit was just starting to come out and powerlifting wasn't a super-big thing yet." Being a strong woman doesn't seem so unusual now, when Brazilian fitness models such as Gracyanne Barbosa, Vivi Winkler and Anne Freitas, whose suspiciously well-developed glutes and thighs pump iron in professionally lit videos, have millions of followers on Instagram. But back then, Kortney liked the way her body broke societal norms just for its strength. Plus, she was a people pleaser. And she was good at it.

Men who saw her ads on a wrestling website would fly her around the United States and even beyond. When checking into a hotel, she'd tell the front desk the deal: "Hey, this is gonna look like *Pretty Woman* part two, but this is what's really happening. These guys are paying me a shitload of money to pick them up and carry them around. It's a trip, I know, but don't kick me out."

Having struggled with body image, muscle fetish was a watershed moment for Kortney. "I truly was fascinated by why these guys got into this," she says. "It helped me in my own journey because I had an epiphany one day when I was standing in a hotel room with a guy who had paid me five thousand dollars for three hours, and he was worshipping my calf muscles. I started to realize that men are programmed to like everything imaginable, and that's for the purpose of procreating. But as women, we are spoon-fed the images on the covers of magazines, as if that is the definition of success. I wanted to go out and tell every woman on the street what I'd learned."

If you're trying to imagine the demographic of Kortney's clients, you might be picturing high-powered CEOs or high court judges inverting their own power trips as a kink, but many were mild-mannered public servants, or still in college and had saved up for a session. She even enlisted one, a PhD student, to conduct an online survey to collect data. "All throughout the Middle East there are men who want to be picked up and carried around—piggyback rides, fireman carries, cradle holds, donkey races with them sitting on your back," she says. "In the UK, a lot of guys are into biceps, which is interesting, and things like arm wrestling."

Kortney had quit meth by this point but joined her mother in popping painkillers, because bench-pressing and donkey-riding dudes was taking its toll on her back. Just as the meth had aided in weight loss, she saw benefits in Vicodin and OxyContin. They seemed to make her operate more efficiently, at least at first.

OxyContin is a strong synthetic opioid—so strong that she'd find herself nodding off in the middle of choking a man out between her thighs. And then there were the performance-enhancing drugs, like pre-workout stimulants, which somehow seemed more legitimate because you could buy them in stores. These got her jittery. "With drugs it was never like I wanted to get fucked up," she says. "I always wanted to be in control. Drinking, not so much. I got drunk and I would turn into the devil. But when I was spun out on drugs, I would improve your property value and fix your credit score. I would go to the gym and get on the elliptical trainer. And you know, the heart rate monitor would be 199 [beats] per minute."

Everything changed when Kortney met a new client in a hotel in Australia and fell in love. British bloke David May worked for Jetstar, but would go on to become chief executive of the rugby team the Gold Coast Titans. His love only had two conditions: whatever Kortney did, she should be safe, and she should be happy. They were wise words to gift someone so wild at heart.

When we meet up in Melbourne for lunch, Kortney shows me the tattoo of Prince on her arm. She's used the singer to cover over the *KO* she got in her youth, because she decided that alter ego had a lot of negative energy associated with it. There's also a new *TT* tattoo, standing for "teetotal." Giving up drugs and alcohol was one of a few major moves to distance herself from her earlier life, not out of shame but in the spirit of evolution. She removed her silicone breast implants, suspecting that their leaking was responsible for the onset of her autoimmune disorder, Graves' disease, and gave away the muscle-fetish gig to become the volunteer strength and conditioning coach of the Titans's under-twenties squad.

Even so, she became the subject of lurid headlines when Australian tabloids got wind of the fact that the Titans boss had married a colorful character. "Exxxclusive: Mrs. Titan's Porn Past," ran one. "Titan Boss Wife Kortney Olson Tells of

Drug Hell" and "Gold Coast NRL Club Hires Fetish Porn Star to Train Under-20s Squad," announced others. As far away as England, there were headlines such as "Ex-Porn Star Helps with 'Cor' Strength."

This unanticipated spotlight sent Kortney into a shame spiral, wondering if she was indeed an awful person. "A year prior to that, there was an All Blacks player who married an actual porn star, and the whole country was high-fiving him—great job, son!" she says of Byron Kelleher and Kaylani Lei. "And then along I come and I'm the scum of the earth."

With all that media doing the rounds, a big-sister mentoring program that Kortney had applied for rejected her application, so she decided to buck up and start her own program. For the next few years she ran regular Kamp Konfidence retreats in the Gold Coast hinterland, aimed at giving marginalized girls the tools to become strong, confident women. (Further news stories debated whether having had breast implants made her the ideal person to do so.)

She also turned to her go-to: her muscle. Kortney competed in an arm wrestling competition and became Australia's first female champion. Don't they say something about success being the best revenge?

I WAS GUILTY of some rote preconceptions about what constitutes a bodybuilder when I began this research. Whitened teeth gleaming in rictus grins; sucked-in stances; stripper heels and posing pouches; skin as brown and gristly as a pork scratching. And the darker side: that screaming bro with the weights at the gym, making a show of dropping them as loudly as possible; misogynistic incel chat on internet forums; tabloid headlines about bodybuilder murderers with Napoleon complexes and roid rage.

Lex Luger is a perfect example. Before his retirement, he was the bodybuilder-turned-WWF-wrestler dubbed The Narcissist. In his memoir, *Wrestling with the Devil* (2013), he describes standing shirtless in front of the mirror every morning, flexing, before heading outside and admiring his reflection again in the tinted windows of his Porsche. In fact, no reflective surface could escape Lex unmolested. "On a couple of occasions, when different friends shopped with me, I'd abruptly stop in front of a store," he writes.

> After I had done this several times, someone finally asked, "What are you looking at?" "Something incredible in the window." Yeah, I was looking at something incredible in the window all right: me. I enjoyed looking at what I believed to be a perfect physical specimen. From the meticulously coordinated Adidas and Nike sports outfits, to the custom-made clothes, to the specific color highlights I had running through my hair, to my bronzed tan, everything had to be perfect.

In Australia, there was Aziz "Zyzz" Shavershian, the "King of the Aesthetics." Zyzz became an early YouTube celebrity in the mid-2000s, urging his Aesthetics Crew followers (a "coterie of mirror-licking narcissists," as *The Courier Mail* put it) to transform from "sad cunts" to "sick cunts." He died, aged twenty-two, of a heart attack in a sauna in Pattaya. Many news reports debated his probable use of black-market steroids, readily available in Thailand.

For some bodybuilders, being ludicrously jacked up is an aesthetic, in the same way that Lolo Ferrari, darling of 1990s television program *Eurotrash*, had the kind of breasts (each containing three liters of saline) that invited open gawking and disbelief. Romario dos Santos Alves, known as the Brazilian Hulk, was a security guard who started injecting his arms with synthol, a mixture of oil, lidocaine and alcohol used by some bodybuilders for immediate "swole" results. It solidified his muscles into boulders that bulged out of his neck and arms in strange formations. His biceps grew to two feet in circumference, becoming so unwieldly that he had to switch to needles traditionally used on bulls, and he nearly lost one arm to necrosis. There are many examples of these unabashedly unnatural comic book physiques. In fact, the Brazilian Hulk challenged the Iranian Hulk, Sajjad Gharibi, to an MMA fight that never occurred, and then there's the Russian Hulk, Kirill Tereshin, who has biceps like Popeye but a torso that suggests he's never been acquainted with a set of weights. It's not presumptuous to refer to Tereshin's injection of his arms with three liters of petroleum jelly as self-harm after it occasioned surgery to remove hardened jelly and dead muscle.

It's easy to gawk and laugh at these outliers. In a 1996 edition of *New Scientist*, bodybuilder and medical student David Huang critiqued a recent news story about steroid use that he felt continued the media's longstanding fascination with "bodybuilder bashing": "If this had been an article on anorexics, bulimics or anorexic-bulimic gymnasts, I am certain the journalistic tone would have been much less snide ... Bodybuilding is often singled out for ridicule because it is an easy target."

Much intelligent and philosophical analysis of bodybuilding has come from bodybuilders themselves, ranging from objectivist Mike Mentzer—heavily influenced by Ayn Rand—who created the Heavy Duty Training System: "It is only within the context of having properly developed your mind that you will be able to truly enjoy the achievement of your material values, including that of a more muscular body," to Melina Bell, professor of philosophy and law at Washington and Lee University, who has said that academia and bodybuilding complement each other. "If more of history's great thinkers realized this," she told *The Chronicle of Higher Education*, "they might have been able to get outside of their minds and kept from going crazy." Plato, who argued for the benefits of balancing mind and body, would no doubt have agreed.

The late postmodernist writer—and bodybuilder—Kathy Acker argues in her 1992 essay "Against Ordinary Language: The Language of the Body" that bodybuilding "can be seen to be about nothing but failure." Muscles are worked to failure; in order to grow, they must first fail. This growth, ironically, happens as the body makes its inexorable movement toward its final failure, death. Some days there is failure to reach the reps and performance of previous days, although the actions and nutrition of a bodybuilder are mercilessly structured, and so ought to produce a routine result of improvement. "By trying to control, to shape, my body through the calculated tools and methods of bodybuilding, and time and again, in following these methods, failing to do so, I am able to meet that which cannot be finally controlled and known: the body," she writes. "In this meeting lies the fascination, if not the purpose, of bodybuilding. To come face to face with chaos, with my own failure or a form of death."

In the art world, there's Cassils, who called their creation "CUTS: A Traditional Sculpture" (2011–2013) an "endurance-based performance." The transgender artist trained with celebrity coach Charles Glass at Gold's Muscle Beach in Venice to gain twenty-three pounds of muscle in twenty-three weeks. It's an inversion of Eleanor Antin's 1972 performance "Carving: A Traditional Sculpture," in which the artist crash-dieted for forty-five days. Cassils additionally used a "mild steroid" to allow them to regenerate muscle tissue faster.

"I had achieved a confusing body that ruptured expectation," Cassils told the online platform *Artsy*, also commenting on the disorientating effect of reaching new terrains of strength and power so quickly.

In pushing past the peacocking caricatures of bodybuilding, I come to develop a real respect for the pursuit and those who commit themselves wholeheartedly to it (because there really is no other way). It seems to me that bodybuilders are often problem-solvers, striving to bring order to chaos. A case in point is Karen Adigos.

I fly to Perth to interview Karen, a forty-year-old fitness instructor who works out of the Rockingham branch of bodybuilder mecca Gold's Gym. There, you'll usually find her in the vast weights room, under the watchful eye of the patron saint of Gold's, Arnold Schwarzenegger, who appears in a giant mural on the wall. Famously, he used to pump iron at the original Gold's, which has stood in Venice Beach since 1965.

Karen is muscular in body, but also in efficiency. I follow her sparkly white Lycra shorts through a tour of the gym. It's easy to forget that bodybuilders don't don mahogany skin and sequined underwear on anything other than competition day. For the other 364 days a year, they simply look like healthy folk in activewear.

Once back in her office, she apologetically shows me a color-coded schedule on her phone. Karen gets up at 3:00 a.m. to do cardio, leaving her partner, Ben, to fall back asleep, then drives the thirty-five minutes to Gold's to see her clients. If she's prepping for a competition—as she is at the moment—she slots in time with her coaches wherever she can, but always gets in a two-hour weight-training session. She finally gets home at around 8:30 p.m., leaving time just to eat and plan for the next day. It's almost as though Karen has come to view everything that filters into her life as data, whether that data is stress or the number of grams of protein in a meal. So she's going to be a hard woman to pin down, but she says I can shadow her workout with her strength and conditioning coach the next day, as well as her visit to a remedial therapist and her posing class. In the meantime, I'm free to use the gym. I've forgotten my goddamn shorts, so I do some kettle bell squats and deadlifts in my flimsy skirt, surrounded by perfectly groomed muscle-men and -women way too intent on examining their form in the mirrors to notice my predicament.

In the car the next day, Karen volunteers the links that she's made between her success in competitions and her childhood.

Karen grew up in the Perth port of Fremantle, having emigrated with her mother from the Philippines as a two-year-old. She never met her father, who served in the US Navy. While Karen's mother worked a night shift, Karen was left alone with a trusted male figure, who began molesting her from the age of five.

I think back to an insight of Kortney's: that stories of chaos or abuse in childhood are not uncommon with bodybuilders. Some big names in the industry have spoken publicly about this kind of history, such as Flex Wheeler and Kai Greene. Perhaps this is why many contemporary courses for personal trainers teach them to look for a client's "emotional pain point." Through some digging, they'll find out whether a client wants to train because they're sick of feeling like a victim, or because they're wanting to work through their anger, or just because they're worried they're not attractive to their spouse anymore, and then pitch the training to them as a panacea for that vulnerability.

Karen says that her abuser stuck to the usual script, warning her that if she told anyone it would break up her family. So she kept quiet. But as she got older, when he turned to physical violence, she started to act out. "At high school I got involved with stupid people and would smoke and try drugs," she says. "I used to shoplift as well. I think that was my way of getting attention—just not the right way."

She slips into present tense, emphasizing sharply. "I'd do *stupid* things because I was *angry* and it *feels* good and I can *forget* about it. Just doing little shit things, you know?"

At the age of sixteen, she formed a relationship with an older girl who introduced her to clubbing, ecstasy and cocaine, and she ran away from home. In her twenties, she fell pregnant to a man she wound up marrying out of pressure. Their relationship grew abusive and fell apart. Plagued by anxiety, and feeling unsupported, Karen had a breakdown.

Through much of her twenties and early thirties, she simply survived, muddling along working in hospitality and then moving into personal training. She often found herself attracting the wrong kind of men because of her unmet need for validation. "You shut off and stop caring," she says. "I wasn't in touch with my mind or my body. You have a lot of self-doubt, no self-confidence. Then I just woke up one morning and thought, *I'm sick and tired of everything*. Sick and tired of being shat on. I'd always had that victim mentality: *Why do things always happen to me?* Now I realized that nothing would fix me unless I accepted things for what they were and started focusing on things that were good for me. And structure was the key." Bodybuilding offered a rigid framework of reps, sets and portions, to which she had to comply to see gains—in muscle, but also in well-being. With them came relief from the unpredictability she'd come to fear in childhood.

We've reached the remedial massage clinic of Simon Lythgoe, in the same building as a CrossFit gym. Buff bodies filter in and out, and a few of them greet Karen. It's a bit of a one-stop shop for lifters.

It was Jane Fonda—another abuse survivor—who coined the workout phrase "No pain, no gain," and that certainly seems to be the case on Si's table. Karen takes off her ever-present waist trimmer belt and lies on her front. He inserts needles, which are hooked up to an electrostimulation unit, into her muscle tissue.

The current promotes the distribution of natural analgesics that reduce pain and stimulate blood circulation, speeding up the healing process. Unfortunately, it hurts like hell, but Karen says she tries not to engage with pain, whether it's pushing through reps of weights or being turned into a human porcupine.

"It's like trauma," she says. "If you absorb it, you just feel it more, so I ride through it."

I think of writer and bodybuilder William Giraldi who, in his book *The Hero's Body*, writes of the "chronic memory" of month-long meningitis that weakened him as a fifteen-year-old—"the successful shame of my body's failing." When Cassils was a child, they had undiagnosed gallbladder disease that caused rotting of their organs and stunted their growth, so as a teenager they turned to weight lifting to rebuild strength. "My body is a lab. I am a machine," they wrote.

William grew up surrounded by overtly manly men, in a New Jersey town called Manville, of all names. His grandfather, father and uncles were "celebrants of risk" who "valued muscles, motorcycles, the dignified endurance of pain." His mother left when he was ten. When he discovered weights, it was sheer relief; thirty minutes during which he forgot to feel even a shard of pity for himself. And that thirty minutes set his future course. "I needed to make my own creation myth," he writes, "to renovate my pathetic vessel into a hero's body."

I love that phrase "my own creation myth." Karen says something similar. "You've got to find yourself again to build yourself," she says, "and I thought that bodybuilding would really make me feel very powerful. I realized I needed to do something to fight. I needed to create some victory for myself."

Over the decades, some bodybuilders have adopted the regalia of the Ancient Greek and Norse gods, from the world-famous Mr. Olympia contest to references to Adonis, Thor and Odin. Others equate their craft with a higher power of a Christian nature, hashtagging their gym-mirror selfies with #repsforjesus. This alignment of the pursuit of physical perfection with God may jar, given the Bible's view of false idols, but it makes sense when you consider that the story of Christ was one of ultimate sacrifice. If you are an athlete dedicated to a lifestyle of suffering to a degree that is utterly perplexing to others, it might well be tempting to draw comparisons to Christ's glorious purpose.

Brad Turnbull, Karen's strength and conditioning coach, does not attribute potency to a higher calling. For him, it simply comes down to mental grit. I meet him as he runs Karen through an hour on the weights. It's "peak week"—nearly competition time—so they've stopped trying to build muscle and are now focused on keeping the muscles "explosive" so that they pop pleasingly when she poses on stage. At each machine she does a hundred reps of fifty, then thirty, then twenty, with forty seconds' rest between each set, and she's further tasked with visualizing the muscle contracting. They call it "the mind in the muscle."

Brad doesn't look particularly physically imposing, but he has the singular intent of a man on a mission. He talks at speed and moves fast, and it strikes me he's no stranger to folding the corners of blankets. He confirms that he served in the armed forces, as a cook in the Navy, though now he balances coaching with his job as a prison officer. Brad got into training when he was sixteen and was competing in bodybuilding competitions by seventeen. As Karen grinds, I ask him where he thinks extreme endurance stems from.

"I believe it's genetic," he says, "because no one can teach you it. I remember being a ten-year-old kid when my stepfather used to work on a farm. I used to go and help him, and if we had to dig a hole, I'd dig it all day long. He'd say, 'Stop now, it's time for a break,' but I'd have to keep going till I'd finished."

Peak week also means fine-tuning Karen's macronutrients, electrolytes and water intake. "Right now we're doing fat loading and I'm thinking to myself what things I could change," says Brad. "I know how much carbohydrates I've had her on and I'll see where she lands on Friday. I'm starting to get a picture of what I need to do. I might need to adjust that. More carbohydrates, less carbohydrates, more water, less water."

I notice Brad tends to talk about Karen as though she's a prize specimen that he's entering for best-in-show: "If I backfill you with carbs you'll lose conditioning ..."; "If I diet you below two thousand ..."; "About three days out from the comp we bring them back down to the normal water intake, which would be three liters, but they're still peeing like they've got six liters in them." It's a bit like animal husbandry, I say. Karen laughs. It is.

Back in Karen's car, I ask what she thinks of Brad's idea that people who can persevere through pain are born with that ability.

She considers. "I think we are born with perseverance but then trauma brings it into focus," she says. Trauma gives that innate sense of perseverance some meaning and purpose.

We arrive at Warehouse Fitness in O'Connor, where Daniela O'Mara is holding private posing classes. In her native Slovakia,

Daniela was a rhythmic gymnast until the age of twenty, before moving into musical theater. Upon relocating to Australia she competed in her first bodybuilding competition at the age of thirty, and rebranded on social media as the Aussie Fitness Princess.

After some cajoling from Karen and me, she demonstrates a posing routine: walking to the front of the stage, holding poses and making spectacularly sassy quarter-turns to show the judges each angle of her physique. Daniela is lithe and moves fluidly, so it's no surprise to learn that before she became a coach she competed in the fitness division, which usually incorporates a gymnastics routine. Her former husband, Mike O'Mara, is the founder of the competition that Karen is entering, the IFBB O'Mara Classic—and at which Daniela will be a judge. Competitive bodybuilding can be incestuous.

Daniela tells me that in the figure category, judges will be looking at shape and symmetry, but also femininity. There should be more of a taper to the torso than with the bikini competitors, and more defined shoulders. "Presentation"—essentially beautification, poise and femininity—is also important.

As Karen practices her routine, Daniela refines Karen's posture. "She is exceptionally sassy for the figure category, which is mainly tomboys, so she's got something special," Daniela says approvingly. "Don't drop your shoulder, Karen."

A WEEK LATER, I'm back in Perth to watch Karen compete at the Hyatt Regency. I arrange to meet her at the hotel's Grand Ballroom after she's done her hair, makeup and tan touch-up. I'm nervous for her. There are only two women in her figure division, and it's not a drug-tested competition, which might give Karen—a natural competitor—the disadvantage. She seems to have made peace with her worries today though, and takes me to the mirrored metropolis backstage for a nose around.

Each competitor has staked out their own area and populated it with bejeweled cases for their bikinis, high heels and snacks. The snacks are body hacks. Coca-Cola or port wine dilates the veins and makes them pop pleasingly because of the high sugar content. Potato chips provide a burst of carbs, the intake of which will have been carefully rationed over the past months, and salt, which dehydrates. Similarly, black coffee, a diuretic, draws water away from the skin surface to make muscle more defined.

Women wearing silk robes and thongs flit between the hair and makeup stations, or take their place at a tanning tent. There's a lot of "pumping up" going on—getting blood flowing to the muscle by using weights—and the last-minute run-through of posing routines.

Some competitors are teenagers. Others are in their forties, fifties or sixties. The uptake of the sport by older people is very healthy. Sometimes the impetus is purely practical: a person who has had to quit another sport due to injury might be able to safely lift weights. Other times it's the transformative nature of bodybuilding that appeals, especially to those already going through a transition period. In middle age, many women in particular find their role changing, perhaps through their children gaining independence, or menopause, or a long-strained relationship coming to an end. I have met a woman who took up competing at forty-seven after leaving an abusive marriage, and another who started at forty-five, feeling that she had entirely lost herself within the confines of marriage and motherhood.

I join Karen's friends at a table. They're all sitting very upright, nursing green juices and protein shakes. No one is taking advantage of the bar, I notice. Like most serious bodybuilders, Karen rarely drinks alcohol. In fact, her language reminds me at times of AA's twelve-step recovery, with its emphasis on gratitude, mindset and structure.

As competition day progresses, I realize that breast augmentation is a necessity in many of the women's categories in order to be judged favorably. At one point, when Karen pays our table a visit, a man from the judging table comes over to say a quick hello. She introduces me—"This is Jenny the journalist"—and he starts to talk about the fitness category, sponsored by and mostly populated by Perth's Best Girls (suppliers of "sexy female pub and party entertainers"). Earlier, I'd seen the competitors in this category doing their quarter-turns during the prejudging, with the free arm that wasn't on their hips undulating like seaweed in the tide. Over the refrain of Destiny's Child's "Bootylicious," the judges called out instructions. "Nice and wide, mate"—that sort of thing.

"You can see they've all got different body shapes—tall, short—so basically you pick the one you most want to sleep with," the man explains, then retreats back to his post.

"That's just his sense of humor," Karen says hastily.

When it is Karen's turn, everyone at our table grabs their phones and jumps up to take photos. Karen had described to me what it felt like to walk on stage in her first competition and her fear of messing up her routine. "You feel like your whole body is cramping," she said. "You're sweating. All these people are look-ing at you, judging you. What are they not going to like?"

You might assume that this kind of scrutiny and the fear of not being good enough would exacerbate a sense of rejection that was instilled in Karen during childhood. She managed to master it, though, by consciously deciding to take on a different mindset—that word again—for every competition since.

"I thought, you know what? I've worked so hard for this day," she said. "Don't look at it like you're being judged. Look at it like you're representing a physique that you've created. Yes, there's still that sense of needing external validation, because you want to prove that you can create consistency. But it gives you a sense of power, I guess. It shows that you're not that quiet person peo-ple don't think has potential. And it's true, a lot of people who have succeeded at bodybuilding have been through the same kind of thing, but they now know their value."

This afternoon, Karen wins the women's figure category. Pop-ping and polished in her gold bikini, she holds aloft the trophy, which depicts two flexing figures on a plinth. Then she puts it down carefully. There is time for a few more victory flexes for the photographer.

KORTNEY NO LONGER competes as a bodybuilder. In her final IFBB show, in 2015, she watched other women getting called out ahead of her who didn't even have visible abs. And she realized she was done with it. Within female bodybuilding, the bulkier divisions were attracting less and less interest, while the bikini division, introduced in 2009 and more akin to a beauty pageant, was becoming the most popular. "It's a lot more appealing to get pretty girls bending over in a bikini to show their hamstring split than some totally ripped-up woman who's taken too many roids," she says.

There are whole websites dedicated to discussing whether athletes are "natty"—natural—or "juiced." Kortney's physique is natural, although years ago she flirted briefly with the steroid oxandrolone, sometimes known under the brand name Anavar, which tends to be preferred by women because it increases the metabolic rate and burns fat while building lean muscle, bulking up the shoulders in particular. Kortney disliked the side-effect of acne. She tells me that while steroids give an athlete a cutting edge, those who take them still work hard, so to discredit them as cheating isn't seeing the bigger picture. Playing fields are never level in sports, for all manner of reasons—genetics, injury, wealth, time and training resources among them.

"Being a drug addict, my biggest concern was that I would not want to stop," she says, "and I was just so petrified of morphing into a man when I really enjoy being feminine. But when it comes to certain types of professional athletes, I say more power to you, because you're out there bashing your body to entertain the rest of the world. I'm typically just like, women, do what makes you happy ... but at the same time, be aware of the consequences."

Kortney probably didn't intend that comment as encouragement to me personally, but the idea of embarking on a Cassils-style experiment in the name of journalism, rather than art, appealed greatly. I'd also been getting the nagging feeling that I ought to have shadowed a bodybuilder in the "swole" ilk —someone who had taken steroids for years and gone harder than everyone else by massively inflating their physique. Mike Bolkovic, who was profiled in the VICE Sports series aptly titled *Swole*, admitted to VICE that, despite having been rushed to the hospital on a few occasions, "I enjoy walking places, especially walking with my girl, knowing that people are thinking, *Holy shit—let me stay out of this guy's way.* I'll be truthful on camera: right before I came here I took a shot because I thought, hey, it's going to make me feel better on camera." It's a stark contrast to Karen's emphasis on mindset.

So, in the middle of Melbourne's coronavirus lockdown, I decide to visit a doctor who prescribes performance and image enhancing drugs. The devil makes work for idle hands.

"Right, yeah—as long as it's an art project," one of my wrestler friend deadpans. He's a few months into his latest cycle of black-market testosterone, which he injects into his deltoids and thighs. He's put on a few pounds of muscle, gets constant erections and his chest hair has spread luxuriantly over his stomach. He's curious as to what benefits *I* will enjoy.

I must admit, the former illicit drug user in me is hungry to experience what steroids might feel like. A righteous gale blowing about your ballast? An unshakeable self-belief that dilates the pupils? Another friend who used to take Anavar and peptides told me that she could suddenly spot the other women at the gym who were also using, as though she'd put on X-ray specs. Really, it was the fact that they were "killing the pull-ups" that gave it away, but I remember that feeling myself from when I abruptly quit alcohol and could suddenly see, with laser beam focus, who else in the bar was a nondrinker—it's about what you redirect your attention to.

That friend recommends I see an antiaging doctor, whose remit ranges from facial rejuvenation and hormone replacement therapy to human growth hormone. Before my appointment, I'm directed to have an exhaustive pathology report done on around seventeen vials of blood.

A few weeks later, in the waiting room, I sit for fifty minutes as the previous patient's session runs over. Once I'm in the consulting room, it becomes apparent that the delay was due to the doctor, who looks pleasingly like a Flash Gordon villain, taking great relish in his work. We look at his screen, scouring the results for my body's shortfalls. The doc tells me that my thyroid, cortisol levels, liver, kidneys, cholesterol—and many more unfathomable things—are all tip-top. In fact, my immune system is so good, he says, that the coronavirus won't stick; at which point I wonder if the phrase "with a pinch of salt" ought to apply to everything.

He leaves his analysis of my hormone levels to last, much as you might save the best bit on your plate. "These hormones are natural steroids," he points out. "As soon as I say 'steroids,' people think ooh, bad stuff."

Naturally occurring IGF-1 regulates the effects of growth hormone in the body. The figure drops as you age (although increases with sustained exercise), but mine is higher than the normal range for my age group. "Ooh la la," the doctor says. 'Tell me truthfully. Are you taking growth hormones already?'

I wonder if he's flattering me, until he muses, "I suppose you could have a pituitary tumor."

Peering at his computer screen, he reads out my free-testosterone figure. "At a seven, it's at the bottom end," he says, in a tone that sounds loaded with *ask me more.* "Your muscles aren't as strong as they could be and you don't feel as good as you could, in terms of confidence."

There's little about that summary that doesn't make testosterone sound immediately seductive. I'm swayed by visions of Linda Hamilton's sinewy arms in *Terminator 2: Judgment Day* (1991), in the famous scene where her character, Sarah Connor, does pull-ups in a mental hospital. Nearly thirty years later, Hamilton tried to re-pop those guns for *Terminator: Dark Fate* (2019) by taking testosterone. Specifically, she told *CinemaBlend*, she was aiming for 5 percent more muscle mass, "and then I turned into an angry man, who was like … My blood pressure was spiking and if somebody pissed me off I was just like [unintelligible noise]."

"What can we do about that?" I ask the doctor of my low score.

"Plenty of things. Beautiful things."

The doctor recommends a testosterone gel for women—generally given to older women with low libido—at a strength of 0.5 milligrams per milliliter, which I must rub into my skin twice a day on my bikini line, where the skin is thin. "If you get it inside you, congratulations," he says. "You'll have a powerful orgasm." [Side note: untrue.]

I turn down an offer of DHEA—a precursor to testosterone and estrogen that has been nicknamed the "fountain of youth drug" and should further boost T levels, but which seems a bit, well, cancer-y—and walk out of the consultation room with my prescription for testosterone and some flash-looking vitamins.

The doctor halts me just before we reach the reception desk. "I like to see people at their superhuman best," he says, conspiratorially.

Yet upon receiving my pump-bottle from the compounding pharmacist and perusing the label, I suspect I'm expecting too much. I've read posts on bodybuilding forums from women discussing their doses of black-market testosterone. These tend to be around 60 milligrams per week. My wrestler friend injects 500 milligrams a week, typical for a male bodybuilder. I'm on 1 milligram a day. I've practically been given a homeopathic dose; in fact, the pharmacist probably just whispered the word "testosterone" into the gel.

I know then that it is going to be a flawed experiment. And so it proves. After just four weeks of half-hearted application, I abort the mission early. There's nothing to report but minor skin irritation from the alcohol-based gel and a vaguely horny feeling whenever I rub some into my bikini line. I can't tell if it's genuine heightened libido or a Pavlovian response to pulling aside my underwear, but in any case, it's nothing I couldn't muster up unassisted.

I can see the appeal of taking up more space, though. I'm reminded of a former bodybuilder who spoke anonymously to *MEL* magazine about the way female contestants are passed over if they are too muscle-bound: "All our lives, women are shrinking, vanishing, disappearing," she said. "Then the IFBB, this organization that should be helping all of us achieve our goals since we're paying them megabucks in competition fees and membership dues, publishes these memoranda saying women should 'downsize' by 20 percent. Bullshit. I use steroids because I want to be 'more than,' not 'less than.' I want to take up space. I'm only five-foot-three, but I weigh 150 pounds. I take up space. I want to see other women take up space, too. I want them to spread out across the stage, as big as training and chemistry allow them to become."

Of course, there is resistance to this kind of boldness. The social media project *You Look Like a Man*—founded by Indianapolis-based Jessica Fithen, who became the heavyweight Strongest Woman in the World in 2019—documents the derisive comments received by female weight lifters and strongman competitors when they post their training videos, because to some men, women building muscle is the ultimate in unforgivable tourism. Click through to the profile of the guys leaving comments, and they tend to either be flexing in a gym with their shirt off or promoting their coaching business. Sometimes both.

Fitness is a field that has more self-appointed gatekeepers than most, which calls for a different kind of endurance from those they endeavor to keep out. As one female strength athlete put it to me, "This industry can be the last frontier for people who can't survive in other fields, and they hide behind it." Worse, she says, people who might politely be called "old-school" tend to fantasize that they live by the law of the jungle. I'd been telling her about a strength coach I approached for inclusion in this chapter, who declared me an "outsider." After detailing his decades of experience and his credentials in various sporting disciplines ("never finishing worse than third, ever"), he fired up: "That you think you can dab your toe in it and learn everything in five minutes is an insult to me, my job and everyone in fitness and martial arts."

The astrophysicists, neuroscientists and academics I've interviewed over the years could have said similar, I suppose, but they seemed to comprehend that being contacted by a journalist for an expert quote wasn't a tactical grab for their turf.

The comments documented by *You Look Like a Man* are designed to decimate the confidence, such as when one random coach, angered by a woman's request that he keep his unsolicited advice to himself, tells her he will use her "laughable" videos as tutorials for his clients as examples of what *not* to do. Jessica turns such "corrections" of form, foul insults about appearance (pointing out "camel toe" or debating whether a woman is on steroids and therefore has an enlarged clitoris) and concerned medical advice ("you'll injure your uterus") into inspirational memes—superimposing the comments over sunsets or mountain scenes. There's even a merch range. It includes a sweatshirt that reads "Probably Steroids" in the same font as the "Enjoy Coca-Cola" slogan, "Take Up Space" and "Big Clit Energy."

Over the years, Kortney Olson has had her thighs fetishized by men who paid good coin to caress their mighty girth, but has also bumped up against hundreds of the aforementioned kind of dumb comments on the GRRRL social media pages. Her approach is generally to ignore stupidity and reward positivity, but she couldn't resist making a video for Instagram about "correctile dysfunction." *Do you suffer from an uncontrollable urge to explain things?* it begins, over footage of her husband Dave despondently kicking sand on a beach in his Oasis T-shirt. As luck would have it, he stumbles across a gym and starts eagerly correcting women's form.

"It's been going on forever," Kortney tells me. "When women are stronger and more powerful and don't give a fuck, then those guys will fizzle out."

The whole point of GRRRL is to welcome women into fitness who might previously have felt excluded by gatekeepers. The women that the label sponsors, or has as ambassadors, have ranged from top-tier UFC fighters, such as Zhang Weili and Rose Namajunas, to amateur powerlifters and strongman competitors and disabled athletes.

"There are women who are really good at sports who don't look a certain way," Kortney says. "They deserve to have more of a platform because they have really good messages, but they don't have that platform because they don't fit the stereotypical athlete. We want a new horizon of athletes to watch in ten years' time because a younger generation saw people who looked more like them and so they weren't intimidated to try something."

Actually, visit any online community of women who are lifting—among them Old Ladies Lift ("Age is inevitable, weakness is not") and Barbells Before Boys ("It's not about what your body looks like, it's about what it can do")—and you'll notice there tends to be a narrative of building confidence that runs in parallel to building the body. Conversations revolve around taking up space, challenging fat phobia and rethinking beauty norms to embrace strength.

Dr. Stefanie Cohen is a Venezuelan 25x world-record holder powerlifter, who weighs around 120 pounds but can deadlift 440. She wrote some thoughts on women and strength that have been widely shared:

Women need iron. Not the vitamin. The barbell. We are trained by the world around us to have fucked up ideas about our bodies; iron unfucks them. We are taught that the only good direction for the scale to go is down, and to agonize ritualistically when it goes up. Iron teaches us the power of gaining weight for strength and gives us another weight to care about—the weight we are lifting. We are taught to think of our bodies as decorative, an object to be looked at; iron teaches us to think of our bodies as functional, our own active selves, not passive objects for another's regard. Whole industries exist to profit by removing from us our confidence and selling it back as external objects. Iron gives us confidence from within through progressive training and measurable achievements. We are taught to be gentle and hide our strength or even to cultivate charming physical weakness until we start to believe our bodies are weak. Iron teaches us how strong we can be.

The phrase "cultivate charming physical weakness" hits a nerve with me. My backstory is oddly similar to Kortney's. We were both sexually abused at the age of seven by an older boy; both raped at eighteen when wasted; both developed a taste for alcohol and speed and embarked on paths of self-destruction. The difference is, I had an instinct to make my physique more waif-like, easier to take advantage of—call it conditioning. Kortney chose the opposite route. From that childhood incident onward, she visualized herself as being powerful. Belatedly, now that I train in a sport, I realize that this feeling of power is intoxicating.

And as the gatekeepers know, the more you experience that feeling, the less you care what people might think, or want, of you.

Chapter Four

ENGAGING IN EDGEPLAY

BDSM

T HE MAN I'M meeting is a strongman coach. He trains people to flip tires, hoist Atlas stones and deadlift three times their body weight. But today I'm talking to him about his other job. As a professional dominant, he has a Twitter account—that I've given a good browsing—in which he posts photographs of himself carrying a naked woman over his shoulder, or standing by some desolate outbuilding, brandishing a self-made leather restraint. "Sir James" is like his villainous alter ego.

When booking Sir James, you'll be asked what experience you have with bondage, discipline and impact play (that's striking, with various implements or appendages), and he'll get very specific about it. This conversation will provide the parameters within which he can move during your visit. He is the dom, after all, so once a session starts, he's in control. His pre-appointment instructions might include "Wear a dress, or a skirt and blouse, that I can take off easily at my own pace."

These are the instructions I'm given, anyway. I figure that the full Sir James experience is a claimable expense for an author writing a book about endurance.

The fetish dungeon is in the industrial backstreets of

Melbourne's Oakleigh South, almost indistinguishable from the auto-repair shops and warehouses surrounding it. I press the buzzer at a discreet-looking door and am met by a woman who takes me to a small reception room. It's separate from the exit, to avoid clients sighting each other. If you're being walked down the hallway to a dungeon, or the medical room, or the cross-dressing room, your fetish provider will also check the coast is clear.

While I wait for Sir James, I flip through the book of services, which include electrical play, genital torture, anal fisting, sensory deprivation, tickle torture, suspension, voyeurism, golden showers, medical procedures, cuckolding, public humiliation and babyism (including diaper change). Facilities include a gyno chair, crosses and stocks for naughty villagers. There's a poster on the wall that warns, *no condom, no sex.* Sex? How suburban.

Sir James enters, so tall he blocks out the light. He's dressed like an off-duty fascist in a crisp shirt, black leather braces, black pants and black lace-up boots, and he has the kind of full beard favored by strongman athletes. He asks me a few questions about phobias and medical issues, and explains the verbal red/orange/green code for stop/mmmmmaybe stop/don't ever stop. For the first time, anxiety creeps in. It's not dissimilar to the feeling when I committed to a bungee jump—the wait at the top platform was the worst part. Let me just hurl myself into the abyss already.

Admin complete, he leads me to one of the dungeons, which is painted black and red. Mirrors line one wall. In a corner, there's a shower. Sir James snaps on surgical gloves. Within seconds I'm in a headlock and bent facedown over a black leather table, being tethered to it by straps around the wrists and ropes around the ankles. He explains a rule. There are no one-word answers: every utterance must end with "sir"—even unintelligible protests.

Over the next ninety minutes, I'm put into various submission holds—against the wall, on the table, across the concrete floor. I warn him I'm experienced in Muay Thai. He responds with a guillotine choke. As it turns out, Sir James has a solid background in wrestling and jujitsu. I've done a bit of wrestling training myself, so we incorporate some moves. I laugh at the sight of myself in the mirror, legs flailing, or face flushed and pressed against the table.

Tradition and common sense dictates that my bottom takes most of the impact work. It holds its own through floggings with a cane, a switch, a studded paddle. Sir James observes it doesn't easily bruise. "We both know you tried," I commiserate, and earn myself more thrashing. He tells me I'm a "brat"—a subgenre of submissive. Somebody who answers back or disobeys orders is a brat. That's a convenient comeback for a dom, isn't it? Especially when "brat" seems to cover both impudence *and* independent thought.

With abrasion now upon abrasion, I press myself against the concrete floor to escape the blows and hinge my legs at the knees to defend my rear escarpments. I'm not a screamer, but I find that the dungeon is a place in which you can yell with impunity. And it feels good.

Afterward, I drop into a service station to buy a can of Coke, because something sugary is advisable after a good flogging. In the restroom I look over my shoulder into the mirror and examine Sir James's latticework on my flesh. A few friends get surprise photos. It's important to make memories, isn't it? We're living in the experience economy now.

A WEEK LATER I'm back, this time in journalist mode. I meet Sir James in the dungeon office, which has a heavy green banker's lamp on the desk and is stocked with bondage magazines. Oddly, one of the pictures on the wall is of a couple having vanilla sex. Making love, even.

Sir James has changed into his civilian wear of a T-shirt and jeans, and is slightly out of breath, having just seen off a client whose partner is sadly no longer interested in bondage. "It was basically a lot of spanking, being tied up and reassuring her that she was a dirty girl," he says.

It's not unusual for a dom to assume the title of Sir, Master or Daddy. Sir James is a "sir" because he feels it has a more liberal authority than the traditional master/slave dynamic. "I don't like my visitors or play partners to be robotic," he says. "I like to engage and dominate them, encouraging them to have a bit of fun fighting back before accepting their fate."

Before he was a sir, he would go out drinking every weekend with his friends, but realized he wanted to do more with his life. Then came an unexpected segue into working as a dominant. "Some people I met through athletic endeavors recommended I try it. My demeanor and imposing body and frame of mind gave me an edge when it came to expressing what a lot of clients want," he says.

He began with a few months of observation and then undertook a year-long apprenticeship, working with clients under supervision. Eventually, he was invited to work as a professional dom at the dungeon.

Most people who come to see him for the first time only know that they want to be engaged in activities where they feel pain. "Something's happened during sex, or they've seen something or read something, and they realize they really want that," he says. "It's like this unknown expression. In a very short period of time, they go from 'I want to experience this. Please don't hurt me *too* much,' to 'I want to go home crying.'"

I understand this desire to up the ante. During our conversation my eyes keep sliding to the picture of the love-making couple, and eventually I realize I'm just looking to the right to search my imagination. Sir James will mention some appalling activity, such as spending an hour wrapped in plastic wrap, blindfolded and shut in a box with only a breathing tube for air, and my initial recoil is swiftly followed by consideration. Clients being highly suggestible—including to themselves—is something he has to keep an eye out for.

"With new people, their minds often race ahead of where they are," he says. "I know I'm going to lose clients because I won't do the most extreme things on the first day. We will certainly work up to that."

He doesn't ask in-depth questions about a client's life, but he'll get to know them intimately through experimentation. Can they be tied up for ten minutes without struggling? Can they adapt to and breathe comfortably in awkward positions? Progress must be incremental.

"A lot of people write and say, *I saw some fetish porn where somebody had their nuts crushed in a vise and were getting punched in the face,*" he says. "They write in and say, *Will you injure me? I'm not going to do that.* There's a difference between inflicting pain and causing permanent disfiguration. It's an industry where as a professional you also have to be honest with yourself: *What do I feel comfortable doing?* And permanently injuring someone is not my fetish."

Has anyone asked him to kill them, I wonder.

"People have asked for things that *would* kill them, but they probably don't realize it," he says. "Like ropes around their neck so they can be tied into certain positions upside down for an extended length of time, or to be choked and held unconscious, or for me to sit on top of them for five minutes."

It's impossible to tell how many of these emails are just people getting off on writing them, but the staff at the dungeon have to assume that a small percentage of potential clients might have a real fantasy of dying.

"If that's the case, we will often direct people to ..."

Your mate Dave?

"A suicide hotline."

THE PURSUIT OF feeling alive—really alive—can bring us close to death, as I discover when I recruit a black belt in jujitsu to choke me unconscious.

I've never so much as fainted before, but having begun to move in fighting circles, curiosity about the infamous blood choke has naturally got the better of me.

It's a common maneuver with those skilled in certain martial arts, and maybe some rogue bouncers. It's also known as the sleeper move, the rear-naked choke, the *hadaka jime* and the *mata leão*, which translates as "lion killer." Unlike the air choke that asphyxiated singer Michael Hutchence, it works by cutting off the blood supply to the brain from the carotid artery or jugular vein, and in just ten seconds can render someone unconscious. Not relieving the pressure can result in death.

I sit with my legs out flat in front of me and my arms up in the air so that the black belt can ascertain the exact moment I lose consciousness. There's an instant, as he squeezes my neck harder between the forearm of his left arm and the bicep of his right, that I think, *Oh. I don't like this.*

And then I'm waking up after what feels like a whole night's sleep, so deeply have I rested. I'm confused to see the black belt at my side. What's he doing here? Then I look down and see my hands curled up near my chin, my fingers pincering the air. I'm having a fit. I'm embarrassed that I've lost control of my body in this way ... in fact, wasn't I just saying something a second ago that I now can't remember? I vaguely recall a sound coming out of my mouth. Then I notice that my mouth, too, is moving of its own accord, as if I'm loudly appreciating a spoonful of soup.

"I'm sorry, I think I'm having a funny turn," I say—the most weirdly English expression I've ever uttered. And then it comes back to me, as though my mind is a computer that has finally finished rebooting. "Oh. You were choking me out."

He nods gingerly. "That was surreal," he says.

Exhilarated, I jump up. It's a bit like the feeling of getting off a terrifying fairground ride and wanting to go straight back on; a survivor's high. No wonder when professional prankster and *Jackass* star Steve-O filmed himself getting choked out by former UFC fighter Chuck Liddell, he jumped for joy into Chuck's arms upon coming to.

"Another one for your bucket list," the black belt says. Then he adds: "I haven't done that before either."

On the way out to a bar that night, I recount the incident to a friend and realize that I'm gabbling in a manic fashion. I'm also driving too fast. I cut the journey short. Exciting as the experience was, I decide against tempting fate this way in the future. Strokes have been known to occur—though very rarely—and while it's fun to dance around the void, I at least try to only dance around each void once.

In a sense, fetish providers are there to facilitate someone's dance, but they've cannily developed ways to make clients *feel* like they're in danger when they're not actually at risk.

"I'm going to pull back the curtain a little bit," Sir James says. "If you put your hand against someone's trachea without much pressure, they will feel like they're choking—but you can ask them a question, they can respond. And if you can talk, you can breathe."

Similarly, being blindfolded will often make impact play feel more violent than it is, and a blunt but cold knife feels shocking, almost painful on the skin, as does being sprayed with icy water. They're not quite the "enhanced interrogation techniques" of Guantánamo Bay, but you can bet that some service provider somewhere would be happy to oblige with waterboarding or rectal tube feeding if you ask nicely.

"You can also overwhelm people by not giving them time to acclimatize, which will often make them hypersensitive," he says. "As long as you don't do this kind of thing to a degree where you're going to cause psychological damage, these are ways of mitigating danger to the person while still giving them the feeling like they're going through something intense."

As a strongman coach, Sir James has a grasp of the fundamental mechanics of human movement that's vital when administering bondage positions and the safe range of motion of a limb. It's also taught him when to push and when to stop. He discreetly surveys a client's heart rate by checking the pounding of their neck, or looking for dilation of their pupils. He'll stay conscious of any change in their mood or in how they respond.

"I've had to monitor quite a few athletes, working intensely with them to find out what their breaking point is," he says. "So if I'm hearing from a client that they love being hit, and they're smiling all the way through it, I still need to be able to monitor that and say, 'Hey, we're getting to the point where you might not recover the way you want to tomorrow.' Their body is flooded with hormones that are making them feel great."

The relationship between pleasure and pain is complex. It's accepted that pain and reward processing engage many of the same regions of the brain, but further explanations span neurobiology, evolutionary biology, psychology and philosophy. The Ancient Greek philosopher Socrates, when unchained by guards in preparation to drink hemlock—his death sentence for corrupting the youth of Athens—is said to have rubbed his legs in relief and remarked on how curiously synergic the two states are: "For they are never present to a man at the same instant, and yet he who pursues either is generally compelled to take the other," he said. "Their bodies are two, but they are joined by a single head."

FOR WEEKS BEFORE her performance, Anna practiced dragging a stone around her backyard in South London. The ropes with which the stone was trussed were attached to the skin of her upper back by two steel hooks. She didn't worry about what the neighbors would think—they were used to such strange sights.

During the week, Anna runs a design studio. On weekends, she goes by flamboyant stage names. She shapes her hair into a Louise Brooks-style flapper bob and dons an ensemble from her enviable wardrobe of fetish wear. She travels the country to take part in performances of *shibari* (the Japanese art of rope bondage, the intricate designs of which might take up to three hours to complete) or flesh hook suspensions (in which she is hoisted aloft for up to thirty minutes by ropes attached to her skin). She usually collaborates with her preferred rigger, Damon, as well as fellow performers, who either facilitate the suspension or are suspended along with her in one synergic super-structure.

For tonight's performance at a fetish club, Damon trusses Anna's near-naked body with ropes. When he pierces Anna's back with the hooks and equalizes the tension of the ropes, she has the usual shock response. Sweat begins to run from her palms. The longer the wait between piercing and actual suspension, the greater the anxiety and discomfort. Some people get nauseous, or even vomit.

Anna drags the stone back and forth across the stage to accustom her skin to the weight of it. She is aware that the audience has pushed right up to the front of the stage, but there are so many lights angled at her that she can't make out any faces. Another woman on stage slices at Anna's back with a knife, drawing aesthetically pleasing lines of blood. Then it is time.

As Damon hoists the stone aloft with a pulley, Anna is raised beneath it. There's a moment, just before her toes leave the ground, that used to feel terrifying—the moment of defying gravity. But it's since come to feel liberating. Once aloft, she spins through the air above the audience, with Damon pushing her feet or working a rope.

"This rock that was my burden actually comes to empower me and lift me up," she explains. "There might be a minute or two where you just have to breathe through the pain and process it. Once you've been out there for about a minute to two minutes, you're fine. All the pain goes—all of it. There's nothing."

It's known within BDSM circles as "subspace" and, crudely put, it's the body getting high on its own supply. The endogenous opioid system responds to pain, producing three families of opioid peptides in the central and peripheral nervous system: beta-endorphins, enkephalins and dynorphins. The pain can induce a euphoric state. Being on the receiving end of strenuous physical abuse as a submissive will often do the same—subs often report a trance-like state and out-of-body feeling.

Jennifer Bene, an author working in the genre known as "dark romance," has written about this reaction. While someone may still feel a cane or belt land on the skin, they're only aware on some level that there is pain. "I find myself leaning back into the strikes for a moment (when the high starts to take over), and then I sort of feel like everything melts," she writes. "Like the way you feel after a really good massage, just languid and soft and warm. Each new strike sends you further out into subspace, and it is a perfect place where my brain is blissfully empty and quiet. Where I feel safe and protected and cared for, because I know my dom is watching out for me and that knowledge allows me to let go and just … float."

Perhaps subspace is like a runner's high—the kind that ultramarathon runners often report hits them when they've pushed through more pain than they thought they could bear. More than a second wind, it's a meditative zone in which the physical shackles drop away. In his book *The Rise of the Ultra Runners*, Adharanand Finn describes his experience: "One hundred kilometers. My body rebelled, my mind almost gave up the ghost, but step by step we pulled together. And for eight crazy miles near the end I was flying … I went from broken to blitzing, from dead to a jumped-up racehorse after an adrenaline injection."

When he confides in other ultramarathon runners after the race, there is no surprise. This is what many of them run for. It reminds me of something Anna told me that made me laugh: "I think people often view riggers as a type of sensation vending machine."

Damon cuts the ropes and Anna drops to her knees like a marionette. The literal comedown is usually followed by a high that slingshots into an emotional comedown, known as "sub-drop." Many liken it to the "bluesy Tuesday" experienced by those who take party drugs on weekends.

"It can be brutal," Anna says. "People in your life need to be very aware that it's going to happen. It's not negotiable; it's part of it. You can't have that endorphin load come out of you and not have the drop."

On a biological level, the endogenous opioid system has been overloaded and needs to rebalance, as does the endocrine system, which produces adrenaline, among other hormones.

The first time Anna performed a suspension, her state of euphoria lasted four days. Now, the crash usually comes sooner, two days after a performance. She has a support group that meets up at the pub for post-mortems. "I can be high as a kite," she says. "Then the crash is really hard. You feel very vulnerable and like you're going to cry at any second. You just want to watch movies and hide in bed all day, but I'm often doing these performances on a Friday or Saturday night and then I've got to be back at work on the Monday. That's the hardest thing for me—to be doing this activity in this almost alternate reality, and then sitting in front of the computer and being Anna again. It's such a messy divide between those two things."

Just as Luke Tyburski, the ultrarunner we met in Chapter One, must plan his next race as soon as he collapses from the previous, Anna's anticipation of her next suspension is as addictive as the act itself—and planning it feels a bit like insurance against a dip in mood.

"My day-to-day existence is focusing on that," she says. "It keeps depression at bay, because that's something that I've struggled with my whole life. But then it reaches a point sometimes where the planning becomes completely anxiety-inducing and you feel that you can't possibly cope with all the things you have coming up."

Before she entered the world of BDSM, Anna says she was divorced from her body, living mainly in her head and neglecting her health. "My perception of my body and mind was that they were two very separate things," she says. "BSDM and suspension have allowed me to realize that they are completely connected. Practicing aerial yoga every day keeps me sane; it's like a compulsion."

She'd already been frequenting goth and BDSM nightclubs, and dipping a toe into different activities, when she went with a friend to a "rope hang"—a casual weekly event where a group would gather at someone's house to practice *shibari*. "As soon as the rope touched my skin, I knew I had found something special that really connected with me," she says.

Part of the appeal may be the thrill of doing what other people could not. In some of Anna's performances, Damon wraps her entire head in rope and then inverts her—suspending her upside down. "I have a lot of people come to me afterward and say, 'How do you do that? I would totally freak out if that was me,'" she says. "I think people who have fears of confinement watch in horror as my head is bound, imagining the person inside the rope panicking. But for me, it's the exact opposite of panic. The rope touches my skin and I feel peace and calm and *right*. All my worries dissolve, my fears disappear. It feels like a blessing."

I think back to a friend in London who'd always joked that she was a Pollyanna: dressing conservatively, making a glass of white wine last all night, getting on well with her parents and holding down a steady retail job. But, when she plugged into a fetish community, Sian suddenly lit up like a Christmas tree. She'd take me shopping to the gay sex stores in Soho, where she bought giant dildos shaped like fists. With shining eyes, she'd regale me and other friends with tales of having to wear a diaper the day after a good pounding, or of being filmed while slapped about the nose with an erect cock. "I said, 'Thank you, Master, may I have another?'" she recalled, her face radiating a sublime light. It was a new dawning of Sian.

I ask Anna if she finds herself dialing things up a notch each time she plans a suspension. "Yeah, big time," she says. "At one show I did four hooks in the back because I took my friend Kelly's weight. She was tied in a hip harness beneath me, an extra 143 pounds. You go into it dealing with the known risks as best you can. For example, I'm aware that hook can hold a 220-pound guy, so two hooks should be fine, but just in case we put in four. We rehearsed all different hand signals because we didn't know how loud the music would be."

Human skin is the strongest part of the suspension system. It's more likely a knot would come untied, or a rope, which concentrates the hold to a smaller area, would snap. If a rope failed while Anna was inverted, she would likely fall on her head. Safety harnesses are an option, but to *completely* eradicate risks strikes Anna as at odds with the whole idea. "That's not saying I want to die. It's just that a big part of our daily lives is being safety-aware and people suing one another. If I bring that into my hook suspension practice it's like The Man's got control of that too. My body is not for your rules."

Back in 1990, sociologist Stephen Lyng coined the term "edgework," now frequently used in BDSM circles, as "voluntary pursuit of activities that involve a high potential for death, physical injury, or spiritual harm." The referent was in the work of Hunter S. Thompson, who described himself as "a connoisseur of edgework," meaning he constantly pushed boundaries. In BDSM terms, edgework could mean breath play (erotic asphyxiation), fire play, blood play, knife play and barebacking (sex without condoms), and it's a step beyond the fundamental principles of BDSM: safe, sane and consensual. Lyng wrote,

"Edgeworkers of all stripes ultimately seek to get as close to this critical line as possible without actually crossing it."

The notion of edgework has been applied to extreme sports, crime, stock market trading and dangerous occupations such as firefighting. Perhaps there are similar attractions in drug experimentation, too: Lyng observed that many who engage in these activities—such as mountaineers—find the experiences yield partakers "permanent knowledge of what it is to feel so totally 'wired' or 'alive.'"

There are two schools of thought when it comes to suspension play involving piercing. One is that "free bleeding" is more natural, and the other is that sanitization is paramount. "When you just let the blood flow, I feel like that's a really important part of the process," Anna says, "but you also get people who prefer to dab up the blood constantly. For example, you get professional body piercers, for whom cleanliness is everything and bleeding is terrible. I think that if you don't want to bleed from having a flesh hook shoved through your skin, maybe flesh hooks aren't for you."

That's a bit like deathmatch wrestling, in which the wrestlers (who generally don't get tested for blood-borne viruses if they're performing on a local level) hurl themselves onto the same barbed wire and thumbtacks, and wind up slipping around in each other's claret. There's a berserk commitment to going all-out, and they're certainly a different breed to the high-flying wrestlers in superhero spandex.

That's not to say more extreme is always good. Anna says that hook suspension has attracted a cohort—men, usually— who treat the ritual competitively, and more as an extreme sport.

"They run around trying to be the most hardcore, without much connection or spirituality attached," she says. "In my mind, it's more of a sensory thing. The people that love doing it, it's almost like one rope, that's all they need, and they melt away. They have permission to let go. The rope is a conduit for surrender."

WHEN PEOPLE CRY in Sir James's hands, their first instinct is to apologize. He thinks that's because in Western society there's a stigma against public displays of emotion. "Even in your own family, you can feel very incapable of expressing your true inner self, at being upset about something," he says. "But crying isn't necessarily a negative thing. Sometimes it's just raw emotion."

It's disappointing for him if a person doesn't leave in a more serene, peaceful state. "You don't want to get to the end of the session and they have a dark cloud over them," he says. "Many people come in to express that malaise, or even to revel in it, and then get it out of themselves and leave happy."

Like the octogenarian who felt as though all eighty of his birthdays had come at once whenever he visited Sir James. He would travel hundreds of miles to Melbourne from northern New South Wales, to indulge in bondage as far away from everyone he knew as possible. "He had almost zero mobility, so it would take a lot of patience, over three-hour sessions, to get him into more obscure positions and cock ties, and to take photos of him, make him feel like he was involved in that stuff," says Sir James. "He'd be really happy but he was still a grumpy old man, complaining about everything that happened on the way there—while tied up naked, upside down."

Even doms can experience mania during play. Sir James describes it as a "top high." "You need to monitor yourself for talking fast, hyperactivity and everything being the 'best ever' during the session," he says. "It could be triggered from adrenaline and feelings of power."

Sir James doesn't claim to know what motivates people to see him. The popular assumption that somebody must be psychologically damaged to engage in BDSM irritates him. Then there's the theory posited by psychoanalyst Robert J. Stoller, author of *Pain and Passion* (1991). In interviewing masochists, he discerned a pattern: they had all withstood painful and invasive medical treatment as children. He theorized that they reenacted and eroticized this trauma, with their adult selves now in control. Closer to home, I know a psychologist who specializes in treating adults with autism spectrum disorder. He's observed through these clients that BDSM often appeals for three reasons: the sensory stimulation; the secure and comforting sensation of bondage (weighted blankets offer much the same); and the idea of having a role with clear rules. There are multiple threads from BDSM enthusiasts with ASD on Reddit that back his theory.

The late Bob Flanagan was a performance artist who used BDSM as the message and his body as the medium. His long-term partner, artist-dominatrix Sheree Rose, called their sadomasochistic dynamic a collaboration, while Flanagan said he felt more like a mad scientist than a guinea pig. Flanagan crossed over to an alternative music audience in 1992 when he appeared in the Nine Inch Nails clip for "Happiness in Slavery," as someone willingly being tortured to death by a machine.

The 1990s were the salad days of artful self-torture. *Body Modification Ezine* was launched, later spawning the Pain Olympics, which escalated to acts such as slicing scrotums and popping out the testicles. The industrial metal band Genitorturers formed in Orlando, Florida, fronted by Amazonian body piercer and pro-domme Jennifer "Gen" Zimmerman. The Jim Rose Circus—which included acts such as The Amazing Mister Lifto, who would hang heavy weights from his penis—found a wider audience by joining the influential touring festival Lollapalooza.

In the 1997 documentary *Sick: The Life and Death of Bob Flanagan, Supermasochist*, Flanagan's response to the question he was always asked—Why?—was: "Because it feels good … because it makes me feel invincible. Because my parents said you can be whatever you wanna be, and this is what I wanna be. Because it's nasty, because it's fun, because it flies in the face of 'normal,' whatever that is." And, he observed as someone living with the painful condition of cystic fibrosis, "The masochist is actually a very strong person. I think some of that strength is what I use to combat the illness."

There's a wealth of anecdotal and scientific evidence to back up this last idea. It seems that constant pain can be relieved by impact play, partly because of the release of endorphins—our natural painkillers—but partly because the brain's focus is moved to a precise area of the body and the volume of those pain receptors elsewhere is muted. There's also the psychological aspect, of giving meaning to pain and being in control of it.

Some of Sir James's clients come to him because they are experiencing pain due to illness, including cerebral palsy and multiple sclerosis. "It can range from people who have period pain wanting me to spank them as a comedown sort of thing, all the way to people with chronic pain," he says. In fact, the dungeon sometimes invites kink-friendly registered nurses to discuss overexertion, emergency procedures, triggers and safe methods of body placement.

For many people, BDSM operates on a deep psychological level, be it the power to subvert long-held feelings of shame, the ability to develop trust in another or find the intimacy that might be missing elsewhere in their lives. "And they'll have an improved mood and better productivity for believing they are experiencing something more potent than the average person could," offers Sir James, "whether it be being tied up, or isolated, or the person 'most used' in sex."

This mentality of 'If I can survive that, I can survive anything' reminds me of something Anna confides. "When you overcome fear, you can apply that to any everyday situation," she said. "It actually made a big difference in my work life, to be able to go: 'Bitch, you overcame gravity: like, fuck! Who cares what this arsehole wants?' You did this 'impossible' thing, so you can do this other 'impossible' thing."

As Sir James says, "In a way, BDSM is more extreme than self-driven activities like running an ultramarathon. You enter an almost meditative state from being forcibly tied up—like, 'I will endure'—and that endurance comes from an ability to survive, rather than an ability to push through and keep running. As someone who has run an Ironman, I can say that there's quite a difference between what I saw in myself, finishing that race, and someone who can survive beatings that even I don't think I could endure."

He also wonders if BDSM can be some kind of replacement for religion. It's a physical catharsis that might resemble a feeling of absolution. "The idea of it being penance isn't necessarily a negative thing," he says. "It's something we do because we want to feel pain that will ultimately make us better, psychologically. Whether that's a smart, logical choice that we would make if we were completely devoid from our hindbrains, who knows, but we can either channel that into something good or into something bad."

I book in one last session with Sir James, to make sure I've got everything pinned down. Leading up to the session, he sends me photos of a variety of outfits he could wear, including a traditional wrestling singlet that he's striking a pose in, but we settle on his jujitsu uniform of shorts and a rashie. I had gone to a kink night called Provocation in a dingy Melbourne nightclub not long before, and couldn't help noticing during the jelly wrestling that many participants seemed to have a solid background in jujitsu—the close-combat martial art that largely takes place on the ground. Perhaps it's not surprising that the sport can attract people interested in exploring the dynamics of domination and control elsewhere, too.

This time we spend the best part of ninety minutes wrestling on mats in a different dungeon room—one with a human-shaped iron gibbet cage in one corner. In the hour before my appointment, I killed some time in the neighborhood by having a massage at a Thai parlor. I knew that my masseuse's good work would soon be undone, but I didn't anticipate that the oil would leave me so slippery. Sir James has to work hard to apply a good grip, often using a knee, or his whole body weight, to pin me. I don't mind. Ever since I can remember, I've contorted so awkwardly in my attempts to fall asleep that I've dislocated my shoulder, or woken with one arm twisted behind my back, all circulation cut off. Rarely does dawn break without a limb having to be violently thrashed back to life. Perhaps some of us seek restraints for comfort, like the swaddled infant. Or maybe we just want a thorn for our paw.

As I sprawl on the floor, Sir James adopts the stance of a trophy hunter above me and flexes a muscle. Later, a friend wonders why I'd want to literally be under the boot of patriarchy, but I find something that Anna said relatable: that she'd spent too long neglecting her body for her intellect. Securing such an experience for myself—with the suite of hormones it releases—feels far more invigorating than the cheap dopamine reward of watching porn on a screen. In any case, once Sir James is done with his victory pose, he joins me on the floor for a lie-down and a casual chat.

When our ninety minutes are over, I shake his hand and say goodbye. I suspect I'll be back for special occasions: birthdays and Christmas, and possibly Eid al-Fitr, Hanukkah and Thanksgiving.

An ordeal as a gift to the self—another facet of endurance that I was not expecting.

Chapter Five

LEVELING UP
Belts and Iron

RICHIE HARDCORE AND I meet at Melbourne's Marvel Stadium late on an October morning. I spot him in the crowd straight away. Hard not to: he's Brylcreemed and buff, and wears a smile that seems kind of sad around the eyes.

We've got good tickets to UFC 243—a massive mixed-martial arts (MMA) event put on by the sport's most hyperbolic promotion company, the Vegas-based Ultimate Fighting Championship. There's a large contingent of New Zealanders in the crowd, since there are three fighters from Auckland's City Kickboxing gym on the card. As we walk to our seats, so many of them stop Richie to say hey that he looks modestly embarrassed.

"I'm not the man anymore," he insists. "I definitely noticed the change when I retired from professional fighting. New Zealand is a small place, and when I was successful I could go to clubs and the bouncers would be, like, 'Yo, what's up, dog?' My fragile ego totally loved it. There was all this external validation that, as someone with a weak identity, I really thrived on."

This is typical Hardcore-brand honesty, built on a yearning to relate and connect. Having hung up his belts, Richie is now a Muay Thai coach, but also a public speaker and activist, and counts New Zealand prime minister Jacinda Ardern as a friend. His talks range from destigmatizing mental health issues to preventing gendered violence to living well. The shirt he's wearing today, arms cut off to fashion into a tank, reads *Fighting Saved My Life*.

I first encountered Richie when he was booked to give the keynote at a New Zealand drug and alcohol conference a year after I had done so. As his interests spanned both addiction and fighting, I wanted his take on why some of us push our bodies to extremes, particularly in light of a UK study published in 2016, led by sports psychology professor Lew Hardy and professor of sports Tim Rees. Of its thirty-two participants, sixteen were super-elite athletes who had won multiple gold medals at major world championships such as the Olympics, and sixteen were elite athletes from the same disciplines who had not. There were commonalities between the two groups, such as being raised to have a strong work ethic, but also a crucial difference: the researchers found that every single super-elite athlete had experienced childhood trauma—whether due to parental death, family breakdown, emotional and physical abuse, bullying—compared to only four of the elite group. Could it be hypothesized that such adversity gave these athletes an edge in terms of mental toughness, ruthlessness and resilience that their peers did not possess?

The most successful athletes can compartmentalize, storing away worry and pain in a part of their brain so it does not interfere with their performance. Children experiencing abuse also do that well. Their schoolfriends wouldn't have a clue.

Of course, traumatic things happen to many of us in

childhood, but we don't all win Olympic gold. Perhaps this can be explained by another of the study's findings. These super-elite athletes' "foundational negative critical events" occurred in close proximity to positive critical events linked to their sport, such as discovering and taking up the sport, or achieving a new level of success, or the introduction of a significant coach—in other words, a cathartic lifeline was offered, at an opportune time, to a child with a lot of hurt emotions.

Richie, as it happens, has lots to say about the link between childhood adversity and sports, and after our initial interview we keep in touch socially. At one point, he sees a video post on Instagram of my stumbling Muay Thai training and makes me a tutorial video—after asking via DM whether unsolicited advice would be okay. The first time we meet, he checks if it would be okay to give me a consensual hug as we part.

We don't reach consensus on everything. He's straight-edge—his adopted surname refers to hardcore punk, of which "straightedge" is a subculture that attracts followers who are typically sober. So he promotes abstinence from drugs and alcohol, as opposed to my harm-minimization slant—although he does support decriminalization of cannabis. And he gives school talks about the dangers of porn culture, so he's vehemently *anti* the kinds of acts I describe in the next chapter. That's his prerogative, but as our long and lively debates on the matter reveal, he can't wrap his head around the idea that some women might enjoy them.

Today's fights start early so that the pay-per-view event can stream in the late afternoon in the United States, but plenty of punters are weaving to their seats with cardboard trays of beer. Richie doesn't drink (some of his other T-shirts state *Do Muay Thai, Not Meth* and *A Sober Mind Is a Powerful Weapon*) not because he ever had a problem, but because of what it did to his dad. Growing up in West Auckland, he'd see his father hit his mother and get hauled off by the cops. Richie started jumping in when things got violent between his parents.

"Are you familiar with that concept about the first thousand days of neurological development and how our personalities take shape?" he says. "Well, my first thousand days weren't peaceful. And eventually, I wound up beating my dad up a few times because I got good at fighting, but that shit fucks you up—it's not a healthy thing to do. And you don't have the language to talk about that. I needed somewhere to put all my hurt feelings. I used to walk around and look at the ground, and I thought I was real fucking ugly. I'd apologize for voicing an opinion. I was equal parts insecure and angry."

Richie's father is now sober, but even back then he had his moments of trying to rectify the damage caused to his son. One idea was to take Richie, then thirteen, to a taekwondo class. "My dad told the instructor, 'I'm not doing a very good job as a dad, can you help my son?'" And Richie really took to it. He discovered he loved having bruised knuckles and black eyes. He loved consensually kicking the shit out of people, if he's honest. Not because he's a violent person, but because it made him feel alive and worthwhile in a way that nothing else had.

"It was the first thing that made sense to me and gave me a sense of belonging," he says. "As my body changed and I started beating grown men in sanctioned combat while still in high school, I realized it was the process. Like, if I do this, the chance of success is higher. If I follow the steps, my body changes, I get stronger, and so too do my self-esteem and spirit."

This reminds me of something psychiatrist Bessel van der Kolk has said. He wrote the best seller *The Body Keeps the Score* (2014), and he believes martial arts to be among the best treatments for traumatic stress because it reinstates a sense that the individual "is not a helpless tool of fate." Working to that principle, there are trauma-informed martial arts programs emerging globally—usually aimed at women who have experienced sexual or domestic violence—such as the Fight Back Project, founded by Melbourne fighter Georgia Verry, and Grapple Isle's Trauma-Informed Jiu-Jitsu, designed by Tasmanian Claire Hayes, among others.

Not that the road to invincibility was smooth for Richie. If he had a bad day's training or lost a fight, he'd be despondent. "Literally, in tears." But Richie found he was apologizing for everything less and less, and not putting himself down nearly as much. Then girls started asking him out. He's now a first-degree black belt in taekwondo and a multiple New Zealand Muay Thai champion.

"Not to sound too melodramatic, but for me personally, having my face full of stitches seemed better than having my heart full of stitches, and I see that for a lot of people," Richie says. "My brother is running ultramarathons in his forties and he used to shoot heroin. I think for every person that's doing ultramarathons or getting their face smashed in doing Muay Thai, they're finding a pathway to peace of some sort."

The UFC 243 headline fight today is Israel "Stylebender" Adesanya versus Robert Whittaker, and it's a spectacle. Adesanya has enlisted his old dance crew, Broken Native—the name of which he has tattooed across his chest—for a fierce, choreographed entrance. It's an intimidation tactic, much in the vein of the Maori haka, that he persuaded UFC president Dana White to bend the walk-out rules for.

Once in the UFC-trademarked fighting ring known as the Octagon, he writes Whittaker's name in an imaginary notebook—a "death note" that's a nod to his love of Japanese anime. Clearly, he's determined to stamp his personality all over this fight, like a dog cocking a leg. (On that note, two years earlier he pretended to whip out his penis and piss on the Octagon canvas, as though marking his territory.)

By contrast, Whittaker paces into the arena quickly, skulking with his hoodie pulled down low over his head. His choice of music, Cold Chisel's "Khe Sanh," is probably designed to remind the Australian locals where their loyalties should lie. But waiting for Whittaker is his new nemesis, who's intent on treating the Octagon like his own personal playground.

Richie has been giving me a consensual lowdown on each fight. For years he coached Brad Riddell, who won his slug-fest of a fight earlier today. While Richie didn't train Adesanya, he's watched him rise through the ranks. "Israel was a skinny kid, and coming in from Nigeria to small-town New Zealand, he got teased and all that sort of shit," he says. "Now he's one of the baddest fucking dudes on the planet. I've been acquainted with him since he was fighting in shin pads, and he built himself from the ground up."

Adesanya himself told the site *MMA Junkie* that "I was like a runt back in high school," and according to an interview he gave to the *NZ Herald*, "You have to be able to talk to yourself in the right way." He describes crying into the mirror one day after being picked on; it became his moment of reckoning. "I was upset and then eventually I just kind of talked to myself and then eventually I just started doing it … I've been doing it for years now."

Adesanya was inspired to train in Muay Thai after watching the martial arts movie *Ong-Bak* (2005), in which a young villager travels to Bangkok to recover the stolen head of an ancient statue of Buddha from a group of thugs. It's a classic hero's journey, and now Adesanya endeavors to make himself the hero of his own narrative.

As sports site ESPN would later put it, Adesanya's ostentatious entrance at Marvel Stadium today "could have been a disaster. If things had gone wrong in the Octagon, Adesanya's dance would have become a humiliating meme." But Adesanya drops Whittaker in the second round with a left hook to the jaw. Moments later, the new undisputed middleweight champion scales the Octagon fence to double-flip the bird at his next opponent, who's seated cageside. It may be just another moment of showmanship, but Paulo Costa—in a shiny disco shirt, looking admittedly quite like the Latino singer Ricky Martin that Adesanya compares him to—looks authentically displeased.

Martial arts movies have a long history of attracting the underdog and promising the kind of legendary elevation Adesanya has experienced. From *The Karate Kid* (1984), *No Retreat, No Surrender* (1986) and *Sidekicks* (1992) to *The Power Within* (1995), countless action films have taught dweebs that martial arts can help you protect yourself *and* save the day.

Teenage Richie loved the *Karate Kid* franchise, which kicks off with new-kid-in-town Daniel LaRusso becoming the target of a local gang. Richie would practice all the moves, even standing on poles and doing the crane kick, trying not to roll his ankle. After walking home from training at the local community hall, he'd launch into the latest batch of VHS tapes he'd borrowed from Blockbuster Video, lying on his bed surrounded by posters of The Cranberries (yeah, he'll admit it) and book quotes that he'd stuck to his walls.

"I've always been over into sentimentality, I guess," he says.

It wasn't only Hollywood movies that roused young martial arts wonks. During the explosion of Hong Kong cinema in the 1960s and 1970s, plotlines tended to be political, but still relatably concerned with the underdog overcoming an oppressor. As the documentary *Iron Fists and Kung Fu Kicks* (2019) explores, the 1967 Hong Kong riots, in which pro-communist youth protested against colonial rule and police brutality, inspired a swathe of bloodier, angrier films concerned with vengeance. These included the excessively gory *One-Armed Swordsman* (1967), in which a young man's father is killed, and the only keepsake he has is a broken sword. In *The Chinese Boxer* (1970), a kung fu student takes on Japanese karate thugs. Set in 1940s Japan-occupied China, it reflected the sentiments of Hong Kong's student-led nationalist movement over the Japanese occupation of the Diaoyutai Islands. It was a similar story in United States in the 1970s, where, at the tail end of the civil rights movement, African Americans embraced kung fu movies alongside blaxploitation flicks, perhaps relating to the vengeful, nonwhite underdog who could bust some moves. Breakdancing takes its cues from kung fu movies.

Movies about boxing tend to document the grizzled or down-and-out protagonist's last slug at redemption. There's 1931's *The Champ*, where a former world heavyweight champion's biggest fight is now with the booze, or 1949's *The Set-Up*, where an aging boxer's manager accepts bribes that he'll lose, or 1956's *Somebody Up There Likes Me*, where a career criminal comes good by winning a title fight—or the titular Rocky, a nobody-fighter and debt collector who gets a freak shot at the world heavyweight championship. By contrast, the message of martial arts movies is clear: with a mentor and some self-mastery, you can hone your mind and body and become utterly unfuckwithable.

WHEN CAMILLA FOGAGNOLO was seven years old, she broke her arm playing on a swing on the family farm. "I landed on my hands, which I shouldn't have done," she admonishes herself.

But you were *seven*, I protest.

I look at her incredulously. We're sitting in the reception of Artgym in Hobart, a gas station-turned-kettlebell-heaven with a 1980s Memphis aesthetic. Camilla is a former Olympic weight lifter and a strongwoman who deadlifts cars and hoists stones at contests around the world.

"I'd done judo for a year," Camilla says, shaking her head. "I should have known how to break a fall."

Ordinarily, a broken bone would be a major life brag for a seven-year-old, but Camilla was raised to be stoic. She was homeschooled by her disciplinarian father, and along with reading, writing and arithmetic, she was taught to be tough. So she tried to smack the bone back into place. When that didn't work, she wrapped herself in a blanket and sat quietly on the couch, shivering from the shock. "Because then maybe it would just be all right, and I would get away with it, and nobody would know."

Camilla and her older brothers, Priscus—now a pro MMA fighter—and Regulus, grew up halfway up a mountain in the Tasmanian town of Dromedary, a twenty-five-minute drive from Hobart. The children would often be left to their own devices during the day, when their father taught in Hobart secondary schools and their mother worked the farm. Persistence and self-sufficiency became necessary tools.

Sports were their only socialization with the outside world. Every day, the young Fogagnolos were put through a drill of qigong-style breathing exercises; an uphill circuit run; rounds of tumbling, somersaults and handsprings; rope climbs; and wood splitting. The regime was masterminded by their father, Roberto, who had grown up learning gymnastics, weight lifting and field athletics in his native Italy. Roberto's own father had been shot in a firing line during World War II (then posthumously made a war hero), leaving the boy to be raised by a single mother who scraped to get by. That sense of hardship was duly passed down to the following generation.

"Looking back, it was a strange setup, because we were always taught that ego is nothing and 'yourself' is nothing," Camilla says of Roberto's Soviet-style ethos. "So even though we were striving to be as good as we could be, we were still meant to put ourselves last."

One of the greatest golfers of all time, Tiger Woods, has described his father Earl's coaching techniques, taken from

Earl's psychological warfare training as a Green Beret. These tactics ranged from Earl making distracting noises when the adolescent Tiger was trying to concentrate, to shouting slurs—all aimed at pressure-testing and cultivating mental toughness. "He would push me to the breaking point, then back off, then push me to the breaking point, then back off," Tiger said. He'd been given a code word if he wanted the abuse to stop, but that word was "Enough"—a word loaded with surrender. Which, of course, was unacceptable.

In his autobiography, *Open*, Andre Agassi described the modified tennis ball machine, nicknamed "dragon," that his father, a former Olympic boxer, built to fire balls at 110 miles per hour at his seven-year-old son. The idea was that his son would hit a million balls a year—around twenty-five hundred a day. To add to the pressure, his father would crowd him and yell at him.

For someone raised in an environment where complaint was not tolerated, Camilla has had a lot to bite her tongue about. She was sexually abused between the ages of nine and ten by somebody the family trusted and, just like the time she broke her arm, she deduced this to be her own fault. As a teenager, she was kicked out of her home by her father for rebelliousness: she was smoking and drinking, and pushing for the same kind of freedoms that Priscus enjoyed.

"I thought I should have the same rights as him and I'd argue with my parents all the time," she says. "There was one big, big argument between me and my dad when he screamed at me for hours. I woke up the next day and I had my bag packed. I sat down with him and said that I'd like to leave for a week and sort my head out, then make an effort to try and be better."

Roberto's response was: "I'll open the gate for you, and once you're gone, you're gone. You'll never see the farm or your brothers or your mother again."

Harsh as it was, his threat was idle: two days later he'd managed to track her down through her boyfriend and they smoothed things over somewhat. But Camilla soon fell into a violent relationship, the shame of which was sharpened by the popular belief that someone so well versed in karate, judo and powerlifting couldn't possibly ever come a cropper to a bloke. She also experienced far too much loss for a young person: the agonizing death of the beloved horse that had become her only form of escape; the overdose of her ex-boyfriend; the passing of the coach she'd had from childhood; then the death of her father.

Ruminating on her life has led Camilla to an epiphany about the relationship between endurance and childhood trauma. "What sparks that ability to endure? Why do some people have it and some people don't?" she asks rhetorically. "I believe that I understand that. I talked to my last weight lifting coach about this quite extensively."

It was Camilla who told me about the UK study that found that its entire group of super-elite athletes had experienced early-life trauma. It explained to her the riddle of the naturally gifted athlete who dabbles with training and quits prematurely.

"You think, 'If you just trained, you would be Olympic level!' We all know people like that, in sports, in arts, in anything," she says. "But they don't want to hurt. They have no desire. Why would they? They've got nothing to prove. As opposed to people who go, 'I'm broken but let's go again tomorrow, and the day after, and the day after'—and if you don't, you beat yourself up over it. You're weak, you've missed out, you've failed."

So it's constant self-flagellation?

"Absolutely. Without a doubt. It is its own form of self-punishment."

Camilla believes there should be research carried out into the occurrence of self-harm and high-level athletes. "I would nearly guarantee that high-level athletes *won't* self-harm," she says. "It's not because we're mentally healthy—because actually, no high-level athlete is okay; even on a physical level they're fighting injuries, overtraining, worrying about nutrition, sleep, all that sort of stuff. If you're training hard, 99 percent of sessions *hurt*. We are already achieving that self-harm by training, by trying to perform at such a high level."

Few people illustrate the idea of childhood trauma promoting mental toughness better than David Goggins. The former Navy SEAL's memoir, *Can't Hurt Me* (2018)—and if that title isn't the howl of an inner child, I don't know what is—details his transformation from overweight victim of domestic violence, poverty and neglect, to the only member of the US Armed Forces to complete SEAL training, US Army Ranger School and Air Force Tactical Air Controller training. He's also a Guinness record holder for the most pull-ups done in twenty-four hours, and runs the world's toughest races for fun. He's so hardcore, he's basically putting Bear Grylls and Andy McNab into early retirement.

Rather like a drill sergeant, David rants repeatedly at his 3.9 million Instagram followers about "callousing the mind," by which he means continuously exposing the self to discomfort to create mental toughness, Earl Woods-style. He's been determined to stamp out the weakness of his younger self, as mercilessly as his own father tried to do. As he wrote in his memoir, which has now sold more than a million copies: "I sought out pain, fell in love with suffering, and eventually transformed myself from the weakest piece of shit on the planet into the hardest man God ever created, or so I tell myself."

Henry Rollins, the tattooed former front man of legendary hardcore punk band Black Flag, who went on to have a prolific solo career of music, spoken word and poetry, was also a weight lifter of many decades and has a similar outlook. In his essay "Iron and the Soul," published on the site *Old Time Strongman*, Rollins describes a pathetic early existence. He was fearful of his parents, was an easy target in his rough neighborhood, and was regularly called a "garbage can" by teachers, who didn't think he'd amount to anything beyond mowing lawns.

His fortune changed when his student adviser, a powerfully built Vietnam vet called Mr. Pepperman who *nobody* messed with, instructed Henry to spend his savings on a set of weights from Sears. He was going to put the boy on a training program—one that also entailed being punched in the solar plexus when Henry was least expecting it. When Henry could take the punch without dropping to the floor with his books skidding down the hallway, they'd both know he was on his way to leaving behind his bully-bait status.

Months passed, and then Henry took a punch that he just laughed off. After school he ran to the bathroom and studied himself in the mirror for the first time since he started training—Mr. P had forbidden him to until the results would be obvious. He saw a jacked body that looked as strong as his mind now felt.

"It was the first time I can remember having a sense of myself," he wrote. "I had done something and no one could ever take it away. You couldn't say shit to me."

Even so, it wasn't until years later that Henry fully realized the gift that weight lifting had given him. "I learned that nothing good comes without work and a certain amount of pain. When I finish a set that leaves me shaking, I know more about myself," he wrote. "I used to fight the pain, but recently this became clear to me: pain is not my enemy; it is my call to greatness."

Camilla has also started to pay closer attention to pain. One day she was training alone at the gym, doing heavy-weight box squats—where you squat with a barbell until you make contact with a box behind you, encouraging you to reach a certain depth and then explode back up from a dead-stop position. She didn't want to do them. There's no sweetening it: they hurt bad. She had five sets of five to do, but there was nobody around. Maybe she could cheat a little.

"Then I thought, *no, I'll keep going*," she says. "After every set, you do another set—of these grinding, shitty, painful reps. I had a little moment with myself. I thought, *Why do we avoid that feeling of pain? It's just a feeling. As soon as people hurt, they stop. Why? Why can't we view that particular feeling as something positive? Like laughter, or sex, or anything like that. Why can't we view it as a positive feeling?*"

ON THE COVER of Chris Fleming's memoir *On Drugs* (2019), there's a photograph of him, early twenties, wearing a muscle tee and looking buff enough to pull it off.

I meet Chris, about twenty-five years older, for coffee in Sydney. He's now an associate professor in humanities at Western Sydney University, so it's a bold but authentic move to publish a philosophical and anthropological take on his own addictive and obsessive tendencies. As he told *The Guardian*, even confessing to the book's existence prompts a flurry of jokes from people about doing "empirical research."

Growing up, Chris worried about inconsistencies around his identity. He was sensitive, but also intent on being strong; into guitars, but also karate. The only constant was that whatever caught his attention would become an all-encompassing obsession. He writes in *On Drugs*, "As far back as I can remember, I've had a strong sense of being permeable, porous, of my body being open to the unpredictable forces of outside matter ..."

He developed a series of obsessions about different pursuits with which he might align his identity. There was fishing (or reading about it—he was also obsessed with newsdealers), dogs (despite not owning a dog, he made appointments with vets to talk about them) and the issue of the lack of seatbelts on buses (the subject of many petition letters). His older brothers, heavily into sports, were creeped out by their younger sibling's love of Bowie and art. One brother walked into the lounge room on a Saturday, bruised and covered in mud from a game of rugby, and caught Chris knitting. From then on, he would introduce Chris to friends as "my half-brother, half-sister," and called him "Cwithie" until Chris was in his early twenties.

"In my mind I couldn't measure up to anyone: the people I was at school with, the men in my family," Chris tells me.

Outside of the home, things were worse. Chris was bullied

for the crimes of being bookish, intellectual, musical and—as was wrongly deduced—gay. He was intimidated, held down and punched, even burned. Boys threatened they would kill him, and he believed them.

"Life for me as a kid was terrifying," he says. "I was always gripped by fears that something was going to happen. Danger was just around the corner. I was scared of everything—of other people, of myself and what I might do."

Chris developed obsessive-compulsive disorder at the age of seven, which hijacked his head with repetitive behavior patterns and punitive thoughts of children being skinned or of people drinking vomit. This only subsided when he discovered self-medicating with drugs.

"I've never been super good at approaching the world with an even keel," he says.

With each of his obsessions, a new world would open up—and that was a welcome thing. "An obsession put me to work and gave me an itinerary, a way of warding things off," he says. "You're pushing something down and allowing it a voice simultaneously. Partly it was also the idea of transformation: by learning about something and engaging with it, I could become someone else."

I find that relatable. When I was an adolescent, newly obsessed with alcohol, I checked out library books on drugs that I was yet to try. Uppers. Downers. Psychedelics. A world of possibilities stretched out in front of me. *You mean to say that if I take this little pill, just like Alice in Wonderland, I will change entirely?* It was an irresistible offer to someone who wanted everything to change, but mostly themself.

As he grew older, Chris's focus moved to becoming stronger, perhaps even stronger than his brothers. An interest in boxing started after seeing *Rocky* (1976) and getting up off the couch to go for a run. And he ran. And ran. And ran. The next day, he decided to go running again. "My dad saw me limp toward the door and said, 'You might want to keep your eye on that—Flemings don't really do moderation.'"

He bought as many American bodybuilding magazines and books as he could find. *Muscle & Fitness. Flex. Unleashing the Wild Physique.* At first, his collection of tomes on muscular development grew much more rapidly than his muscle mass. He was initially enamored by the promises of these magazines—the articles that vowed to unlock secrets, the advertisements depicting beefcakes who gained their mighty physiques through magical potions. Chris marveled at the idea of transformation through ingestion. Then he discovered the book *The Matrix Principle* (1991), cowritten by Dr. Ronald Laura, which mixed philosophy with strength training, and something really clicked. Chris had been experiencing some cognitive dissonance over building a tough façade around a tender temperament. Ronald Laura offered Chris some reconciliation of the conflicting aspects of his identity. After all, Ronald himself was a world-renowned bodybuilder, bench-presser and arm wrestler who was also a Wittgenstein buff with a PhD.

At sixteen, Chris decided to study karate, because martial arts, steeped in discipline and structure, offered a relieving sense of order to his busy brain. "The belt system is like a computer game. You level up," he says of karate. "In life, things aren't so clear. When do I become a better writer? Well, I know

I'm a better writer than when I was ten, but I don't go through gradings, so I can't tell precisely. The grading system offers something incredibly tangible. It gamifies life and progress in a way that very few things do. It offers concrete goals and everything becomes very manageable and quantifiable."

Once acquainted with throwing hands, he became a bouncer at various Sydney clubs. The tough-guy persona felt like a sham, but at the same time, it seemed the natural extension of his progress into bodybuilding and martial arts, and a way to flirt with machismo. He may not have had an innate "brute force and ignorance," as Rory Gallagher sang in 1979, but his attentiveness to his studies worked in his favor. "Throwing a punch or grappling are extremely unnatural movements," he points out. "You've got to put a lot of attention into it to actually be able to do it properly. When I worked as a bouncer, it became really evident that very few people can actually fight. Most guys end up on the ground."

While he admired the clarity of martial arts, Chris grew to dislike the punitive system, in which pupils were expected to show extreme deference to superiors and belittle those below. "You see martial arts as this alchemical thing of 'I'm going to turn this base metal of myself into gold,'" he says, "but it's a very tarnished gold when you get there. You're just you, wearing a black belt. I suddenly realized I didn't want to be bowed to, which was shocking. I'd wanted respect and for people to think of me as deadly, and now it felt very awkward."

When someone with a fragile sense of self has their ego bolstered, a kind of monster can be created. Master Ken is the creation of American actor Matt Page, and began life as the protagonist of the web series *Enter the Dojo*—which Matt describes as "*The Office* meets *Karate Kid*." And actually, anyone who's seen the latest in the Karate Kid franchise, the comedy *Cobra Kai*, will be familiar with the concept of martial arts mastery turning dark in the hands of people with rampant egos.

As a martial arts instructor who has created his own discipline of Ameri-do-te, Master Ken—all arched brow, puffed chest and bulging biceps under his bright red gi—bullies his students into one injury after another. "Better to be tried by twelve than carried by six," he lectures one, who is reluctant to use excessive force to permanently disable their opponent. On the "Master Ameriken" Instagram page, he invites real-life martial arts instructors to demonstrate a technique, so that he can pronounce it "bullshit," and outdo his guests with ridiculously complex maneuvers.

Actor Matt has black belts in Okinawan kenpo and kobudo, and is adept at aikido, boxing and stick fighting. He didn't so much as dream up Master Ken as see variations of him across the multiple dojos he studied at ... and just a touch in himself. "Master Ken is a way to embody all the things that I think but I can't say as myself," he admits. "In the context of a character who's very arrogant and oblivious, he can just blurt out whatever crazy or egotistical or uninformed thought I have in my head and it fits."

The essence of Master Ken is an arrogance that hides a lack of genuine self-belief. Austrian psychotherapist Alfred Adler, in *Understanding Human Nature* (1981), posits the theory that children with a "belligerent approach to life," or "very weak" children, are prone to developing a fantasy world. Eventually, their powers of fantasy may become a means to avoid reality. "Feelings of inferiority, inadequacy and insecurity determine the goal of an individual's existence," he writes. "Here are found the first indications that the awakening desire for recognition is developing alongside the sense of inferiority. Its purpose is the attainment of a state in which individuals are seemingly superior to their environment."

This is where striving for goals can take on a problematic slant. "Their goal is so constructed that its achievement promises the possibility either of a feeling of superiority or an elevation of the personality to a level that makes life seem worth living … We orient ourselves according to an artificially created fixed point, a point that has no actual basis in reality: in other words, a fiction."

Master Ken dreams up scenarios of street fights and gun battles for his students. And he has no hesitation in fighting dirty (his motto is "re-stomp the groin," since stamping on the genitals is his finishing move), using methods that are ineffective and dangerous in a real-life situation. Matt reflects, "I don't know how much Ken has actually been in combat versus him viewing the world as a dangerous place. So much of his mentality is preventative or in preparation, because it really seems to me that a lot of traditional martial artists spend their entire lives training for a situation that statistically will never happen. They put twenty or thirty years of training into this: 'When someone points a gun at me … When someone pulls a knife … When I'm attacked by two attackers of equal size and skill, they will attack me in this way and then I will react in this way …'"

He assumes that some deep-rooted anxiety motivates practitioners like Ken—and that, he says, is a part he can relate to, having been picked on at school. "If you're ever in a situation where you feel helpless or you don't feel in control of the situation, that's very scary," he says. "That was definitely my experience, having been knocked around a couple of times. But violence is unpredictable and you can spend all this time training and then you could fall down the stairs, you know? There are variables that you could never have anticipated. There's this perpetual desire to be in control of a situation that is elusive."

Chris Fleming has ditched the martial arts, but he still works out, and has a tendency to overdo it when he does. "I can barely stand afterward," he says.

But you could argue that as an academic it's in his job description to be an overthinker, and so his tendency to push a pursuit or idea to its limits has its benefits. "My work is still tied into my identity in a really big way," he agrees. "Before I gave up drugs, I'd identified as a nineteenth-century intellectual poet inebriate, staggering around. And the drugs *did* sort out my identity issues in some way, because when I was taking them, I finally thought, *This is me.* They brought me an artificial self-acceptance."

Chris felt that he needed drugs to do his job in the same way that bodybuilders feel they need steroids—they were just the tools of the trade. But his habit landed him massively in debt and destroyed his marriage, so eventually he went to rehab. And gradually, he learned not to try to outsmart the sober wisdom of his mentors. He's now written nine books, covering philosophy, literature and cultural analysis, with a tenth and an eleventh on the way. The way his mind takes topics to extremes may sometimes have been a weight on his shoulders, but it's also allowed him to carry entire universes in his head.

AS RICHIE HARDCORE and I left Marvel Stadium after Israel Adasanya's victory, we talked about social media. We could both tell when we weren't mentally match-fit because we uploaded too many Instagram posts. Mine tended to be when I was lonely; Richie's, when he was anxious. He said he knew the signs well. While he was still a professional fighter, he broke up with his wife. Soon after, he retired. "And I had this huge fucking space in my life that I filled with depression and a lot of sugar, and ridiculous amounts of posting sad memes on Instagram at two in the morning."

Richie and I are hardly alone in our use of social media—plenty of athletes post inane motivational quotes or photographs of themselves executing a kick against a mountain backdrop. It makes me wonder if seeking online validation is almost inevitable for goal-oriented people. Instagram interactions activate the same reward pathways as aiming for goals, after all, delivering a ding of dopamine.

Not long after we part, Richie is "canceled" on Twitter, not for the first time. It's become common for someone prominent who uses social media to talk about different causes to be leapt upon in an "Oh-ho!" fashion if they're deemed to do anything hypocritical; the more woke, the more they can be broke. Last time was back in 2016, when Kim Kardashian posted a nude to Instagram and Richie commented under someone else's post about it, "We need to teach healthier ways of validation."

And yet, as one indignant tweeter pointed out, he would happily be pictured in a workout photo with his shirt off. This time, I can't discern what the outrage is over. There are a few dark threats from a handful of people claiming they will expose his misdeeds, but no follow-through.

Nonetheless, it plunges him back into the anxiety so familiar from childhood.

The police move to prosecute the woman deemed the instigator for breaching the *Harmful Digital Communications Act 2015*. Similar charges against her concerning other people, dating back a few years, are revealed. Richie decides to turn the whole shit show into a mission—he wants to understand as much as he can about cancel culture. Reading the relevant work of Jon Ronson, Douglas Murray, Ayishat Akanbi and Peter Pomerantsev gives him strength, due to the knowledge that what happened to him is part of a broader cultural trend. Maybe he isn't so much callousing the mind as poking the bruise, but as a journalist I can understand his motivation to take control by turning an ordeal into a talking point.

Our mutual distress drives home to me how fragile people like us still are underneath the armor. Sometimes, as much effort will have to go into reinforcing the fortress as went into building it initially, particularly if the wounded child's Achilles heels—lack of respect, abandonment, shame—have been targeted. Perhaps some types are drawn to the state of struggling. A condition such as anxiety might feel better utilized if put into the context of an epic battle—a tournament or a fight night or even a thorny issue. The boxing ring or Octagon becomes the real arena for the internal war.

The martial arts movies would have something to say about this, of course. They would say that there will be continual trials and fearsome foes, usually resulting in a temporary defeat, or the loss of reputation, public mockery and humiliation. The individual must exercise discipline, drawing on their skills rather than fighting with their emotions. Because a key tenet of martial arts is that you never stop learning.

Chapter Six

THIS IS HARDCORE

Porn Stars

RUMOR HAS IT that after Bridgette Kerkove retired from porn, she changed her name and found God. It's not an unpopular retirement plan in the industry.

She's been at the back of my mind for the past twenty years, dating back to when we both worked in pornography. I was a subeditor for the American adult magazines *Club* and *Club Confidential*, also writing most of the content, including interviews with the top performers. Bridgette was riding the crest of the wave that was gonzo. Gonzo porn was similar to gonzo journalism, in that the pornographer inserted themselves in the scene and provided the point of view—usually with a handycam. It was irreverent, veered wildly between humor and disrespectfulness, and did away with artifice, such as sets and plots. With the industry accessible to anyone with a camera and some hustle, a more extreme element wound up decimating the landscape of popular porn.

Enter Bridgette.

Patricia Felkel was born to a large Catholic family in California in 1977. As a sixteen-year-old private school girl, she met Skeeter Kerkove: twelve years older, covered in tattoos and rider of a Harley. For Patricia, raised by deeply religious parents, he was basically catnip.

By 1999, Patricia was going by the name Bridgette, presumably as a nod to Brigitte Bardot, whose bouffant blonde hair she now had in common. According to one of numerous ungentlemanly interviews Skeeter later gave about his wife, she was about to become the highest-grossing woman in porn, making on average a film a week that year. Perhaps her most infamous achievement, though, was the zeitgeisty gonzo act of taking a hundred and three chopsticks anally. I remember sitting at my desk and reading about that in *Adult Video News*, the industry's trade magazine—and stopping mid-chomp of my focaccia.

Skeeter started off by inserting seventy at once in a condom, then added to them until his wife was at capacity. This was a record-breaking event, as someone in France had previously managed only seventy-four (disclaimer: as is the case with many porn records, Bridgette's achievement was later revealed, by her, to be greatly exaggerated). Even so, record-breaking feats—such as number of participants, most semen ingested and biggest breast implants—were as '90s as my choice of lunch.

Someone with such a capacity for endurance as Bridgette was in the right place at the right time. Gonzo budgets were small, exploits extreme and turnaround fast. As one notorious pornographer, Rob "Black" Zicari, sloganeered at the time, "Pussies are bullshit," and girls like Bridgette frequently accommodated two or three penises anally at once. Black later did time for films depicting simulated rape.

I didn't mind working for porn magazines. It sparked my

morbid imagination about what I could or could not endure—perhaps in the same way that we read newspaper reports about grisly incidents—and the writing was simple enough to be conducted while extremely hungover; essentially, taking something out of one hole and inserting it into another. But while the pages we commissioned were relatively tasteful shoots of some of porn's most incredible-looking women, like Bridgette, Jenna Jameson and Janine Lindemulder (there was the occasional insertion of dildos and butt plugs, but they were expensive-looking), the gonzo advertisements at the back of the magazine were something else.

Skip the next paragraph if you still have a dewy-eyed view of humanity that you'd like to retain.

Here, lesser-known women drank cocktails of cum, saliva and vomit, had speculums slotted in their rectums so as best to suck someone's urine out of them with a long hose, and threw prolapse parties, with their rectums as the party pies. My brain conducted mental gymnastics, trying to allow for the fact that these exploits might not be as appallingly painful as they looked, and to convince myself that this could fall into the realm of "healthy, fun-for-all fetish." Bridgette's butt-cutlery, by contrast, seemed almost quaint, but it was still a thoroughly odd thing to do—neither sexually satisfying for Bridgette, one presumes, nor erotic for the beholder.

And yet, I was on my own mission of endurance: the pharmaceutical kind. Often, I'd sit sweating out a hangover at my desk long after everyone else had gone home, waiting for a porn star with a willfully misspelled name to pick up the phone in Los Angeles. More often than not I'd be stood up in favor of plastic surgery, rehab or a bender, and I'd eventually head over to the unlicensed sex shop my boyfriend worked at, where we'd tuck into a bottle of GHB, which he also sold. This "liquid ecstasy" would give you a cheap, heavy high within twenty minutes, but really it was like playing Russian roulette because it could just as easily shut down your nervous system sufficiently to put you in a lengthy blackout. There was some weird, bloody-minded satisfaction to be had in putting my body through its paces.

Was this really so different to Bridgette's reasoning for pushing herself to her limits? The most marked difference between us, in fact, was that she raked in the money and got to walk the red carpet at the Adult Video News Awards in a fabulous dress, while I slumped at my desk and looked at the slides.

It was around this time that I sat down in a Soho café with Grace Quek, a.k.a. porn star Annabel Chong. The documentary *Sex: The Annabel Chong Story* (1999), about how she came to make the porno *The World's Biggest Gangbang* (1996)—which kicked off a whole gangbang series—had just been released in selected UK cinemas.

Annabel, a former gender studies student at the University of Southern California, explained that she was exploring the idea of the female as stud, citing the mythology around Roman empress Messalina, who—popular and probably politically malicious rumor had it—enthusiastically bedded half of Rome. But it felt as though Annabel was retrofitting her film with a motivation. In other interviews, she had mused that her 251-man feat was more like team sports, which were part of the fabric of American society. It was about communal bonding, spectacle and statistics, not about sex.

That made more sense. From a young age, Americans are

encouraged to pursue athletic achievements, to break records, to win. Why would American porn stars and directors escape that kind of conditioning? And if the gangbang is the sport, then the star at the center of it—be they a straight woman, a gay man, trans or otherwise—is the athlete. Speaking to the *Turner Entertainment Report*, Annabel said of the gangbang, "It's like running a marathon … the pain is part of the high, part of the adrenaline."

Twenty years later, Annabel—now Grace again—is a software developer whose LinkedIn profile claims she enjoys playing linebacker for the LA Warriors women's football team and competes in Masters Track and Field Championships.

Just as Bridgette Kerkove's chopstick count was exaggerated, so too was Annabel's cock count. She eventually admitted there had only been seventy men, but she was penetrated 251 times. Similarly, the next movie in the series, starring Jasmin St. Claire, was advertised as featuring three hundred men, but actually there were only thirty milling around. In her memoir, *What the Hell Was I Thinking?!!* (2010), she dubbed it "among the biggest cons ever pulled off in the porn business."

Jasmin later retired from porn and became a wrestler, and even cofounded her own promotion, Pro-Pain Pro Wrestling. In her memoir she notes "a big part of being a wrestler is selling, making it seem like you got hurt really bad," which is known in the wrestling industry as "kayfabe"—making something staged seem real, from injuries to rivalries. With *World's Biggest Gangbang 2*, she'd pulled off the ultimate kayfabe.

On the day of Jasmin's gangbang, Annabel was invited on set to metaphorically pass on the baton. Journalist Evan Wright, writing for *LA Weekly*, reported: "I experienced a sense of numbness on Jasmin's set—as I would on many others—that I can only compare to accounts I have read of combat. It was the sense of being in a group of people deliberately and methodically engaged in acts of insanity."

Soon, such scenes would be commonplace. As porn stud Tyler Knight wrote in his 2016 memoir *Burn My Shadow*:

> Directors for other bukkake movies and gang bang scenes rove up and down the line handing out business cards. One director poaches talent for a gang bang scene with an overdue pregnant woman. His scenes resemble a school of swarming piranhas stripping a cow to its bones. The scene will shoot close enough to Northridge Hospital in case the woman goes into labor.

Director Mike Quasar worked for the production company on Jasmin's film, as well as on the third in the series, *The Houston 620*, named after the star, Houston. Predictably, he tells me that the advertised 620 guys were actually 180.

"It was one of the most absurd things I've ever been involved with in my entire life," he says, on the phone from his home in Woodland Hills, a neighborhood that borders the porn metropolis of San Fernando Valley. He's had a long day on set and I can hear the ice cubes rattling in his tequila. "It was certainly a moment where I stepped back and went, *Okay, I've made poor choices.*"

Mike calls himself a "reluctant pornographer," but the Canadian has the animated curmudgeonliness of veteran comedian

Marc Maron, and once we start talking about the industry, he's off on a roll. I tell him I look back almost nostalgically at Annabel and Jasmin's record-breaking era (which is also the era of the annual KSEXgames, ambitiously intended to be an adult-themed version of the Olympics, and at which Mike, as host, would make observations such as: "When Gen's not competing, she enjoys recreational drugs and chinchilla breeding"). Because if porn then was like extreme sex Olympics, now it's like factory farming, churning out unmemorable girls for immediate consumption.

Mike agrees. "People often ask if porn has got too extreme. You know, porn was actually much more extreme back in the late 1990s, early 2000s," he says. These days he's in the thick of the trend for stepfamily porn, as shown in a recent tweet: "I wake up every morning with a hangover. Then I go film a stepmother banging her stepson who's strangely only eight months younger." Despite the taboo of almost-incest, this is ridiculously vanilla content when compared to his work of decades past.

"Oh god, so much of this I blocked out," he says. "I'm going to have to go back to therapy if we talk about it. The thing you have to understand about me is that much of what I film is of no interest to me whatsoever. I shot the world's biggest gangbang, but I wasn't like, *Oh, this is gonna be so great, there's gonna be a girl surrounded by six hundred registered sex offenders ...*" The ice cubes clink again.

"Once you get out of missionary position you've lost me," he insists.

I offer Mike my theory—that porn performers feel the same kind of pride in their abilities that an athlete might. Most people wouldn't, but also *couldn't*, pull off the pretzling and dilating that these women and gay men put their bodies through weekly. And those on the receiving end are surely a thousand times more hardcore than those muscle-bound performers paid to dish it out (men who'll momentarily pause a scene of double-anal penetration in order to position a cushion under their own knees for comfort).

"I literally had this conversation two hours ago with Joanna Angel, when we were shooting today," Mike says. "She was talking about when she goes to work for Kink [a BDSM production company], and she looks at it like it's going to the gym: 'How much more can I take? Can I do this?' It's all about what she can tolerate. So it's not even a sexual thing, it's literally like an endurance test."

For six years, Mike shot for a site called *Throated*, which specialized in deep-throating, with plenty of spit and gagging, but is moderate by current standards. When he hired girls, he would show them some scenes to make sure they understood the nature of the acts to be performed. "But that was an endurance thing too," he says. "It's like, okay, how long can I hold this penis in my throat before I have to breathe? How long can I do this before it makes me throw up?"

"Face fucking" has since become a leading genre of porn, often making headlines for its use of spitting, choking and slapping, the practices of which have infiltrated many unwitting women's Tinder dates. To the novice, these films are identical whoever makes them—they share the same acts, after all. But they're not. Some production companies employ pro actresses who perform their roles with relish and a fair degree of humor. Others specialize in videos that seem to be expressly made by men who hate women, *for* men who hate women. Their female talent tends to be Midwestern cannon fodder: homely teen-age girls who haven't done their research and are essentially ambushed on set, girls whose eyes brim with tears of humili-ation halfway through their ordeal with a two-man tag team. Sometimes they're subjected to racial or religious slurs.

Rough, degrading sex isn't by default misogynistic, but it's noteworthy that if you open a browser and seek out correspond-ing sexual acts in gay porn, the vibe may be aggressive and performatively debasing, but it's never this hateful.

Some of these hetero production companies make a mockery of consent. It's common for BDSM production companies—an example being Kink, which has its ethical tenets on its site—to interview the submissive performer afterward, partly to demonstrate that she's okay, and partly for her to demystify her lifestyle-love of rough sex and bondage for the vanilla viewer. But in the exit interviews from some other production compa-nies, the female performer is alarmingly void of expression. She answers flatly that yes, she is okay. Yes, she enjoyed that. Yes, she'll say hi to her dad.

Mike's uncomfortable with the direction in which the genre has gone. "To me it doesn't feel like it's role-playing," he says. "To me it literally feels like people being taken advantage of. I'm not trying to be a hero, but at the same time there are certain things that I just think are wrong, you know? A lot of that stuff has nothing to do with endurance or a lifestyle, it's truly just to do with breaking a human being."

And yet, stats from Pornhub reveal that it's largely women who are sticking terms such as "brutal" and "forced" into search engines. Cognitive dissonance may give us an uncomfortable feeling when we're ordering coffee in a takeaway cup or not challenging a taxi driver on their racist beliefs, but when it comes to watching porn, cognitive dissonance is *hot*. Pornography makes hypocrites of us all.

"It absolutely does," Mike agrees. "I understand that there's context to everything—like, you don't want Harvey Weinstein opening his bathrobe and inviting you into his room and pulling your hair and spitting on you, but I guess maybe you might want your boyfriend to do that if that's what you're into. It just flies in the face of the era that we're in right now. We're in this culture of hashtags like #MeToo and #TimesUp, and yet the second-highest traffic material is women being abused by men."

He argues that no matter what women are searching for, most pornographic content is still geared toward men. "I know I'm an incredibly cynical person, but the end result is a man on an iPad, balling up a tissue and throwing it into the trash, no matter how you want to intellectualize what you do and talk about enlightenment and freedom and discovering parts of yourself. Anything else you want to describe porn as is just hubris."

IT SEEMS FITTING that when I finally get Orion Starr on the other end of the phone, we both have croaky voices. Mine's because it's five in the morning in Melbourne. Hers is an authentic New Yorker rasp. But it's also a temporary effect of the sexual activity she's most known for, and that's what we're here to talk about.

Orion has worked for the production company Facial Abuse,

and she has a different take to Mike. "It was the most exciting thing," she says. "It's not your regular hardcore porn scene, it's real extreme degradation. That's just the fetish people have, and in order to make a great scene you have to enjoy what you do. I like a lot of crazy, taboo stuff; I'm just an extremist, I guess. I like to do things that people wouldn't normally do and I like to make a statement doing that. I also like proving people wrong."

The main reason I tracked down Orion is that she tests her limits both by dishing it out and by taking it. To her, they are two sides of the same coin. When she's not being deconstructed by cock, she's a professional cage fighter, and fights in leading MMA promotions such as Bellator. Orion is not the first adult performer to be attracted to martial arts—Blaten Lee, Priya Rai, Brittney Skye, Aby Rulloda and Adrianna Luna all dabbled in fighting—but she's by far the most successful.

Last week she posted a nude on Instagram, with the caption "This is what lethal looks like." In it, she's holding the camera phone up to the bathroom mirror. Her bleached hair is parted in the middle, her body angled away so that her vulva is only just visible. The tip of her tongue rests to one side of her mouth, showing her pierced bottom lip. Her nipples are pierced, too, with steel bars, and on either side of her pierced belly button there are tattooed stars. She has a ram's skull tattoo on her chest, and the words across her ribcage run in reverse in the mirror: *SEX AND VIOLENCE.*

Orion has filmed with Facial Abuse more than any other company because it's based in New Jersey, whereas most shoots would require her to fly out to Los Angeles. "It's this old building with separate studios and offices in it. It's pretty suburban," she says, when pressed for details. "I bring a few outfits, then I do my makeup and get ready in the dressing room."

I want to get technical. How much water does she have to down in order to throw up with optimum mess on set? "You have to drink tons," she answers vaguely. "I drink half a gallon every day anyway." I'm getting the vibe she wants to switch the conversation to fight training, for which she points out she must stay reliably hydrated. But not yet.

Orion would typically be on set for four hours for such a film, basically two scenes: the disparaging introductory interview and then the sex. She insists that during the breaks the tag team of men—who, when the camera is rolling, snarl at her to open her legs wider like the stripper she is—snap back to being the sweetest guys. The problem, she thinks, is a lot of girls just accept a booking from their manager without weighing up the consequences. "For me it's not just about the money—I enjoy it," she says. "I'm a sexual deviant. When I was eighteen I started going to fetish parties and doing dominatrix work. I wanted to get more involved with being an all-round dominatrix *and* a sub, because I like to try both ends of the spectrum. I like to be dominant sometimes and sometimes I like to be submissive. I have a very high pain tolerance."

Her attitude toward punishment reminds me curiously of the book *Why We Fight* (2019), in which journalist Josh Rosenblatt writes of his forays into MMA training as a forty-year-old. In particular, he marvels at how quickly he becomes beholden to bravado, dining out on his injuries. "How right it felt to give in to my bloodiest instincts after all those cerebral, dormant, placid years, to feel my body fighting for its own preservation, to abandon my veneer of civilization and decency and experience the life-affirming thrill of putting my life, and the lives of others, at risk," he writes. "I soon found myself looking forward to getting punched in the head and choked into submission, and I started to recognize and long for the odd mixture of horror and envy that seemed to appear in people's eyes whenever I explained at a dinner party or the bar why I was limping or how I got this black eye or that broken finger."

As a fighter, Orion is tough, sharp and focused, yet something of a scrappy underdog. She's like the Tonya Harding of MMA, likely to never be accepted entirely because of her porn career. And yet, that career probably gave her the resilience for cage fighting. After one high-profile loss, London's *The Sun* described her as "humiliated" and Brisbane's *The Courier-Mail* as "brutalized," but then, her adult movies on sites such as Pornhub are listed with descriptors such as "Orion Starr dumps her guts." Orion is unphased. "People talk a lot of crap about me," she says. *"She's probably just a drug addict with tattoos, into devil worship,* blah, blah, blah. But I really don't care what they say. They're just hating because I do what they can't, you know what I mean? They don't have the guts to do it. So. It is what it is."

Orion was always a thrill-seeker. As a kid, she loved rollercoasters and amusement parks, watched horror movies avidly and dressed up as Freddy Krueger for Halloween. In her spare time now she cosplays as a Viking, or the DC Comics villain Harley Quinn. As a fighter, she's adopted the bad-guy nickname "Rebecca Carnage Rampage." She had twenty-five kickboxing fights before making the move into MMA. "I've had just as many fights as I have years of life," she says. "It feels like I was kicking and screaming and punching things when I came out of the womb. I guess I was born to be a fighter. I've always had a killer instinct for it."

On one of her Instagram accounts—she has around six, for different alter egos, including fetish model and cosplay enthusiast—Orion hangs shit on future opponents, or mocks those who have dropped out or who lost. *"Love this shot. You see her face getting wrecked…,"* *"Getting ready to fuck her world up."* Someone schools her: *"Great match, but respect your opponent if you want to become a good fighter."* Orion retorts: *"Fuck that bitch. Who says I'm nice?"*

When she wins, her gloating is glorious. Perhaps it's her geeky love of cosplay coming out, but she's fully embraced the theater of MMA. "I literally jumped up and down with my first win, screaming my head off," she says happily. "A lot of people secretly just want to see you fail, so it felt like, *Oh my god, I just literally made everybody fucking mad.* I was jumping up and down, screaming like an orc. It was so great. The girl [her opponent] had made a slick remark to my coach, then I noticed when I passed by her dressing room later she was crying in the corner." She laughs. "So I made her cry." She laughs again.

I don't find Orion's duality—of being both aggressor and submissive—odd. To understand it better, it's a question of moving our focus away from what participating in extreme sex acts does *to* a person to what it does *for* the person.

If I put myself in that position, I can see I'm proving my ability to survive—perhaps even thrive. My throat survives battering. My eyes survive the spit that spatters them. My neck survives the thumb prints. I'm playing chicken with my fantasies—the ones most people keep in their heads and don't let spill out onto mattresses. Maybe I'm working through the wrongs that have been done to me in decades past, obeying some internalized script. Or maybe I just need to feel *something*. Sometimes I might find myself wondering about the motivation of the person inflicting this upon me. And then perhaps I decide that it's better off being none of my business.

There's a prevalent belief that porn stars must have been molested as children. Howard Stern, the shock jock who frequently has adult performers on his show, almost always asks about this, including of Bridgette Kerkove. Bridgette said no, "Everything was good."

If you consider that, according to some statistics, one in four women in the general population has been sexually abused, then many women in the porn industry will have been. But a study published in *The Journal of Sex Research* finds only a minor increase of sexual-abuse history among performers, compared to the general public. Of 177 female performers interviewed, 36 percent had been abused, compared to 29 percent of a control group. That prompted *Slate* to report on the story with the headline "Porn Stars Molested About as Often as Accountants, New Study Finds." The theory that childhood abuse is a gateway to porn aggravates many high-profile performers when it's raised in interviews. If you read their memoirs, the most common theme is childhood neglect and a corresponding need for attention.

Growing up, says Orion—"if you want to get into that"—her mother would "get wordy" with her. "And I was bullied a lot. I was pretty much alone most of my childhood, always sitting at lunch alone, up until I got into high school." She brightens.

"Then all that stopped because I developed and everyone stopped picking on me, like, 'Oh my god, she's attractive.' And I was like, 'PAH! Now you want me, but before you didn't! Now, yeah, you want me. Do you remember all those times you used to call me this, this and that and laugh at me in the lunchroom? Yeah, I remember that.'"

Orion's outburst reminds me of a passage in Jasmin St. Claire's autobiography, in which she describes getting into porn to take revenge on abusive exes and to anger her mother. (Jasmin, incidentally, considered being interviewed for this chapter, but graciously declined when I described it further, explaining, "I don't want to be put into a book with people like that.") Tera Patrick, a former teen model from San Francisco, had fallen out with her disapproving mom; Australian performer Monica Mayhem wanted to stick it to her heavy-drinking mother and those who'd bullied her; Penny Flame, who began her career after answering an ad in the San Diego State University newspaper, wrote about a mother who was always drunk; and Ashley Blue grew up in a Californian home with parents who were addicted to drugs.

"That's probably what really drove me, aside from I've been in really abusive relationships, physically and mentally," Orion says. "It just builds up over time, like, 'I'm so sick of this. I just want to PUNCH somebody.'"

A week after I talk to Orion, I proudly post a video to Instagram in which I'm whaling my way through some kickboxing pad work. I receive a private message from her.

Have u ever even had one fight?

Is Orion *dissing* me? Deflated, I point out that I have

not—yet—but that this is my aim.

Oh i have 25 [kickboxing] fights plus 2 MMA fights

I write back that I know this, as I interviewed her the week before and we talked about it.

Oh i didn't realize ur the same girl, she types back. *My bad. Lmaoooo.*

EVER REALIZED THERE'S a two-month-old Tupperware container of leftovers in the fridge and given it a sniff out of curiosity? You're not alone. Ever recoiled in disgust and then willingly sniffed it again a few seconds later? You're one of the freaks eFukt caters to, because eFukt capitalizes on the eroticism of disgust.

Founded by Deven (just "Deven") in 2006, the website is dedicated to collecting the most gross-out porn on the internet, divided into categories too offensive to mention, which—if you've read this far—is saying something. Thirty seconds on that site will have you convinced humanity is hurtling toward hell.

Rachel Herz is a psychologist and cognitive neuroscientist, well regarded for her work around emotion, memory and smell. In her book *That's Disgusting: Unravelling the Mysteries of Repulsion* (2012), she explains that disgust is a neurological bedfellow of lust, in that the same brain regions—in particular, the insula—are activated by erotica and by repulsion. Less scientifically, this explains why, mere seconds after an orgasm to something sickening is achieved, an individual's laptop lid tends to be hastily slapped down. She references a 2005 German study in which one group of twelve participants had sadomasochistic tendencies and one group did not. The group that purported to be disgusted by images of men being whipped had the same regions of their brain activated when viewing this as when viewing maggots or non-sadistic erotica. For both groups, it was only images of geometric patterns that failed to set the fMRI scanner alight.

Whether we find this palatable or not, disgust is an aphrodisiac. Even oysters, widely considered to have aphrodisiac properties themselves, are often construed as hideous and onerous to swallow, Herz notes. "Sometimes we are perversely attracted to people whom we actually loathe or find physically revolting," she writes. "This is because lust is fueled by an animalistic passion that shares many commonalities with repulsion. Lust can also be provoked by the thought of what is obscene or forbidden."

Think of the Germans and the Japanese, two nationalities stereotyped as being tightly buttoned, and yet who make the best (or worst, depending on your viewpoint) pornography. Japan in particular specializes in inventively grotesque genres, including bukkake, in which multiple men ejaculate on a performer's face, and gokkun, in which the performer drinks copious amounts of semen from a receptacle. Perversely, genitals are always pixelated, in response to Article 175 of the Japanese penal code, which stipulates that it is illegal to share indecent materials. Leading Japanese porn star Ken "Shimiken" Shimizu theorized in an interview with the website Tokyo Night Style that these restrictions are directly responsible for the industry's leaning toward unusual fetishes. "Japan's censorship has created many sexual subcultures you see today," he said. Similarly, in his book *The Anatomy of Disgust*, William Ian Miller points out that Freud recognized disgust was not just there to prevent pleasure, but to heighten it and even create the conditions for it. "The argument is largely economic," William writes. "Disgust helps create conditions of scarcity which build up demand and increase value."

Both culturally and individually speaking, disgust sensitivity is on a scale, whether it be the country that is comfortable with manga porn at newsstands or the friend you have who loves popping other people's zits. In both examples, there is a high disgust threshold.

Whereas eFukt often capitalizes on porn stars' misfortunes— such as semen exploding from a woman's nose or some other particularly "comedic" scene—some performers like to explore the frontiers of disgust deliberately. Ashley Blue retired about a decade before Orion Starr entered the scene. In her brilliantly lurid memoir *Girlvert* (2011), written under her real name of Oriana Small, she analyzes her three hundred-movie career and her motivations.

Brunette, corn-fed and cheerful of countenance, Ashley had a wayward girl-next-door thing going on. "I have always had a high threshold for the gross, the vulgar, the sickening," she writes. "For me, it is a source of happiness and excitement."

Ashley became bulimic at around thirteen, the same age that she became sexually active. She got into the habit of sticking her whole fist down her throat. "I loved it," she writes. "It was exhilarating, I could feel a rush in my entire body, a rush of fluids out of the stomach."

In the podcast series *This Is Really Happening*, there's an episode called "What if You Had a Fetish for Disgust?" that features a soft-spoken young woman called Gwen. Gwen talks about how throwing up feels like the literal purging of the shame she felt constantly, growing up in a very religious family. She became plagued with anxiety in her teenage years, which manifested as self-disgust. Once Gwen accepted that disgust was a permanent part of her makeup, she decided to become friends with the emotion. She has a playmate, Dick Wound, who "forces" her to vomit, which further absolves her of shame, but also feels astoundingly intimate. She says of their activities, of which vomiting is the most printable, "I think they're meaningful and connective and powerful."

By the time Ashley had made a name for herself, fisting her own mouth had become a kind of on-camera signature. "Only in porn would a person's wretched habit of shoving her hand all the way down her throat be considered a talent," she writes. Much later, she would subvert her on-screen persona by starring in the series *Girlvert*, in which she played (with relish) a mean girl, forcing other female performers' mouths onto cocks, making *them* gag. The star of titles such as *Gapeman 2*, *Oral Hygiene*, *Irritable Bowel Syndrome*, *American Bukkake 26*, *I've Been Sodomized* and *Piss Mops* observes: "The life I'd created for myself was just a trough for me to gorge in. I couldn't get enough."

It seems some people are just more inclined to this kind of game of chicken with themselves. As we know from Chapter One, it's called sensation seeking, is connected to impulsivity and is linked to the activity of dopamine in the reward system of the brain.

Consider cocaine. There are two compelling reasons why many porn stars like the drug. The first is that it means they can go without eating for up to fifteen hours, flushing the system enough to tackle an anal scene. The second is that their already highly activated reward pathways are keen for more stimulation—something that can only really be tackled by abstaining and resetting. It's why "chemsex"—a drug fueled sexual bender, most associated with gay men—tends to play out in marathon sessions until an individual crashes; an Ouroboros of self-destruction.

Ken "Shimiken" Shimizu was outed as an adult video performer early in his career. In the face of public shaming, he decided to take an unapologetic stance and cheerfully admitted to everything, even scatological work. As a result, he won public favor. One television network even launched a new segment, which translates as "Let's Fix Shimiken." Its premise: as a high-risk sexual performer, perhaps Shimiken could be coaxed away from porn with a different extreme activity? He was sent on missions such as skydiving and bungee jumping.

Ashley Blue's reward system seemed to be firing on all cylinders. She was suspended on her first day of high school for smoking, and was the first girl in her school to have sex in the eighth grade. As a teenager, her modus operandi seemed to be to go one harder than her peers. Such a rule-breaker and exhibitionist was almost inevitably attracted to gonzo porn. "I wanted to live fully, extraordinarily, not just eking by with some weekend gangbangs from time to time," she writes. "I realized I had never pursued much in my life with pure gusto, courage, and passion, and often felt caged, dull, and bored. Now, considering the far reaches sex could be pushed to, I felt free."

The nature of dopamine is that the more you rodeo-ride your

reward system, the more reactive it becomes, which means the more compelled you feel to raise the stakes. Take the performer Asa Akira—whose motto is, "If it's for everyone, it's not for me." She's given much thought to the subject of porn, both as host of *The Pornhub Podcast* and in her memoir *Insatiable* (2010). In the latter, she recalls going to a Fourth of July barbeque early in her career and listening to other female performers bragging about their endurance:

> "I did anal for Jules Jordan last week, and Mandingo fucked my ass. I can't believe it fit!" one of them humble-bragged.
>
> Not to be outdone, another girl exclaimed, "But have you ever done double anal? I can pretty much fit anything back there now."
>
> "Donna put an entire double-ended dildo in my ass once for *Jay's Deep Anal Drilling*."
>
> What the hell are these girls bragging about? I thought. Having a big asshole is a good thing? I'd never end up like that.
>
> Alas, the curse. I had said it, even if silently, even if just to myself. That word. Never.
>
> I am totally like those other girls now.

The Facial Abuse team, responding to the public's desire for ever more extreme content with scenes involving toilets, dog bowls and waterboarding, are only copying what highly sexed people have been doing since childhood: incrementally drip-feeding the excitement because the brain's nucleus accumbens quickly adapts to novelty.

That's when an interest in violence—a secondary map in

the brain—can overlap with sex. Norman Doidge, who wrote the groundbreaking book about neuroplasticity *The Brain That Changes Itself* (2007), describes committed porn surfers as creating a "neosexuality," with each orgasm reinforcing the behavior as surely as training a dog with treats.

"Because plasticity is competitive, the brain maps for new, exciting images increased at the expense of what had previously attracted them," he writes.

> Sooner or later the surfer finds a killer combination that presses a number of his sexual buttons at once. Then he reinforces the network by viewing the images repeatedly, masturbating, releasing dopamine and strengthening these networks ... Because he often develops tolerance, the pleasure of sexual discharge must be supplemented with the pleasure of an aggressive release, and sexual and aggressive images are increasingly mingled—hence the increase in sadomasochistic themes in hardcore porn.

This desensitization through tolerance affects performers, too. In his memoir, Tyler Knight remembers being on set and weary at the idea of mustering yet another erection. "I purse my lips together. Shut my eyes. Exhale. Go to my fantasy wank bank? Please. The shit I've done, that motherfucker's long overdrawn. I peaced it out and replaced it with my growing Flip Book of Horrors that's now as thick as a dictionary ... I pull the flip-book off the shelf and I flicker fucked-up movies on the screen behind my eyelids." And the founder of eFukt certainly isn't immune. When asked in an interview if he masturbates to videos on his site, he replies, "I'm pretty sure eFukt gave me erectile dysfunction. I can't even remember the last time I got hard from watching porn."

The consumer's increasing desire for extremes has created a supply-and-demand relationship between endurance and economics. For performers today, pornography doesn't so much offer the opportunity to explore their limits as to commodify acts of endurance. It's why some women have moved into the territory of OnlyFans: a content platform that facilitates a direct exchange between performer and consumer through a subscription, pay-per-view or tips. As well as controlling their own finances, performers call the shots with the content, which is often filmed on a smartphone and sometimes made on demand. There's more of an intimacy to curated content—appealing to consumers who'd prefer an online girlfriend to a gaping aperture.

Back when I was working in porn, I couldn't have envisaged any of this. These days, there's little chance that Bridgette Kerkove would make column inches for her acts of endurance, just as no media company would devote the resources to pay me to be hungover at my desk, writing about it. So may you be celebrated here, Bridgette. Your chopstick achievement remains seared into my brain—an extreme feat in an era yet to tip over into the abyss.

Chapter Seven

THE ART OF SUFFERING
Wrestlers

"T HERE ARE PEOPLE who think that wrestling is an ignoble sport," wrote Roland Barthes in his 1957 collection, *Mythologies*. "Wrestling is not a sport, it is a spectacle, and it is no more ignoble to attend a wrestled performance of Suffering than a performance of the sorrows of Arnolphe or Andromaque." It is this "Exhibition of Suffering," he concludes, "which is the very aim of the fight."

Sixty-two years later, Alex Mann positions my phone on a Melbourne pub table, hits record and leans forward. I press a heavy red staple gun flush against his forehead. "You ready?"

"Yep," he says, squeezing his eyes shut.

I fire a staple into his skull and he groans in pain.

That's pretty firmly in, isn't it?" I observe.

"Yeah, it is, yeah," he wheezes, peering into the camera.

He digs out the staple with my car key. Packing a staple remover would be against wrestler protocol.

Belatedly, I wonder aloud if I should have participated in this. Alex has a brain injury from being repeatedly struck on the head with a DVD player while wrestling as his alter ego, KrackerJak.

"It doesn't make a difference," he assures me. "You're more likely to get hurt taking the body slam or the suplex than you are stapling yourself or stabbing yourself with a kitchen fork. It's all just meat, that sort of stuff."

Alex is a hardcore wrestler, which means his fights are known as deathmatches. In these sadistic soap operas, opponents flout rules and use trash cans, ladders, fluorescent lights, trestle tables, chairs, mousetraps and other repurposed household objects to inflict ultraviolence upon one another—and, let's face it, on themselves. With the staple gun, he's demonstrating that such antics are far more painful outside of the ring, or "the theater in the round," as he calls it (of which Barthes would surely approve). In the real world, adrenaline and endorphins are disappointingly slow to flow.

He's had to get creative with pain lately. While trudging the road to recovery—which means avoiding wrestling—he's developed some performance-art routines for burlesque clubs, such as The Twelve Unnecessarily Violent Days of Christmas, in which he repeatedly staples his body. Then there's the Painful Pollock, for art spaces, whereby he swings upside down, slices open his face and drip-bleeds onto paper. These activities harness the transcendence of pain in the wrestling ring, plus he quite enjoys decontextualizing violence in this way, removing it from the arena of imminent threat.

While pro-wrestling is one of the most injurious sports (or, more accurately, it's sports entertainment), it's generally only hardcore wrestlers who leave blood smears across the ring. Early in his training, Alex assessed his strengths and limitations, and decided this was the style he was best suited for.

"I'm not an athlete and I'm not tremendously acrobatic," he says. "I can operate at heights but I don't fly like an eagle, so that limited me in terms of some of the really out-there stuff I wanted to do. Instead, I was left with the gougey stuff, like having someone hold me down and repeatedly staple things into me, or cut me open."

He settled on the name KrackerJak for its onomatopoeia— "It's a violent, crunchy sound, like stomping on a plastic cup"—but he began to create the persona that is now inextricably woven into his identity before he even considered wrestling as a possibility. As a kid growing up in Warburton, country Victoria, he would gawk at the pumped-up characters of fantasy and sci-fi (surely never better than in 1987's *Masters of the Universe* movie, with the ultra-swole Dolph Lundgren as He-Man). "There was such a masculinity to it," he says. "You don't read the campiness of it when you're six. It's like, bad dudes in leather. You think, *What a tough guy. Look at that big moustache. Look how big their chests are. What a real man.*"

Eventually he discovered wrestling through Super Nintendo's *WWF Super WrestleMania*. The game came with a booklet that listed all the characters at the back. It appealed to his drama-nerd side, as did the fight scenes dressed up as sports, so he started to watch wrestling on television. This was in the early 1990s, just before the World Wrestling Foundation (WWF)— now known as World Wrestling Entertainment (WWE)—was investigated for doling out anabolic steroids and human growth hormones. It meant wrestlers such as Lex Luger, Hulk Hogan and Rowdy Roddy Piper could maintain the myth of being pleasingly larger than life.

Wrestling was everything Alex liked about acting ... but bigger. You got to create your own superhero or supervillain and interact with other characters, and to write your own script. So he began lifting weights and training with "Red Hot" Ricky Diamond. His first fight, in 2000, was at a street fair in a suburb of northeast Melbourne, outside a chicken shop. Alex was one of twenty wrestlers in a lunchtime Royal Rumble-style pile-on. "I had two minutes in the ring," he says, "but it was enough. I was sold."

I understand a bit about what he means by that. In 2012, as a thirty-seven-year-old journalist, I took a metro train out to an unlovely suburb to profile Melbourne City Wrestling, whose members trained in a ring set up in the backyard of George "The Hitman" Julio. I squeezed past an Alsatian on a chain and a shed cluttered with ancient weights, to a larger shed lined with photographs of the then sixty-seven-year-old Julio as a younger wrestler. As the trainers demonstrated the basics in the ring—back bumps, handstand rolls, whips off the ropes, arm drags, clotheslines and a few flashy moves like the sunset flip and scoop slam—it wasn't long before I'd asked for a go myself. Tommy Hellfire and Andy Phoenix didn't mess about. After I received the minimalist instruction of tucking my chin into my chest, I was flying through the air and landing on my back with a loud smack.

It felt like I'd come home. I returned to the suburb of Sunshine week after week, exhilarated to feel pain in parts of my body I'd never felt pain in before, and pumped beyond belief at the frenetic exchange of energy. True, my fellow novices were twenty years younger, with tracksuit pants stained with bong water and other blemishes of youth, but perhaps the ringside lights and some well-cut spandex would conceal my comparative maturity.

As rookies, we'd help set up the ring in far-flung suburbs. Most of the time it was inglorious: sparse audiences with fists buried in family packs of Doritos, chanting taunts and making greedy grabs at well-oiled biceps as the wrestlers made their entrances or, worse, sitting impassively. But occasionally it reached some crazy zenith. Like at one match, in a vast RSL in Sunshine, when the loud talk spilled into the next room, where a karaoke session was in full swing. That was where I first saw KrackerJak wrestle. He and Carlo Cannon crashed the karaoke stage, but not every onlooker realized that the shocked suburbanite on the mic was a wrestler herself—then known as K.C. Cassidy, now as Peyton Royce and doing very well as a WWE talent.

After six months of training, I threw in the towel. It was starting to seem inappropriate and, all right, a bit pathetic, grappling with teenage boys; not that men in their late thirties harbored the same reservations when I was a teenager. Added to that, I was feeling the pressure. There were so few rings in Australia at the time. The other rookies were hungry for a career and versed in wrestling lore. I never sat glued to televised wrestling as a child; I'd just fraudulently talked my way in as a journalist. But I've always had faint regrets about walking away.

Thankfully, after that first match in Fairfield, Alex stuck at it. He decided that KrackerJak should be the goofy underdog, prone to moments of alarming irrationality: the loose cannon who could go off at any moment. He adopted a hammy cadence, a riff on US wrestler Road Warrior Hawk's delivery, "where you try to make your voice sound like a circular saw starting up." He wore his hair wild, sometimes in bunches, and a black-and-red spandex jersey with *BASTARD* across the torso. He slapped on fake tan before matches to make his muscles more defined under the lights. "Like with everything else in wrestling, a lot of my decisions make me look absolutely ridiculous in day-to-day life, but for fifteen minutes in that ring I look fucking mint," he says.

His wins may include being a three-time WrestleRock Champion, two-time Warzone Wrestling Champion, Melbourne City Wrestling Heavyweight Champion and Professional Championship Wrestling Heavyweight Champion, but as the underdog, KrackerJak should suffer. To hand the mic back to Roland Barthes:

> In judo, a man who is down is hardly down at all, he rolls over, he draws back, he eludes defeat, or, if the latter is obvious, he immediately disappears; in wrestling, a man who is down is exaggeratedly so, and completely fills the eyes of the spectators with the intolerable spectacle of his powerlessness.

Alex thinks a lot about suffering. Even as a kid, the action heroes who appealed to him were those who went through hell. There was something about Steven Seagal swanning off without a scratch that seemed untrustworthy and inauthentic. Not like Jean-Claude Van Damme getting chopped in the nuts and slammed repeatedly against a shipping container in *Double Impact* ... or having his head held underwater in front of jeering bikini babes in *Lionheart* ... or being tied between two trees and mercilessly stretched into the splits in *Bloodsport*.

"Or Stallone," Alex offers, of the actor with the epically woebegone face. "Stallone suffers heaps in his movies. He digs wrestling and I think he understands that idea of the underdog, and the suffering you go through physically, which creates sympathy and which your character learns from."

Suffering in sport is not merely a noble journey of physical sacrifice, but its own masochistic melodrama—a way of thrashing out complicated internal issues in the crudest of external ways. In his book *Welcome to the Suffersphere*, cyclist Jon Malnick opens with Karl Marx's oft-quoted "the only antidote to mental suffering is physical pain," going on to explore the addictive nature of that physical pain. "We start coveting it, craving it, almost as if a hospital X-ray exam might reveal the existence of a suffer-shaped hole somewhere deep inside," he writes. "We try to assure ourselves that there's nothing inherently wrong with this, with seeking out bodily suffering for the calming sense of spiritual purification that follows. It all has much in common with scratching a stubborn itch. The more you scratch, the more you itch."

While wrestling characters have to adapt their personalities and motives according to storylines—switching from "babyface" good guy to bad guy "heel," for instance—Alex found it easier to keep suffering at the core of KrackerJak once he'd decided to work within the cartoonish deathmatch genre. He took inspiration from Ash Williams, the luckless antihero of the *Evil Dead* horror films. Even when Ash transforms from victim to avenger, he's constantly covered in his own blood, often by his own clumsy hand.

Deathmatches duly started to influence KrackerJak's appearance, most visibly in the deep scars all over his body. As a teenager, Alex had been a fan of the hardcore wrestler Sabu, who wore a kaffiyeh headdress and was billed as being from Saudi Arabia (although he was actually Terry Brunk of Staten Island). "Sabu always had terrible cuts all over his body," says Alex. "He'd get ripped open in matches and then just Krazy Glue the cuts shut. I thought that was cool so I went for a more strategic version." He gestures at his bicep. "Like, 'All right, I want two lines here, so I'll get you to use the cheese grater on me in a match.'"

As a veteran of twenty years, Alex's skill set is appreciated. Throughout his recovery, he's kept his hand in with a variety of roles that straddle the office and the locker room: commentator and promo-class teacher for Melbourne City Wrestling; cohost of an ABC podcast about wrestling, *Behind the Belt*; and sheriff of Melbourne's WrestleRock.

He also now manages his brother, Nick, who wears a flesh mask and goes by the ring name of Gore. As Gore, Nick plays the brute to Alex's agitator. He flexes his muscles like the bully kicking sandcastles on the beach, lounges back on the ropes and then explodes forth in comedic timing to flatten someone, or spin them in the air before slamming them down. At one rumble, it takes four wrestlers to topple him over the ropes, swarming around him like helicopters around King Kong.

"I still get my suffering thing in, and I get to protect Gore as well, because I'm more expendable than him," Alex says, sliding into storyline mode, one that's a bit Frankenstein's monster, a bit Marvel. "He has more of a mystique to preserve, whereas I can be his weakling and take the shots. In some ways I'm meant to be the brains of his operation."

There may be fewer endorphins geeing him up when he's hobbling about with his barbed wire-wrapped cane, but occasionally he'll cop a cage door to the face from one of Gore's opponents, or break his finger grabbing someone's ankles through the ropes. It will have to do for now.

MANAGING NICK HAS emphasized to Alex the complex nature of violence. Prior to wrestling, Nick won championship belts in MMA and kickboxing. "Like, legit fighting," Alex says. "There's a point of difference between me and my brother, which is that he obviously has a switch that he's able to turn on and off, allowing him to inflict authentic pain and force somebody else to give up. I never had that capacity. In wrestling, there's this weird miasma of consent. So when Mad Dog [McCrea, another hardcore wrestler] says, 'I want you to attack me with a box cutter,' I'm like, 'Yeah, sure.' He said it's okay and I'm willing to inflict the violence upon him that he needs."

It was this miasma of consent that wound up backfiring, as it often eventually does, in what turned out to be KrackerJak's last match. In a plotline harking back to Greek mythology, whereby gods are killed by their sons so that their sons may succeed them, KrackerJak had challenged his wayward protégé, Lochy "Loverboy" Hendricks, to a match. If KrackerJak won, Lochy would return to the fold and get back on the straight and narrow. If Lochy won, KrackerJak would retire from wrestling forever.

It was choreographed so that KrackerJak would lose, because at thirty-eight, Alex was feeling the wear and tear. He had plans to announce his retirement and then embark on a legend cycle, like WWE stalwarts The Undertaker and Sting. In that guise, he'd pop up every three or four months, pump up a storyline, help forge the reputations of new talent, then gallop off once more to tend to his vegetable patch.

All week, he'd been preparing: hammering nails through plywood to build a twelve hundred-strong bed of nails, ordering forty packets of thumbtacks from Woolworths and prepping his weapons. But he was feeling oddly unenthused. He was up until near dawn the night before, applying his preshow tan, packing his first-aid kit of Steri-Strips and tea tree oil, and editing the video that would play pre-match to bring non-regular punters up to date with the storyline.

Call it a premonition or call it fatigue, but once at the theater, there was none of the usual racing up and down the stairs backstage and slapping himself in the face to psych himself up into his gregarious alter ego. He felt like he was walking through mud.

Alex and Lochy had arranged a few old favorite maneuvers, but the DVD player was a new idea—untested, because who wants a dry run of being smashed over the head with nine pounds of steel? He'd told Lochy beforehand to just hit him until he went down, although—having a theatrical background—he'd privately decided on the rule of three, plus one more as an exclamation mark. There was no safety word. He just had to fall over.

The first time the DVD player came down on his head, it rattled him a fair bit. Even without the blood trickling down his face, he would have known he'd seriously misjudged. In the past, he'd used fan heaters and other steel implements, but they were more hollow. If he'd taken the trouble to unscrew the DVD player and have a poke around, he would have realized that he would struggle to bend the machine over his knee.

For the second and third hits, he braced his forehead on his forearm to try and prevent his neck from compacting. His main concern was the bulging disc at C7 in his neck, which had forced him to take a year off in the recent past. But he couldn't bring himself to raise his arms farther and protect his head. Not with six hundred wrestling fans all invested in his glorious demise.

With the fourth hit, his brain rang. He'd experienced that sensation before, upon having Japanese kendo sticks broken over his head, but this time it was so much heavier. None of the force passed through the DVD player. His head became the crumple zone.

Alex finally went down. Lochy pinned him and gloated, then Alex got up to stumble KrackerJak's farewell lap around the ring. "I knew it had worked, but even in the moment that my career ended and I looked out at the audience to see people crying, which meant I'd broken through that veneer of them watching a show, I felt nothing," he says.

At this point, Alex didn't know he was in trouble.

"And then I did what everyone should do after a traumatic head injury: I drank heavily."

The next day he was due to give a farewell speech at the Melbourne City Wrestling Christmas party. He headed to the restaurant. By the time others arrived, he couldn't stand or keep his head aloft, so he sat at a table and rested his head on two napkin dispensers, stacked one above the other. "Everyone just thought I was hungover. *I* thought I was hungover."

It took another month for his balance to go. Making any kind of rapid movement now made his equilibrium lurch violently to the right. MRI scans revealed post-concussion brain damage had affected his body's ability to tell which way is up. His rehab has followed the same path as that of a stroke patient, trying to rewrite the neural pathways. "It's like exposure therapy, basically," he says. "I've got to keep making myself dizzy and dizzy over and over again."

Such injuries are a daily risk for wrestlers. Had he not been hit over the skull with a DVD player, Alex could just have easily executed a dive through the ropes during training and hit the floor badly, or made an ill-timed impact with another wrestler, or any number of misfortunes. Even when things don't go wrong, the damage adds up.

"They've done tests in the States and they've worked out the regular wrestling match has comparable trauma to the body as a small car accident," says Alex. "We all end up with stronger skeletons because those tiny vibrations damage you and then you grow back stronger, but there's a tipping point where the wear and tear just overwhelms you and stuff starts giving up. In terms of my ability to tell a story and the psychology of it, my understanding is at the top of my game, but my body is not. My body, in terms of what I can ask of it, probably peaked about ten years ago."

When a wrestler falls over and lands—as loudly as possible and over as large an area of the back as possible—it's called a bump. In industry lore, each wrestler has a theoretical bump card, and once it's full, their career is finished.

"Everyone's bump card is different," Alex says. "Sometimes you can take a really bad one doing something simple and that's it, you're done forever. My bump card is much fuller than someone starting out, so even when I do start training again it's going to be about the cardio and the skill and the technique, because I can't be taking fifty body slams every Thursday night. I have to be more precious."

Peer behind the curtain of professional wrestling and it's difficult to see why anyone would want to take such gambles. As WWE Hall of Fame inductee Diamond Dallas Page has put it, wrestling's not fake, because you can't fake gravity.

High-profile injuries include Sabu suffering two neck breaks, Joe Thurman and Buff Bagwell breaking their backs, Mick Foley getting part of his ear ripped off and X-Pac rupturing his anus. Bret Hart received a severe concussion and had to retire shortly after. "I was mad for being there and mad for being in this situation," he told a neuroscience symposium in 2019. "I remember when I hit the ground, I could see a million stars." Weeks later, his younger brother Owen—who had himself broken Stone Cold Steve Austin's neck at the 1997 SummerSlam—died after falling from a harness as he descended from the ceiling during the WWF's pay-for-view live broadcast *Over the Edge*. A handful of other wrestlers have died from brain trauma in or out of the ring.

Even more prevalent is death from combinations of painkillers and other prescription drugs, street drugs and anabolic steroids. Young, fit wrestlers have a habit of tapping out for good between their thirties and fifties; in fact, one 2014 study found that mortality rates for professional wrestlers are 2.9 times greater than in the general US population. Stats such as this gave the WWE an obligation to establish its Talent Wellness Program in 2006, which involves cardiac, brain and drug testing (things used to be very different: in 1993, WWE boss Vince McMahon was charged with routinely obtaining anabolic steroids for his roster of wrestlers), but since then illicit drug use has continued to flourish. It's unsurprising. WWE wrestlers, unlike other athletes, have no off-season, and need to power through show after show while living on the road. The demands of their occupation are more comparable to those of musicians or long-distance truck drivers. And for the many bodybuilders who found their way into wrestling, steroids and GHB—a nervous system depressant that is reported to aid fat loss and muscle growth—were already part of the diet.

In her breakneck-paced memoir, *A Star Shattered* (2016), former WWF diva Tammy "Sunny" Sytch recalls trafficking prescription drugs from Mexico for her fellow wrestlers. "I couldn't believe how quick and easy that was," she wrote. "The bag contained one thousand Vicodin, one thousand Percocet, three thousand Somas, two thousand Xanax, two thousand Valium, five hundred Rohypnol, testosterone preloaded syringes, vials of Winstol, and Clenbuterol tabs … When you get away with that much, a feeling of exhilaration overtakes you, a complete rush of adrenaline. I was so proud of myself."

Lex Luger's memoir, *Wrestling with the Devil*, describes the culture at WWF as encouraging of taking painkillers along with coffee to power through gym sessions when the body was about to give up. Inebriation wasn't just behind the scenes, though. There have been televised matches in which wrestlers were dangerously impaired, such as "Victory Road" in 2011, in which Sting had to hastily pin a staggering Jeff Hardy, and "SummerSlam" 2002, in which Bret Hart had to hiss instructions and mime facial expressions at British Bulldog Davey Boy Smith, because the latter had been smoking crack for weeks.

Times have changed, of course, and even the indie scene has been cleaned up. There are wrestling academies springing up around Australia, and more promotions, put on with greater polish. Promoters are teaming up with breweries and music venues, reaching out to new audiences. The current generation of wrestlers are hungrily seeking out pathways to WWE (which Alex believes is now churning out cookie-cutter wrestlers—"like rock eisteddfod with bumps"), so they're more career-minded and less hedonistic. "I'm not making enough money to kill myself on cocaine," he says, a touch wistfully, "but anyway, I don't drink or take anything before I wrestle, besides an amazing amount of caffeine. It's unprofessional, because you've got to be tight. There's timing, there's safety. I don't want to be half a step slower and then not catch someone and they break their collarbone."

But not being able to wrestle at all due to injury is almost unthinkable, so it's not surprising many choose to numb the pain and power through. Some of those who have found themselves permanently retired have suffered a severe identity crisis, having lived with a larger-than-life alter ego for years. In her memoir, Sytch—whose image in 1996 was downloaded more than that of any other celebrity, according to AOL—describes putting on weight and being unable to work because of pancreatitis from excessive alcohol consumption. "A once confident, outgoing, beautiful woman, who was lusted after for years by men all over the world, and now a depressed recluse, too afraid to go anywhere, fearful that she might be recognized," she writes.

Going to the grocery store was a scary thing. Walking the mall was terrifying. Going to the gym was brutal, because people expected to see the body I had in the nineties and my pre-pancreatitis curves. I grew deeply depressed and self-conscious. My self-esteem was gone. Do you have any idea what it's like for someone to recognize you, and then ask, "What happened to you?" Those same people don't even bother to try to hide the confusion and disgust in their face. It feels awful.

In Christopher Bell's documentary about steroids and human growth hormones, *Bigger, Stronger, Faster* (2008), his brother, "Mad Dog" Mike Bell, won't stop chasing the first high of his wrestling dream long after the phone's stopped ringing. Mike died at the age of thirty-seven, the year the documentary was released, of a heart attack induced by a household inhalant called Dust-Off. He had once told Chris he would rather be dead than average.

That inability to accept oneself as anything less than god-like is summed up in the movie *Fighting with My Family* (2019), in a fictional speech by WWE coach Hutch, played by Vince Vaughn. "Your brother's a journeyman," Hutch tells the protagonist, Paige, just as Bell reflected that his brother had only ever been the WWE "jobber."

There are stars and there are journeymen who take the hits to make the stars look good, and your brother's a journeyman. He's the punching bag. He's the guy with the bad shorts with no fanfare. I bring him out here and then what? We put him on the road for two hundred days, he's chasing fame that's never going to come to him. His wife starts screwing the garbage man because he's never around, his kid can't remember his face … and for what? Maybe he'd get a shot at a pay-for-view event, and he would try so hard to make an impression he'd probably let a real star throw him off a thirty-foot cage onto a concrete floor. He'd have his shoulder bone just kind of spliced right through his rotator cuff, tear it clean in half, and then the doctor would say, "That's it, your wrestling career's over." But why stop then? He wouldn't stop. So then the wife would leave him and take the kid and then he would just keep chasing the pipe dream until he was four thousand miles away from anyone that ever loved him.

In *The Wrestler* (2008), Mickey Rourke plays world-weary pro Randy "The Ram" Robinson, who lives in the reflected glory of his 1980s alter ego. "I'm the one who was supposed to take care of everything," he tells his daughter after the heart attack that finally puts an end to his career. "I'm the one who was supposed to make everything okay for everybody. It just didn't work out like that … And now, I'm an old, broken-down piece of meat."

Where *do* retired wrestlers go, other than rehab? Sometimes they're relegated to less physically demanding roles, such as valets and managers, commentators or WWE ambassadors. Sometimes they line their pockets by signing up for the legend circuit—usually nostalgia matches with fellow former big names. Some—like Road Dogg and Lex Luger—find God. Then there are those who move into porn. It is a well-trod path: both professions require alter egos, ultra-fit bodies, show-manship and an ability to give and take punishment.

Sandra Lee Schwab, a.k.a. Tiffany Million, blazed the trail. She began her career in the 1980s wrestling promotion "Gorgeous Ladies of Wrestling," now made famous by the Netflix dramatization *GLOW*, before performing in adult movies. Wrestlers Tylene "Major Gunns" Buck and Shane Douglas also made films, as well as Tammy Sytch, whose *Sunny Side Up: In Through the Backdoor* (2016) begins with the disclaimer, "This video is not sponsored, endorsed by or affiliated with World Wrestling Entertainment, Inc."

Most famously, there's Joanie "Chyna" Laurer. Joanie and her boyfriend Sean "X-Pac" Waltman released their sex tape, titled *1 Night in China* (it was actually filmed in China), in 2004, through the same company that released Paris Hilton's sex tape, *1 Night in Paris*. Both wrestlers had excelled in the WWF's late-1990s Attitude Era, in which music was louder, women were more sexualized and men looked like juiced-up members of the band NSYNC.

Joanie, who had been dismissed from the WWF, made five additional porn films, some of them vengeful—such as that in which actors mimicked WWF's boss Vince McMahon, wrestler (and Joanie's ex-boyfriend) Triple H and others. She died in 2016, with alcohol, painkillers, sleeping aids and antianxiety medications found in her system, and her brain was donated to a leading researcher of chronic traumatic encephalopathy. CTE is a degenerative brain disease often found in athletes who have suffered repeated blows to the head, such as boxers, NFL players and hockey players. It can cause depression, aggression, confusion, memory loss, impulse control problems and impaired judgment—but where those symptoms begin and an individual's preexisting attraction to high-risk behavior end might be impossible to ascertain.

Joanie's mother had maintained hope that her daughter could get sober. Not long before Joanie's death, she sent her an email. It said: *Get away from this Chyna persona—just be Joanie. If you're just Joanie, you're gonna be okay.*

THE SECOND TIME I interviewed Alex, there was a darkness beneath the bombast. It was as though he were a Marvel character on the cusp of turning villain, after a crescendo of crushing misfortunes and injustices.

He'd taken another major physical blow. Playing a wrestler in an indie film—something he thought would be relatively safe—he landed "like a sack of shit" during a basic move, which he put down to being out of practice, or maybe to his stiff cowboy boots. It snapped the anterior cruciate ligament around his knee joint. Alex's scenes were duly cut, and he estimated it would delay his return to the ring by another two years.

"KrackerJak is inextricably linked with me," he despaired. "I've not made any other characters that I've poured as much time into. He was a character that I was bouncing around in my head before I had even gone into wrestling, and I've grown with him. So many people—two generations of wrestlers and wrestling fans—know me as the real-world blend of that character, that it kind of feels like I can't just switch it off anyway."

A comeback seemed so far off that it was almost abstract.

The third time we talk, Alex is in his house in the hinterland of Melbourne—"the Bastard Compound," as he calls it—with his hair in a jaunty side pony, wearing a sleeveless Melbourne City Wrestling shirt that shows the latticework of cuts on his arms. I mention he seems more cheerful and he confesses he's made a concerted effort, exercising first to energize himself. "The last time we met I'd driven four hours and had just spent nine hours doing renovation on someone's house, on one leg," he points out. "Wrestling had never felt further away."

When the pandemic hit, suddenly everyone was in the same boat. Careers stalled, storylines fell apart, bodies went to seed, testosterone cycles went unappreciated. The forced hiatus has been a great leveler. If Alex can fully recover from his knee injury and be the sage elder while others in the scene freak out, he can make his grand comeback.

His last public appearance as KrackerJak was at the comic convention Supanova, where Gore took on the glowstick-waving JXT, and Krackers helped by wielding his staple gun. It was early March, days before coronavirus caused lockdowns around the world. Krackers wore a full hazmat suit and mask, which added to the audience's sense of alarm. It didn't seem odd that a character as paranoid and highly strung as KrackerJak would be a prepper, but as ever, the line between KrackerJak and Alex was blurred.

"It was vigorous bet-hedging," says Alex of his outfit choice, which he also wore around his local town. "Shit went down in the first two weeks of March and I bought a bunch of supplies for Bastard Compound. People were not cool with the suit, which was partly an act of precaution and partly performance art. But also, that performance was my way of reconciling with my own uncertainty about whether this virus was seriously contagious or not."

The reactions from the general public, even those used to seeing his relentlessly scarred arms about town, were intense. "Some people got angry. Like, I went into Bunnings to buy some supplies and there was actually some authentic hostility toward the suit. I had people stopping me and they'd be like, 'Are you genuinely scared, or is this a joke?' I said, 'Well, let me put it like this: if you're dead on a ventilator in a month from now, then I was dead serious. But if everything's fine, then it's a gag.'"

He and his partner, Josie Hess, a filmmaker, made a web series called *Social Distancing*, in which they took an acerbic view of conspiracy theorists and "freedom fighters," such as the Melbourne wrestler who announced his retirement during the pandemic to focus instead on spreading the word of QAnon. When he was arrested by police at a protest, he was caught on camera rising from the ground while bleeding from the forehead. Did he "juice" himself with a hidden razorblade, as he's been known to in the ring? Only he can say for sure. He, of course, denies it.

Alex continues to film shorts for his Bastard TV channel on YouTube, and again some of his own real fears have bled into the performances. In one episode, Krackers visits a psychologist and examines his anger issues. In another, he tries to satisfy his need for self-harm by having a nurse extract around a pint of his blood into little vials and spray it all over him. (That wasn't faked—a real nurse, Alex's friend, did the honors.)

"I've managed to worm a bit of creative self-harm into the

Bastard TV episodes," he says, "but not having matches robs you of the experience of getting out in front of a bunch of people and being loud. I can stomp around the house shouting, but then it's just unpleasant for one person. There's not the immediate call-and-response thing that you get from performing in front of a live crowd."

As Alex is clearly mourning the loss of ultraviolence in his life, I ask him if inflicting it and receiving it has some kind of cathartic payoff. He flip-flops in his response. "Absolutely. Yes. Truly, it is cathartic," he says at first. "I find my desire to do incredibly violent things does scale according to how unhappy I am in my life. If I'm feeling tremendously content, I don't necessarily want to get out of the comfy bed with my girlfriend and fall into barbed wire. Whereas when you're feeling particularly tortured, that sort of transcendent suffering you can go through in a performance can give you a bunch of endorphins that you weren't going to get any other way. I don't have any other avenues in my life where I scream aggressively at people as loud as I can."

Yet his real-life psychologist has given him something to chew on. "It came up in therapy that engaging in that behavior just reinforces the neural pathways that in turn reinforce your capacity to get angry or violent. I used to think it was like letting off steam. Now I think it's playing around in an area of my life that's easier to get to the more I do it. But it feels so fucking good."

In the meantime, he's strengthening all the body parts he can. Bone mineral density thickens when subjected to abrupt stress. Muscle tissue reknits around micro-tears. The transformation continues. Real superhero stuff.

Chapter Eight

ANGER IS AN ENERGY

Fighters

"**N**AME A FIGHTER** that everybody could objectively agree is not attractive," Eugene S. Robinson challenges me. "I'd be surprised; I can't think of one. I'm not saying they're all Calvin Klein models, but it's rare for me to see a fighter that I don't process as handsome."

Eugene's Skype handle is "Handsome Man."

Since taking up Muay Thai, I've been wondering what the necessary attributes of a fighter are, as venturing into the ring seems to be the ultimate test of self. What powers a pugilist's urge to go toe-to-toe with someone intent on knocking them out, thus risking serious injury, brain damage and even death? Maybe impulsivity. Maybe some spite. Maybe even a kind of death wish bravado, or a long-held fear of having something to prove. But surely, more than in any other sport, all roads lead back to rage.

I decide that Eugene, the author of *Fight: Everything You Ever Wanted to Know About Ass-Kicking But Were Afraid You'd Get Your Ass Kicked for Asking* (2007), and a long-time hyperbolic commentator on the world of biff, ought to know.

Eugene loves, loves, loves a fight, be it in the street, on the mat, in an underground fight club or on stage in his guise as front man for San Francisco experimental rock band Oxbow (just itching for a heckler to kick off). He writes with a fighter's flair—"Topographical maps of the evening's fun had spread out all over my suit in bloodied rivulets"—and acts as nimbly as he thinks, agreeing to an interview the moment he reads my message and participating in it on the fly, while driving home after a run.

Is his hypothesis right—that to be a fighter requires a lantern jaw rather than a burning grudge? In the past week I've seen two veteran fighters, Ken "The World's Most Dangerous Man" Shamrock and Dan "The Beast" Severn, make cameos at a wrestling match. Ken and Dan are action-figure handsome, all thrusting chins and barrel chests. Dan even has a Burt Reynolds-style moustache. But they seem to be ridiculous outliers of masculinity. So instead I sift through a mental Rolodex of cauliflower-eared, railroad-nosed bad boys and choose Chris "The Crippler" Leben, whose wild benders have lent him quite the ruddy bloat.

"If I was a casting director, I would cast Chris all the time," Eugene protests. "Classic Middle America look. Nobody would call him a bad-looking guy."

Many kids are drawn to martial arts because of their anxieties over not measuring up. By contrast, Eugene argues that combat athletes—boxers, kickboxers and MMA fighters—bear the burden of being too handsome, which naturally leads them to become targets in bar rooms and parking lots. "You have to develop a carapace so that people don't fuck with you," he explains. "I mean, that's how *I* grew up."

Which illustrates well that we all bring our own subjectivity and experiences to theories on why people fight.

Eugene was born into a complicated family and raised in Brooklyn in the 1970s. His grandmother became pregnant with his father at the age of thirteen, and her rapist—Eugene's grand-father—was a lifelong criminal, up to the neck in extortion, gambling and loan-sharking. Eugene's troubled father dis-owned him, and his relationship with his mother was fraught. Sometimes she was "all Diana Ross cool"; other times she was hot-tempered.

"I was a fairly good kid and stayed between the lines in a lot of ways, but then my mother's relationship with my stepfather started to go down the toilet," he says. "My mother wasn't a hit-ter, but she was a ranter. She'd follow me from room to room, arguing about something or other, and if I looked upset she would *go* at me. I ended up suppressing and suppressing, devel-oping an unhealthy relationship to anger." Or, as he puts it in his book, "vast wellsprings of rage."

For Eugene, "animal anger" became a calling, "but well before that, it started out as an emotional need." And he gets seriously tetchy if he doesn't see that same base instinct rampag-ing through the veins of other so-called fighters.

Like the time he was loading out after a show in Maine and a couple of dudes tried to rile him in the parking lot, one of them hurling a can of beer. "I finally said, 'If you want to fight me, there's one thing you could do and one thing only: say one more word to me.'" When the man did, Eugene stepped down from the van onto the curb and the guy got a sense of his stature. "I saw fear in his eyes, and that's when I got angry for the first time, because I wanted him to have the strength of his conviction," Eugene says. "I want you to be fully fucking committed to this prospect." Irked, Eugene knocked out that man, and the other ran off.

Or the time he took part in a jujitsu competition and was matched with a man clearly content with just winning a participation ribbon. On his way to the mat, Eugene heard the schmuck's wife urging, "Come on baby, you can do it."

"Like you do your best and that's all that matters!" Eugene spits. "That half-measure thing gets on my nerves. I just smashed the guy, threw him down, side control, got him in a Kimura, tapped him out. And I was like, *Goddamn you. Stand up! Walk! Do not go gently into this good night!*"

It's a stance a million miles away from the dojos of traditional martial arts, upon whose walls there will usually be a pledge that the techniques learned within will not be exploited, and the ethos is to leave the world a better place, not smash it to smithereens. Eugene adds hastily, "But don't mischaracterize my attitude as, *Oh, I don't have time for the weak.* I just don't like quitting. That's why I've been in the same band since 1988. And the last five years of my marriage were like, 'Fuck it. If she can take it, *I* can take it.'"

He laughs uproariously. "You can't lose if you don't quit."

THROUGHOUT OUR CONVERSATION, Eugene refers to the "emotional content" of fighting, and yet when he talked to the famous interviewees in his book about "bloodlust" and "an emotional delight in domination," he found them unwilling to deconstruct their urges. He puts that down to professional fighters being so accustomed to what they do that they no longer examine the emotional underpinnings; nor is there much time in their schedule for introspection. "And if there is, it's not something that you're going to share with the journalist," he says.

So I'm lucky to find someone as frank as bare-knuckle boxer Christine Ferea, who also has a long career in Muay Thai and MMA behind her. Christine agrees to an interview, but wants to know a few things first. Who am I? Why did I become a journalist? What is my interest in combat sports? How did I find her?

It's a logical approach for someone who has to study an opponent so closely that it borders on obsession. Bare-knuckle boxing is conducted over two-minute rounds, so there's no time to feel out the other fighter in the ring. Instead, Christine stalks an opponent for months beforehand by watching their old fights, observing their temperament and tics, and reading their insults on Instagram. It makes for a strange kind of intimacy.

With Christine having hit thirty-seven, everything is riding on this bid for a legacy in bare-knuckle, as her Instagram posts scouting for men to spar with in the Vegas area suggest. When we speak, her most pressing concern is Helen Peralta, a Dominican Republic native, raised in New York. The two last clashed in August 2019, at the Mississippi Coast Coliseum. Both ended with swollen faces: Helen in her gladiator-style shorts and tight braids, with a cut at the corner of her eye that had already caused the lid to bulge into a slit; Christine with her *MISFIT* shorts, sharp undercut and a contusion on either cheekbone.

It was a close battle, but the unanimous decision in Helen's favor marked Christine's first loss in the sport. Naturally, she's hungry for a rematch, but the event has been postponed because of the pandemic.

"What's the plan?" I ask, meaning I assume it will be rescheduled.

"Kill her," Christine says. "Make sure she doesn't get up for about thirty seconds after I hit her."

Christine has the backstory of a fighter in a telemovie: a street kid, in and out of trouble and eventually prison, who found her calling in a jailhouse fight gym and thus avoided her dismal destiny as a homicide or overdose statistic. Her aesthetic is still very much "street thug"—a hangover from childhood, when her family moved from San Jose to a neighborhood in Las Vegas where gang culture was rife. Local guys targeted her brother, and Christine found herself rising to the bait in his defense. "I would be like, 'Dude! They're going to keep fucking with you! I'm going with you—you roll with me and my home-girls.' I didn't know better, I just thought that was the way. You know, to get respect."

Christine didn't consider herself a gangbanger, so she gave herself the graffiti tag "Solo Rider." Later, her first fight name would be "Solo" before she changed it to "Misfit," because, "You know, I'm a tomboy, I'm gay, I'm not a regular female, I'm a fighter. I want that name for all the other misfits out there that have felt misplaced. We can prosper, we can succeed and there is a place for us, you know what I mean?"

She keeps her parents out of her story, other than to say that she came from a "broken family," but she will admit to a destructive lifestyle. "I assaulted police officers, had cops knock my teeth out, so I did a year in jail with no teeth. I was eighteen years old when I first got locked up, then went in there with all the older people, people on drugs, people with connections, and I was in and out until I was twenty-three," she says. "Honestly, I felt more safe when I was locked up or in rehab, or in the suicidal facility I was put in a few times. Then I would get out and I couldn't get my shit together."

Many prominent fighters grew up on what is poetically described as the wrong side of the tracks—though of course their stories of neglect and family violence have gained attention over those that are more pedestrian. "Even if they didn't come from physically abusive backgrounds, a lot of fighters do come from crazy places, and it goes for all social classes," says Christine. "Just because you didn't come from dirt, doesn't mean you didn't go through something. A lot of us fighters felt so weak and defeated at one time."

Former MMA fighter Ronda Rousey and Australian pro-boxer Sylvia "Hightower" Scharper have both spoken about how losing their fathers at a young age led them to channel grief into aggression. "I think from when my dad died, I always adopted the attitude of 'You can't break me,'" Sylvia reflected in the documentary *Relentless: The Sylvia Scharper Story* (2019). After her father's death, Ronda traded swimming, which allowed too much time for sorrowful introspection, for judo, which required 100 percent focus. In an article she wrote for the *Herald Sun* newspaper, she explained, "I had so much bottled up grief and anger and self-loathing, and for some reason I found an outlet that saved me—fighting."

It's as though what goes on in the ring is the fighter's opera: a condensed story of every test and emotion they've survived.

In psychology, it would be put down to repetition compulsion or traumatic reenactment—the idea of recreating a painful early-life scenario with the unconscious desire to achieve a different outcome so as to emerge the victor.

Christine's opera crescendoed with the discovery of that fight gym in jail, as she peered inside and checked out the five-foot-nothing Filipino girls going through their drills. "I was thinking, *I'll beat all these girls*—not knowing that they actually knew how to fight. I was kind of fat, I guess you could say, and they beat my ass. They would catch my leg and sweep me or give me a teep [front kick] to the face."

Fighting was an outlet that Christine desperately needed, because she was fast becoming locked into an institutionalized mindset. Whereas most of us remember where we were when the planes hit the Twin Towers on 9/11, a young Christine didn't even know about the significance of the date until years later, when she saw a movie about the attack. Another day, her father took her to the local skid row to observe the homeless people talking to themselves. "That's gonna be you," he warned her.

"I was just looking for power and respect," Christine says, "but when you get to jail you see how cops treat you and you can't do anything, and you're eating Top Ramen noodles ... Life is not what you thought it was. Then, one time, I was in the yard, laying on somebody's lap looking at the older ladies who have been in and out of prison their whole life. I was like, *This is my last fucking time.*"

When she was released this time, Christine attached herself to a local fight gym, and quickly recognized in the training regime the same kind of structure she'd found comfort in behind bars. "It would have been the perfect life for me if I would have just went to the military, if someone would have guided me back then," she reflects. The *death before dishonor* tattoo on her neck is common among military personnel. "Some of my family are marines, and I wanted to be one as well, but I couldn't because of my record. When I was in locked up in jail at night, I felt more sane. I think it was the fact that I knew what was happening day-to-day."

Once seen as the scrapyard for fighters, bare-knuckle boxing is gaining legitimacy as a sport, in the way that MMA transitioned from what in the 1990s Senator John McCain called "human cockfighting" to a multi-billion-dollar industry. The promotion Christine fights for, Bare Knuckle Fighting Championship, had a coup when it signed blonde and undeniably beautiful Ultimate Fighting Championship (UFC) star Paige VanZant, and Christine admits it's no longer feasible to be the underdog with a chip on her shoulder—she has to work harder on networking with promoters and playing nice.

But with her rap sheet of impulsive and aggressive behavior, I wanted to know how Christine learned to prevent her temper tripping her up in the ring. How does someone utilize their ability to hurt someone without flying into an uncontrollable rage?

"When you get your ass beat, that's how you're taught, because I came in wild, trust me," she says with a laugh. "If you see my amateur fights, oh my god. They're ugly, crazy and raw. Before I got into the ring, I used to think about all the bad things that had happened to me. Sometimes you get lucky with it because the other person isn't that smart, but if they're smart they'll use it against you. When you're angry, you're just swinging, so if the other person has good defense they can side-step or cover and let you tire yourself out going crazy. Then it's their turn."

Anger is thought to be both a primary emotion and a secondary emotion, because it conceals something else: grief, shock, sadness, shame. A person with a fragile ego can similarly protect that through rage and outrage, like the Wizard of Oz behind his curtain, manufacturing a maelstrom of thunder and lightning with levers and a loudspeaker. There's something so invigorating about the first rush of anger, because it sends us a message of righteousness. It bubbles up from what's sometimes called our reptilian brain, which primes us for fighting, fucking, fleeing and feeding. Getting angry can have a cascade effect, triggering dopamine, epinephrine and norepinephrine. With the limbic system so activated, it becomes harder for the frontal lobes to function, and rational thought is inhibited. If someone has been raised in an environment of drama and conflict, this may feel like a comfortable place. And violence can become as intoxicating as a drug.

In the early days, Christine's anger would stymie even her training. When she got tired, she'd get frustrated, and then she'd break something: her shin, her rib, her hand. She realized she had better start paying better attention to what the vets were doing—working hard, staying humble.

The flip side is that professional fighting calls for a pantomime of feuds—which necessitates anger and ego, even if that's embellished a few notches. At press conferences and weigh-ins, "trash talk" reigns, probably made authentically grouchy by the dehydration headache brought on by a weight cut. Before he became Muhammad Ali, Cassius Clay was fined $2,500 for shouting, "Hey sucker! You're a chump!" at Sonny Liston and ignoring several warnings to pipe down. Trash talk is so integral to the UFC in particular that the "staredowns" verge on Mexican soap opera, culminating in shoves, slaps, hurled tables and destroyed backdrops.

Of the women, in 2015, Bethe "Pitbull" Correia taunted Ronda "Rowdy" Rousey—whose father committed suicide—with: "Under pressure, she is proving weak. When her mom put pressure on her, she ran away from home. When she lost, it was because of drugs. That's not a superhero. She is not mentally healthy … I hope she does not kill herself later on." At the weigh-in, Bethe yelled in Ronda's face, "Don't cry." The tables were turned during the fight, in which Ronda knocked out Bethe. "Don't cry," Ronda told her.

Six months later, it was Ronda's turn to trash-talk Holly Holm and fall foul to the same ego trap as Bethe. Ronda called Holly a "fake-ass cheap-shotting bitch," warning her, "You're getting your ass kicked tomorrow, and I'm really going to enjoy the beating I give you." In the event, Holly knocked out the previously undefeated Ronda with a headkick.

In 2017, Joanna Jedrzejczyk and Rose "Thug" Namajunas made headlines when, during the media call, the reliably theatrical Joanna zeroed in on Rose's family history of mental illness. "How are you going to be a champion and deal with all of those things? … You are mentally unstable, and you are broken already, and I will break you in the fight." Ringside, the commentators remarked of Rose, "It's hard to get a read on this young lady … she's just dead-faced." Within minutes, Rose defeated Joanna with a deadly combination of a jab, a knee and a right.

At their weigh-in, Christine had told Helen Peralta, "You ain't ready for me, I can see it in your eyes." She clarifies to me: "I can be whoever I want as my character. I wouldn't go out in the streets and be like, 'I'm going to fuck you up, dude,' but I use it for the fight game and I'm ready to release that." For Christine, the trash-talker is her alter ego. For some fighters, it's their actual ego, and that's why they end up getting in their own way.

"I had a big ego—and I still have ego—but I've learned to control it," she explains. "I watched fighters I looked up to and they would say, 'Leave your ego at the door.' They would even have that on a sign at the gym. I'm a person that studies things, so I went home, like, 'What does ego mean?' I didn't even know what it meant. So I would look it up and figure out how to leave it at the door."

WHEN I TAKE up fighting, it quickly becomes apparent that my ego will be my gnarliest opponent. I'm forty-three when I start, with a career in journalism based on independent decision-making, so I'm far less amenable to being told what to do than a twelve-year-old. I've had a tendency to avoid activities in which my performance would be anything less than above average. And my history of addiction implies I'm the sort of person who conceals vulnerability with bluster. As they insist in AA, such people are "egomaniacs with low self-esteem." Yeah, right.

It's a testament to my ego—and the need for special

treatment—that I pay for a personal Muay Thai trainer about thirty times more frequently than I attend a Muay Thai class. One of my trainer's names, back in his MMA fighting days, was "The Human Bear Enclosure." Since then, Nick Mann has stacked on another sixty-six pounds of muscle in his reincarnation as a pro-wrestler called Gore—yes, brother of KrackerJak. He walks like a blockbuster bad guy, arms held at bay by his swollen lats.

Ordinarily, trainers scream motivational slogans at you: sentiments that spill over into their social media accounts. *Hardships often prepare ordinary people for an extraordinary destiny* was doing the rounds on the 'gram for a while. Some added weight by attributing it to CS Lewis, although it's actually just a line from a movie version of *The Chronicles of Narnia. There's no losing, only learning!* is a favorite with those trainers teaching fighting skills.

Nick disagrees with that sentiment. "There's definitely losing," he says, and he's not about to let me sign up for an inter-club—a friendly bosh that doesn't go on your fight record—until he's satisfied I won't embarrass him. Nick's Instagram profile is nihilistic in tone, and suggests that training is merely a prelude to death. One post is of a trash can, with the suggestion you put your hopes and dreams in it.

Muay Thai is the "art of eight limbs," a combat sport that originated in the sixteenth century and is often utilized in modern MMA. As I pirouette around, throwing legs, Nick keeps his face expressionless as a bouncer—which he is. One Twitter user, who noticed him working security around the Octagon of the UFC event I went to with Richie Hardcore, posted a photo of him, describing his look as "*Die Hard 3* henchman." I ask Nick what he and the other bouncers talk about, standing outside a door for eight hours. "Girls, fighting, movies, how much you hate patrons," he says. "Obnoxious stuff."

Things get more inventive as our sessions continue. Sometimes I'm made to shadowbox with thumbtacks taped to my heels, to keep me on the balls of my feet. Other times, as I do sit-ups, he crouches next to me and smashes me in the guts with a kickpad. Each time he's about to slam the pad down, I hear him take a sharp breath, maybe for effect.

For the past few months we've worked on pads—he holds them, I punch and kick them—and it hasn't been necessary to think for myself, nor hold back on the power. Today, we're sparring for the first time. *Playing*, he emphasizes. But like every other wet-behind-the-ears student before me, I'm pistoning in hard and fast. My fights have hitherto been limited to drunken brawls at taxi stands and in featureless hallways; things I can barely remember, but nevertheless I've congratulated myself for hands thrown, no matter how untechnical. Now it's the opposite. Control apparently trumps enthusiasm.

Nick catches every kick and blocks every punch, and occasionally sweeps me to the canvas, ramping up my frustration a notch on each occasion. In between, he'll drop his arms to his sides, which is something he's told me never to do, so this action must be interpreted as insolence.

"You're telegraphing all your moves and any time you *have* made contact has been a fluke," he says.

My response is lost to the furious revving of V-8 engines from the garage next door, which happens periodically.

A couple of times, he backs himself against the ropes and buries his head in his guard—his forearms—obligingly leaving everything else open. Faced with this invitation and the self-efficacy it requires of me, I panic. His grin is just visible through his wrists. Rather than calculate my opportunity, I whale at him ineffectively. Despair turns to hopelessness turns to blind kicking. Sometimes I kick upward—like a lever—between his legs. That's not a move.

In pro-wrestling terms, if you go too rough on your opponent, they might give you what's known as a "receipt." It's an act of retaliation, twice as hard, to smack you back down to size. *"Watch it,"* it says. In round two, Nick starts issuing his receipts as I flail in impotent rage: repeated chops to my left leg, which I should be noticing is a pattern. They're much harder chops than our official "just playing" capacity, and I make that known by spitting "Fuck!" each time one lands. At this, he goes even harder.

Receipt. Such an innocuous word, not at all loaded with spite.

Eventually the buzzer sounds. Nick leads me by one arm till I'm against the ropes. Unable to avert my gaze, I let my eyes glaze over.

"You're getting too emotional," he says.

I'm not, I think indignantly, as emotions swarm all over my body. He must mean "angry." Although, come to think of it, I could cry right now. But he doesn't know that.

"You need to be cold, calm and ruthless," he continues, up in my face. "If you come at me like that, you leave me no choice but to respond."

So fighters must have "heart," as they say, and yet, their hearts must be devoid of emotion. Devoid of the purest, most cleansing hatred I think I must ever have felt forge through my veins. In my last book, I wrote about my abundance of this particular emotion. *The rage. The fucking rage! It's always there, inflating inside me, like the Hindenburg awaiting a match.* Rage has propelled me in all my ventures, a boundless energy that is as productive as it has been destructive. Why does Nick not appreciate the powerful raw material I'm working with?

But it's not a conversation for today. Today I'm just focused on keeping my face steady while taking off my shin guards.

When I leave the gym, pain radiates from my thigh, up through some mysterious new elevator-of-awful in my torso, and into my chest. Halfway down the road, I give up on hobbling and get an Uber.

At home, I cry into a neat gin and smear myself in Tiger Balm, and think: *There's no better way to learn how fragile you really are than building up your physical and mental strength for months, only to have it crumble at the first test.*

Muay Thai was supposed to be character-building. I had taken it up when I was called on to make a statement about a historic sex crime, which would be a lengthy process over which I had no control. Making this report, I decided, must also signal the end of the passive state of "victim" I had internalized.

Walk tall, I chastened myself, wandering aimlessly through London after I'd completed the police interview. *Taller. See how different that feels? Wow. Bring on the new era!*

It felt forced, but I don't like having no control. And unless you're unlucky enough to be sick—or maybe *until* you're unlucky enough to be sick—you can at least control your body. That's why people who have experienced abuse, inconsistent parenting, medical procedures or some other lack of agency when young tend to be drawn to self-harm, substance use and eating disorders. I knew this, which is why I was determined to weaponize my body more productively, much like the people profiled in this book. Other women I meet when training have similar reasons, growing up in homes of family violence being one I hear repeatedly.

But my idea of Muay Thai serving as anger management was way off. For now, at least, it's making me even more frustrated.

I find the work of Sylvie von Duuglas-Ittu, an American Muay Thai fighter based in Thailand who has hundreds of fights to her name. Somehow she's also found the time to create a huge, free online resource, www.8limbs.us, which analyzes not only the technical side of Muay Thai but also the psychological. Sylvie writes about the difficulties people face in their personal lives that push them toward this combat sport—but that then causes them to struggle while practicing it.

After receiving a lot of correspondence from followers about their vulnerabilities, she decided to write about being gang-raped as an eleven-year-old and the "emotional amputation" she employed to get through the ordeal: "The hand gripping the right leg is too tight, it hurts, but it's not my leg—it's gone, it's theirs, let them have it. I remember pain that I could not describe because it didn't seem to be localized. As if pain was happening as an event that I was witnessing rather than it being attached to me."

Sylvie doesn't believe that this experience is *why* she fights, but that it affects the way she processes fighting:

To this day I rage when there are moments of dominance that are infused with sexuality while training with men in the ring … The instinct to dissociate from my body in order to protect my mind, for example—like a lizard discarding its tail in the claws of a cat—is still something I find myself doing. I will "take" a lot of pain or strikes or damage and not show affect, but I also shut down mentally and emotionally.

In another post, she writes about the emotional severance that fighters call upon, and how in the past she has beaten herself up for not achieving it—whether that be wanting to cry after taking a humiliating beating during sparring, or in a fight itself:

It's a terrifying feeling that my automatic emotional response—one that comes from real violence and real fear and pain in my lifetime—is holding me back. I'm not saying don't feel, but the rules of the ring (a space that we "seal" at the start of fights to demonstrate separation) are such that admitting your weakness or showing the effect someone is having on you—someone who wants to hurt you—is in no way going to help you … You have to practice choosing a different response under pressure until you choose it automatically.

In a more clinical fashion, Mike Tyson has observed: "You can't be disturbed by anything. There's no emotion involved. You can't feel sorrow, you can't feel pity, there's nothing you feel. The job has to be done."

There can be a dark side to compartmentalizing your life in this way, like a flawed Venn diagram in which the circles never overlap. Pick up any biography of a notorious athlete and you're guaranteed to read about a double life that escalates in scale—extramarital affairs, dodgy business dealings, drug use—fanned by praise and accolades, until there's an inevitable crash. In their book *The Upside of Your Dark Side* (2014), researchers Todd Kashdan and Robert Biswas-Diener attribute some virtue to what psychologists call the dark triad—narcissism, Machiavellianism and psychopathy—which they say lies at the core of every fictional antihero, from James Bond to Batman. Each element of the triad represents a tightrope for the athlete. "Lean too far one way and you hurt other people; lean too far to the other side and you become incapable of taking risks, or being truly effective," they write.

Is that what I want for myself? A cleaving of empathy and feeling? *Yes*, an inner voice retaliates. *It is.*

AT THE SIX-MONTH mark, my body suddenly feels profoundly different, like I've woken up in one of those 1980s body-swap movies. Similarly to architect-come-BDSM-club-performer Anna, who describes how she had neglected her physicality before discovering the joy of flesh-hook suspension, I've previously only existed in the loops of my mind. Now I can hear the neural pathways squelching as my body pivots and hinges in foreign movements. In the right light, I have six abs, and am strong and sinewy. What was it Guy Ritchie said about Madonna? "It was like cuddling up to a piece of gristle." Good.

Muay Thai has become my singular pursuit. I've collected bruises like my imagined trophies, and watched endless YouTube tutorials on how to escape headlocks, or vintage fights between flashy, satin-trousered American kickboxers, bouncing like hares on their hind legs, pitted against stoic Thai heroes who conserve their energy for vicious low kicks. If I miss a daily gym session I feel distressed, and I make sure there are sessions available for every day of any planned holidays or interstate trips. I've recruited a nutritionist and calculated macros, and gone to watch live fights, paying particular attention to the female amateurs. I've got little journalism work done, and the paltry money I have earned has lined the coffers of trainers—as well as Nick, I've strayed to sample the styles of some of Melbourne's top fight gyms.

I remember the surety with which I knew, as a child, that writing was my calling; something I intrinsically understood. There was joy to be found in the rhythm of sentences and the instinctive application of grammar. There was never any doubt that I would become a journalist, as I bashed out a newspaper for our street on a typewriter. By contrast, everything about martial arts is a challenge. My mind doesn't automatically transpose the drills I learn on pads to options I can use in sparring. Nothing makes immediate sense, and every victory is a grind. In the fight gym, your journalistic reputation counts for naught, and nobody's heard of *The Guardian*.

So far, I have been coasting on *Sehnsucht*, a word that some psychologists apply to the idea of fantastical goals. Sehnsucht is the tone-deaf singer talking about auditioning for *The Voice*, or the woman in a disintegrating relationship buying bridal magazines. Mine is to get on a fight bill in my mid-forties with no sporting background. Fantasy, of course, preserves the individual from reality, but sometimes Sehnsucht can be viewed more positively, in terms of encouraging the individual to set smaller, stepping-stone goals on their starry-eyed path to the improbable. Those goals shouldn't just be about buying expensive Yokkao shin guards, though.

The root of the problem is that I have been floundering without purpose since the publication of my addiction memoir. In *Woman of Substances*, I was the case study around which my research into the drivers of addictive behaviors was stacked; but the problem with memoir is that by publicly closing the book on an era, you effectively just kill off your protagonist—one you spent a lifetime crafting. That same agitated spirit I'd eulogized in the book now needed to find a new home, like a demon that's just had a crucifix thrust at it.

While going to the gym up to three times a day to thrash the bag is far more immediately cathartic than writing, suddenly I am investing all my self-worth into this new construct, and hungrily seeking validation on Instagram. Some rock pig friends think my progress is stupendous, as opposed to those from the fight world, who know what a spinning hook kick is *supposed* to look like. Regardless, I buy an iPhone case that sticks to gym mirrors, to document all my stumbles, bad footwork and pissweak punches, as though it won't count if nobody sees. Mortification and pride vie confusingly for domination, and the more I post, the more adrift I become. I'm shocked that I've emotionally invested everything—as jilted romantics say— in this person I barely know. And yet I am announcing to the world, *THIS IS ME.*

I determine that matters have reached the point of existential crisis, and phone a reality TV-producer friend. Esther is used to deciding—within minutes—what a person's identity should be. Rather than relegate me to one, she has a kindly piece of advice: "Stop going to the gym so often."

But that won't do at all.

BECAUSE NICK WORKS out of a boxing gym, Misha's Boxing Central, there are no kickboxing partners for me to spar with, so he calls in some favors. I take the train into Footscray to get in the ring with Sarah, a wrestler and jujitsu competitor who practices Muay Thai to keep up her striking game. We've met before, and I like her a lot. Still, when Nick starts us off with some kicking drills and she struggles to get into the swing of it, I'm pleased.

Not for long.

Sarah's over forty pounds heavier than me. When we start our first round of sparring, her face contorts with vicious focus as she throws her punches. I've only ever sparred with one girl, Shona, who has more of a K-1 kickboxing style, slipping and weaving like a boxer. Whereas Shona looks casually for an inroad, Sarah seeks out the shortest route to my head, which she finds by smashing directly through my guard. Her hooks give me instant headaches.

"I've got a headache as well, don't worry," she says good-naturedly when I mention my ailment between rounds, in case she or Nick think we should stop immediately.

One of her front kicks to my guts feels okay-ish for a second, but a few seconds more and I think I'll puke. More than once,

I think to myself, *What the fuck am I doing here?* There's that feeling of despair: she's bigger than me and better than me, an impossible equation. On a primal level, it feels like my best hope is survival. Is this what a gazelle experiences when chased down by a cheetah?

Still, I bore my eyes into hers each round, even though Nick's drilled it into me to focus on the opponent's chest to better get a read on their limbs. I can't help it, though. There's a rush of competition flaring in my brain that I don't think I've enjoyed since primary school—at which point it was the terrible twin of my ego, the great destroyer of friendships. Past puberty, I learned to smother it and schooled myself not to care about the things my peers were striving for.

Take her out, it says now.

In between rounds I blink the sweat out of my eyes and stay stoic, careful not to double over or hold onto the rope to steady myself.

"I'll look after you, but I'll hit you hard too," Sarah warns as we go into the next round. She's true to her word for the next ninety minutes, which feel like fighting for my life, not for practice.

The first thing you have to learn as a woman fighter is not to automatically apologize whenever you strike someone. A person as experienced as Sarah doesn't say sorry; in fact, she'll compliment you when you connect with her nose. Shona had the same even temper, her face remaining neutral on the occasions I'd get to punch it. Sometimes, as she punched me, she'd offer helpful advice about how to get out of the way next time. I marvel at the idea of being able to dig that deep to find such grace. Did Shona and Sarah have an easygoing temperament to begin with, or did they have the ego and rage systematically knocked out of them over time?

In her book *Kill the Body, the Head Will Fall* (1997), Rene Tenfold observes that even with "glove-shy" punches there's "the sense of shock at being hit, not because of pain, but more from the invasion of privacy, the body shock of it." Rene doesn't mention the additional insult of your trainer singling you out for criticism, like your mother being tolerant of naughty guests at your birthday party but sending you—you!—to your room.

"*CHIN DOWN*," Nick yells at me for the fifth time, leaning in over the top rope. "Good job, Sarah."

I mumble a curse through my mouthguard, which I know Sarah won't approve of because she's a good sport and has been taking instruction from martial arts trainers since she was practically an infant. As we remove our shin guards, I thank her more humbly for coming.

Afterward, Nick and I sit in his car outside the station.

"Part of it is being humiliated and hurt and your coach shouting at you. It's all part of the training," he says. He fiddles with his phone to send me the video footage he took.

"I don't want to see it."

"Just analyze it. Don't look at it like, 'I'm so stupid and I'm not making any progress.'"

I look at him sharply. "I didn't say that."

Later, he sends me a post from the blog *Humans of Fighting*, about stoicism being instilled in Thai fighters from a young age. Nick thinks my theory that rage is the pugilist's fuel is overgeneralizing. Take the Thai fighters, who might have been training since childhood, to support the family. He writes: "When you see a Thai boxer who's had three hundred fights, they're not frothing at the mouth when they get in the ring. Their fight IQ is on a completely different level so they can just think tactically: make them miss, make them pay, block, counter." He sends another post from a Thai fighter: "It is not my trainer's job to care for my fragile ego, or my need for affirmation. His job is to highlight my weakness and challenge my limits … My trainers never giving praises is part of the conditioning."

That seems counterintuitive to me. I grow two feet taller when Nick throws a scrap of encouragement. And aren't fighters generally people who weren't told "I'm proud of you" enough as kids?

There are all kinds of training styles, needless to say. There's the noncommittal "good job" of the casual trainer who won't be taking you through to a fight; there's the type who showers you with so much encouragement as to feel embarrassingly undeserved; and there's tough love. Having achieved black belts in taekwondo, gongkwon yusul, hapkido and arnis in Australia, the Philippines and South Korea, Nick's experienced all of these training styles, but mainly the last, when he was a young buck determined to break through, sometimes literally living in the gym. As a trainer, he oscillates between them. Sometimes it's an unreadable expression, perfected by years of turning people away from nightclubs; sometimes it's "You're a grown woman! You want me to hold your hand?" Once, he came out with "Nobody else would agree to train you," which was probably unintentionally self-deprecating.

Before too long, I will have to spar under scrutiny again, sacrificing my self-respect anew. I think about how best to forge through this second, painful adolescence. Maybe these knocks to the confidence could be likened to hypertrophy, the process of weight lifting: you put the muscle tissue under stress and cause micro-tears. It's only through gaining and recovering from these tears that the muscle grows.

THE MORNING AFTER my dark night of the soul, I wake from fitful sleep and find that none of the appliances in my bedroom are working. Maybe it's the universe trying to tell me I've had my lights punched out, because I feel like I'm in a fog. I'm drained and depressed, and I can't figure out what's wrong with me—it's not like I've just been in a car crash; not a literal car crash, anyway. I wonder if I have mild concussion. I turn to the fight section of Reddit. In a thread titled "Crashing emotionally after sparring," BirdyDevil says something interesting: "As crazy as this might seem, this sounds similar to a phenomenon known as 'sub drop' in BDSM. Considering the hormones, mental state, physicality, etc. of sparring, it makes sense that the states could be similar. I'd suggest looking up sub drop and some of the aftercare tips, and try implementing a few after your sparring sessions, it just might help."

The "aftercare" of BDSM play that BirdyDevil refers to would require the individual's sparring partner or trainer to cuddle with them on the sofa while watching gentle things on Netflix. That's a bit much to ask. I remember what Sir James told me about his clients at his sex dungeon: one motivation might be simply the knowledge that they could survive beatings.

That in turn reminds me of something I read in journalist-turned-fighter Josh Rosenblatt's book. Josh explores what he calls the great paradox of fighting: that fighters tear their bodies apart to feel more alive. "Self-creation through self-destruction is something of a silent mantra in the fighting world, understood by every fighter no matter how subconsciously," he writes. He wonders if his propensity for drinking comes from a similar drive.

Are they mirror reflections of each other: one self-negation through pleasure, the other self-affirmation through suffering? Is it the ultimate act of resignation and acceptance of death to tease it and touch up against it? Or are excessive drinking and cage fighting acts of inoculation against the pain of the knowledge of death? Is that what fighting is: a dress rehearsal for the inevitable? Or is it rebellion against that inevitability?

Most of us have a basic grasp of Freud's theory of the death drive, or Thanatos, named after the Greek god of death by Freud's peer, Wilhelm Stekel. But as Sam Sheridan summarizes in *A Fighter's Heart* (2007), there are multiple theories about aggression, only one of which—catharsis theory—posits that it is a death instinct turned outward. Beyond that, the frustration-aggression hypothesis favors the idea that violence is a knee-jerk response to provocation. Social learning theory blames the parents and environment. Then at the opposite end of the nature-nurture spectrum, there's the idea that there's a physiological and neurological explanation. Here, some researchers point to the interaction between hormones, adrenaline and activity in the frontal lobe; and if we throw in traumatic brain injury from repeated knocks to the head, we know that a common side-effect is impulsivity and the inability to control emotions.

Yet fighting has always had a role in civilized society. In 648 BC, pankration—the ancestor of MMA—was introduced at the Olympic Games. It became a spectator favorite, overtaking boxing in popularity, on account of having few rules: no biting, no eye-gouging and no messing with genitals. Strangling, disemboweling and caving in the face were fine. If you've ever seen *Mad Max Beyond Thunderdome* (1985), the motto of that gladiatorial arena applied: "Two men enter, one man leaves." On occasion, a corpse was crowned the victor.

The prize money grew, attracting men prepared to fight to the death, who were immortalized by poets. They were considered godlike and given names that translated to the likes of "Man Subduer" and "Mr. Fingertips." (The latter may sound friendly, but it was given to Sostratos for his habit of breaking opponents' digits as an opening move.) It was advantageous for these gory games to be endorsed by the city-states of Ancient Greece. Spectatorship of pankration, as with the Roman gladiatorial fights and village-square hangings, was a way of controlling the masses, a permissible blowing-off of steam.

A cluster of dystopian-future movies ran with that notion. *Rollerball* (1975), in which opposing teams try and take each other out permanently, imagines a national sport created by shadowy corporations to demonstrate the futility of individual effort. In *Death Race 2000* (1975), a government creates a violent road race to pacify the general population, with extra points given to killing innocent pedestrians. *The Running Man* (1987) depicts a sadistic game show in which the competitors are enemies of the state, set in a world where culture and communications are censored. While Donald Trump didn't go as far as commissioning such a show, he and his family are longstanding supporters of the UFC, even hosting an event at the Trump Taj Mahal in Atlantic City in 2001 when the sport's promotion was struggling. In 2020, UFC president Dana White joined Trump on stage at a "Keep America Great" rally.

Why are human blood sports so appealing to watch? On *The Guardian* vlog "Modern Masculinity," journalist Iman Amrani asks MMA fans milling in a sports bar why they love to watch. One suggests the motivation is little changed since ancient times: "We fight every day. We fight to stay in our job, get paid, get through the days, so watching someone push through getting beat on and they come out on top, that's a rush." Sanctioned violence acts as a metaphor for the struggles in our lives, which explains why so many boxing idioms have infiltrated our language: *Roll with the punches. Throw in the towel. Saved by the bell. Come out swinging. The gloves are off. Have someone in your corner. Take it on the chin.* Other fans remark to Amrani that pugilists are superhuman in comparison to us mere mortals, while fighter Kelvin Gastelum tells her, "I think there's so much fake stuff going around in the world today that people are looking for genuine entertainment, something pure, something real."

I enjoy watching the UFC, but as I try to engage with the crowdless streamed fights during the COVID-19 lockdown, I realize how much the baying, jeering and howling feeds into the overall experience. The psychology is similar to laugh tracks on sitcoms: we're being given permission to feel, and in doing so we pass on that permission to others.

Me, I want to cry—even more so when watching women fight. It feels somehow as though there is more at stake for me personally; a powerful testament to how we live vicariously through sports. The skill of the UFC in particular is that I lap up the orchestrated drama I'm fed through press conferences, preview reels and staredowns. By the time the actual fight occurs, I've invested fully in these fighters' hardships, feuds and sacrifices. I'm glued to their strut to the cage, their pre-match rituals—kissing crucifixes, tuck jumps, miming writing the opponent's name in a death note—and their antsiness as they pace the Octagon. Only then is there the incredible prowess of athletes at the top of their game, heightened by the blood spatters on the canvas and the risk of witnessing serious injury. I get emotional at good sportsmanship and excited by bad sportsmanship. And it's fast, furious and over so quickly—sometimes just a few taut minutes of drama, before both fighters pick up the story on Instagram: the victor to post the precise moment of a beautiful KO, and the loser to write something about being "humble in victory and gracious in defeat."

THE INTERCLUB, AT times called a "smoker," is a rite of passage. It's either the step before an amateur fight, or a heightened sparring experience—heightened because there's a small crowd and the anointment of a winner, and the individuals are representing their gym or team. The two rounds are short, no head kicks or elbows. Those who go too hard will be given a warning by the referee, but even so, vomit, blood and tears aren't unheard of. On the blog *The Muay Thai Guy*, guest poster Rob Fagan observes:

"Almost every smoker I've ever watched was the purest form of total mayhem I've ever seen … it's an arena for each fighter to try out every move they've ever learned in the gym, ever. This translates into the real world as a big jumbled mess operating at very high speed and demonstrating extremely low precision. In other words, a lot of smokers look like something a cat hacked up a half hour after giving itself a bath."

A year into my training, Nick and I arrive at Ultimate Muay Thai in St. Albans for an interclub run by the Victorian Amateur Martial Arts Association. The room's packed for a full day of bouts between members of gyms across Melbourne. I get weighed in to make sure I'm sitting in the 130–140 pound weight class we registered at, then Nick scans the list to see who I'm up against.

"What's her name?" I ask, to gauge how tough she sounds.

"Her name's Dead," he says, and wanders off in the direction of the sausage sizzle.

The whole time the interclub has been looming, it's been plaguing my thoughts. I think back to being a terrified newbie, studying YouTube videos on how to skip—after the time that the gym's owner stopped what she was doing to watch me lolloping over the rope—and practicing shadowboxing in the truck stop bathroom opposite the gym, because it felt as exposing as one of those dreams where you're naked.

But since then, I try to remind myself, I've become bigger, faster, stronger. I've become one of those screamers down the gym, a different-sounding primal yell for each limb as it connects with pad, bag or person. And I've grown to love sparring. Like sex, it can be all polite prodding and apologies, or completely exhilarating and exhausting, and occasionally devastating. These days I'm much calmer, more strategic. Sparring is a game of chess, albeit one where you might suddenly flip the board out of spite. There's the deep pleasure of realizing, *Hey, I'm in with a chance here*—and the even greater pleasure of occasionally realizing that your opponent has no chance at all.

Who would have thought that these sequences of foreign movements could bring such joy? As a kid, I had boundless energy, racing around the playground like a greyhound, always determined to be fastest and the last one standing. But in high school, girls weren't supposed to be energetic, so that zest was lost to sitting on brick walls and smoking. Later still, I sedated my restlessness with drink and drugs. What if I'd discovered fighting? What a gift to that girl. So I make up for lost time now.

I've been to this gym quite a few times, joining in with the fighters' class some afternoons, where I've been humiliated by everyone from an eleven-year-old girl (eleven-year-olds doing Muay Thai have typically been doing taekwondo since they were embryos) to the old-school trainer who likes to literally add insult to injury, making Nick's demeanor seem very Julie Andrews. It's a fairly typical fight gym in its makeup: there's a bank of rowing machines and treadmills at the rear, one wall lined with heavy bags. Today, the mats have been removed from the floor to allow for rows of seats. And, of course, the ring, with its backdrop of flags from around the world.

Wandering around, I spot Shona outside with the members of her gym, and I lie on the grass next to them, content just to listen and quietly panic. Periodically, I make a trip to the bathroom. "Is this your first?" people ask one another in the queue. One girl has been in the ring already and is sporting a bloody nose.

A few minutes before my name is called, Nick warms me up: clap push-ups, roundhouse kicks against his arms and tuck jumps. My mouth is dry, but no water can slake my thirst. He massages my shoulders as we wait at my corner, manipulating my noodle arms, which taper off into comedically bulbous boxing gloves, because at interclubs you must wear the larger, more friendly sixteen-ounces. Then he pushes down the top rope and I climb over.

Back in the school playground, I'd take my place milling around whatever fight had broken out and secretly thank my lucky stars that I hadn't been born a boy. Who could bear to suffer both the shock of contact and the humiliation of a mob of kids encircling you, shouting, "FIGHT, FIGHT, FIGHT!" And yet now, here I am.

We touch gloves—a moment of respect before trying to take each other's head off. My opponent is a collection of moving targets that need to be smashed. Jab, jab-cross, roundhouse kick. Front-kick her if she gets too close. Hope she doesn't pull me in for a clinch, since I haven't got my head around that yet. Nor do I know how to fight intelligently, so when I counter, it will be like I've spun a random limb generator.

The canvas is too skiddy. Eight seconds in, she catches one of my kicks and I get dumped to the ground. I hear a bit of a shame-job "ooh" from the crowd and think it must surely all be over for me now. There's just the faintest flash of the disgrace I've brought to Nick, who's in my corner behind me, but then I'm back on my feet and retaliating as viciously as I can get away with.

Between rounds, Nick pours some water in my mouth as

though I've been sparring for hours and not ninety seconds, then we're back at it. The referee circles us at a distance, murmuring, "Lovely effort, girls. Good job by both." Once we level up to amateur, we can expect no such niceties. A few times my head snaps back from a punch, but I register only the motion of it and the smattering of applause from my opponent's gym members. I can hear her hyperventilating, and I realize she's more rattled than I am. Every time I get a punch through her guard to her face, I'm buoyed. Then the final bell sounds and we both stop abruptly, to embrace in relief.

Despite the early sweep to the canvas, I'm declared the winner. The second the referee drops my hand, my opponent and I bowl past him to hug again. I'm overwhelmed by an immense feeling of love and gratitude toward this stranger. Only she knows what we've just been through—and in showing up, she allowed me to take part in this wonderful sanctioned release of aggression.

This feeling of love might partly be attributed to stress bonding, but after a few punches my body is also flooded with opioid peptides. Then there's oxytocin. A 2019 study led by psychology professor Yuri Rassovsky of Bar-Ilan University found that salivary levels of oxytocin—colloquially known as "the cuddle chemical" and released when an infant lies on its mother's breast—are released during jujitsu training, and lesser amounts during striking sparring, so we might assume that Muay Thai, which combines striking and grappling, releases oxytocin to some degree, further bonding us to our opponent.

I'm reminded of watching Christine Ferea's first bloody fight with Helen Peralta, and witnessing the moment after the final bell rang and they stopped trying to hammer each other to Hades. Over a few brief seconds, the two clasped hands and locked eyes with a curious sort of delight and excitement. When I interviewed Christine and mentioned this, she grinned and mimed pulling someone into a hug. "It's like, 'Dude, come here, I've been dreaming of killing you forever!'" She laughed. "I have nothing but respect for anybody that has the courage to go toe-to-toe with somebody ... I don't care how bad you suck or not."

A year later, in an interview with World Combat Sports, Helen Peralta complained: "She was respectful for about a quarter of a second. Then the moment her ass got out of the ring she started running her mouth again."

WHAT DRAGON ARE you fighting? Mine is shame, and that's what my ego is protecting. I experienced so much of it when I was younger that I fear being ground back under its thumb. Better to flail in defiance.

And yet I keep putting myself in shame's way. If I'd wanted to test my confidence, I could have just joined Toastmasters, but instead I decided that, upon finally gaining the respect I've always craved—as an adult in my profession—I ought to humiliate myself in a new arena, inviting mockery and pity from peers, enemies and strangers. On the plus side, being injured in the ring is the lowest rung on my personal ladder of worry.

In December 2020, a few weeks after Melbourne's second, longest lockdown is lifted, I'm invited to take part in a fight night put on by leading promotion "Warriors Way," in a showcase round. The evening will be livestreamed, with organizer Mark Castagnini hoping that "Lockdown: 2020 We're Not Done Yet" will demonstrate to the whole country the quality of fighting in my state of Victoria.

Gyms have been among the hardest-hit businesses during the pandemic—none more so than fight gyms, which rely on contact. So I don't have long to prepare, but all through lockdown I kept training, using my heavy bag, and taking online Muay Thai and strength-and-conditioning classes. By now I've done two interclubs—a win and a draw. Even so, the inclusion of Nick and me on this fight card as "Team Luna," when we are not associated with a fight gym, is a surprise. I haven't leaned on my journalist credentials, and no one knows who the hell we are. We're like the masked bandits of the bill.

Two weeks before fight night, I notice electrical tendrils sparking my toes every time the word "livestreamed" flickers across my frontal lobe. Fear finds new ways to infiltrate my body, its ghostly fists rattling my bowels like Jacob Marley and his chains.

And then, one week before, a change settles upon me. I realize that everything I'm feeling should be embraced as part of the experience. Being on an actual fight card this time, albeit third from the bottom, I can appreciate the idea of legacy, knowing that everyone that has gone before me has felt all the things I'm feeling. I realize that no matter what the outcome, I've earned my place on the lineup.

I've been sparring with some professional fighters who have volunteered to kick my arse, and I'm pleased to see I hold my own. We work at it right until the day before the fight. Ordinarily you'd have up to a week's rest before a fight, but as nobody has been able to spar for four months, there's little choice but to go all out. I've eliminated alcohol and sugar, and dropped more than four pounds to be sure I make weight, because I'll have my period and that can cause a fluctuation of this much.

As Nick keeps reminding me, the instructions we've been given are to demonstrate technique and control; but all my sparring partners have advised me to go in full-force or risk my opponent doing so first. What I do know for sure is that sparring at 100 percent feels like an epiphany—like taking flight for the first time. The adrenaline and apprehension as you duck under the ropes dissipates when the buzzer sounds, and competition flares in the brain as you advance. A curious crowd inevitably gathers, comprised of whatever class is filing in, watching as they wrap their hands. There's the primal, powerful feeling of seeing your sparring partner tire quicker than you; vampiric, you feast on their energy the moment they show any weakness. Or the elation is derived from just surviving a round in which you were outwitted and overwhelmed, and copped some good ones.

On the day of the fight, a storm looms heavy into late afternoon. I feel exhausted and disconnected, like I'm looking at the world through the wrong end of a telescope, and I can't be sure if the symptoms are psychosomatic or real. Proponents of polyvagal theory would believe my dorsal vagal system has decided that if I was fully present I would be overwhelmed, threatening my chance of survival, and so a level of depersonalization or even dissociation is induced. Nick's idea of a pep talk is to forward me a video of someone prolapsing their sphincter, which he thinks I might find interesting. But when he and I arrive at Hammers for the weigh-in, the storm outside breaks and the familiar surroundings of heavy bags and mats ground me. My energy returns in a rush, and I can't wait to get in the ring.

We're directed to an upstairs area allotted to the red-corner fighters. Blue-corner fighters are corralled elsewhere so that we can't bead each other. I'd looked up my opponent, Clara, on Instagram earlier and found only her work page, featuring righteous hand-tooled heavy metal and leather goods, including a bag that's a homage to Motörhead, whose album *Everything Louder Than Everyone Else* I adapted for the title of this book. I'd definitely like her … but I can't right now. All around us, jittery combatants are lying on the floor and being ministered to with liniment oils to warm up the muscles, or working through drills with their professionally dead-eyed coaches, loud slaps of legs on pads resounding through the room.

Nick wraps my hands, then holds up his own so that I can snap out jabs, crosses and hooks. He braces his biceps for kicks and pulls me in for clinches. I can tell he's being careful to keep his demeanor jokey and relaxed, and he's unusually tolerant, letting me call the time of each drill. I'm grateful. When he deems the occasion is right, he has the patience of a parent: figuring things out with me, counting for me, letting me practice on him like a punching bag, offering little lines of explanation that I'll retain forever, because they coincide with a penny finally dropping.

I remember Richie Hardcore—who had the same coach for eleven years—telling me, "It's a very unique thing, when you spend hundreds of hours holding pads for someone, and you see them break down and want to give up, and you encourage them to work through those difficult challenges." From the point of view of the fighter, "when you're in the corner with someone and they're putting Vaseline in your fucking eye and they're telling you instructions, I don't know if it's more intimate than sex, but it's very intimate. You don't hear the thousand people in the crowd. You hear this one person in front of you on this fucking deep, primal level. If you are attuned well, as a unit, you have complete faith in your coach. It's profound. I can't think of anything like it. Maybe being a mother carrying a child."

Nick agrees when I repeat that. It seems to me, to get sentimental about it, we have a nonverbal language that I can only compare to musicians communicating through music. It's a purer kind of language, direct from your source, unfiltered. True, sometimes it verges on physical comedy, but it's the most authentic kind of connection I've experienced.

Maybe the remedy for ego is gratitude. I'm grateful for this sport. I'm grateful to the women who have offered me their faces to punch in these past two weeks for my own benefit, and to the people hustling to put on this evening to bring the community some hope, and for the sanctuary of the fight gym where, upon walking in, a different mindset is encouraged to settle.

"Give me your gum," says Nick, holding out a hand. My name has been called.

I'm directed to an X taped on the ground, to shadowbox for the video cameras pointing at me from the ring. Thank god for all that practicing in the mirror of the truck stop bathroom. I conclude by smashing my gloves together aggressively, and stride up, ducking through the middle ropes. That seems obnoxious later, when I watch the footage and realize that Clara has followed the Thai tradition of bowing respectfully before lifting the bottom rope—considered the appropriate way for a woman to enter—and bowing four more times in the ring, to each of the four sides.

I'd caught sight of Clara minutes earlier. Her immaculate fight braids were shiny and bouncy. My newfound gratitude was elbowed out of the way by my ego, mightier than ever in the heat of battle. *Ha! Her hair's going to be the best thing about her performance*, it scoffed, out loud, to Nick.

When the first bell rings, Clara delivers a jab and a fast low-kick combo, and it's on. I immediately feel as though I'm dominating the round, because I barely register her strikes. Straight away I've entered into the subspace. It frees me to think aggressively. Clara tries to angle out and I block her path, with Nick relaying instructions in a guttural tone like I'm a sheepdog: "THAT'S IT, CUT HER OFF."

After the first round I head back to my corner, confident that I've dominated enough already to have scored a win. I lounge on the ropes and listen to Nick, kind of. This is going amazingly.

I'm Orion Starr, warning: *This is what lethal looks like!*

I'm Eugene S. Robinson, scoffing: *You can't lose if you don't quit!*

I'm Christine Ferea, bragging: *You ain't ready for me!*

Wow, I'm feeling good.

But the second round is tougher. Whatever Clara's coach said to her, she listened, and I'm unable to back her up to the ropes. We fire legs and fists in the middle, even-stevens.

The judges call a split decision, a draw. What a bummer— this is neither a glorious victory nor a heroic failure, and I can't quite believe it, because the whole world knows I won. I try to control my face as the referee holds both our wrists aloft, but watching the footage later, I see my eyebrow shoot up in the universal language of "Pardon?"

Still, I'm on a righteous high. Thankfully I can't hear the concluding remarks of the commentators: "I just want to mention that Jenny's forty-five ... so it just goes to show that any time is the right time to start when it comes to training and it comes to fighting," they chuckle, ribbing each other about their own inevitable trudge toward my age.

After I've changed, Nick and I go out to a nearby Korean barbeque restaurant to decompress. I can't eat, but I plough through wine, drinking for the first time in two weeks. I just assume this is the right thing to do, even though I don't really feel like alcohol. Nick indulges my boisterous assessment of the fight; now is not a time for serious analysis.

Later, back at home and thoroughly drunk, I message my parents to let them know that I was robbed. Robbed! Dad tells me I sound like Trump. A friend and I sit on the sofa with a bottle of wine and watch the video of the fight, and my high wears off. "It looks pretty even to me," my faithless friend says. I crane forward to my laptop and observe the skill with which Clara waits out my flurries and then counters, delivering technically proficient kicks at odds with my street-brawler style.

We replay the footage a few times and I realize that what I could see in the ring—the doubt and fatigue in Clara's face as I advanced—is not what the judges were looking at. I think back guiltily to my conversation with her after the fight, when we grasped each other's arms with shining eyes and congratulated on specific kicks. I'd secretly been thinking it was cheeky that she only singled out a couple of them for commendation.

A few days later, I'm battling the ever-encroaching sense of shame again: How could I have thought that I did so well? What must the people I messaged afterward think of my obnoxious blustering? Could I not have worn my hair more fetchingly?

I'm reminded of Les Murray's glitter-bomb of a poem, "Performance," which begins:

I starred last night, I shone:
I was footwork and firework in one,

And ends:

As usual after any triumph, I was
of course inconsolable.

Although, you know, I *enjoyed* the naked aggression. Because it felt fucking great. I can reason with myself that there is a certain breed of fighter who is an obnoxious arsehole—even if they come to evolve beyond this—and that type is necessary to the ecosystem and equilibrium of the sport. As Maximus Decimus Meridius, played by the ever-humble Russell Crowe, put it in *Gladiator*: are you not entertained?

Chapter Nine

THE FIRST DEATH
Retirement and Reinvention

PROFESSIONAL ATHLETES ARE a useful lens through which to contemplate our own reinventions. They've embarked on a career trajectory that is stratospheric, but also short-term (unless their chosen sport is lawn bowls), and so loss of identity is guaranteed. Depending on their outlook, their outcomes vary wildly, from a tabloid-worthy fall from grace, to retraining in a new profession that capitalizes on their skills, to becoming a revered elder.

There are a lot of lessons to be extracted for the transition periods in our own lives. Maybe you are reading this freshly separated, or newly sober, or recently let go, or *feeling* let go. Maybe you are hurling yourself into a new pursuit while making self-deprecating jokes to people about a "midlife crisis," or project-managing yourself through some kind of trauma. Whatever the case, with any great loss comes the gift of reinvention, because rebuilding is far more likely to happen when everything is in rubble.

Many of us construct our identity around the attributes we're told as children we possess, such as "artistic," "sensitive," "bright"—or, if our parents aren't careful, "crazy," "hopeless," "worthless." Over time we become almost singularly defined, perhaps by the thing we most excel at, or by our job title, or by our role as a parent or spouse. But everything in life is temporary, and so we all lose our sense of identity from time to time. Certainly we might expect to do so when we go through some kind of major life transition, like hitting puberty, or having children, or when the kids leave home. Sometimes it's for more unexpected reasons, such as serious injury or life-changing incident, and in those cases we have few cards to play because there's no way we could have prepared. That was the experience of Chloe Bayliss.

When animals are wounded, they often go to great lengths to hide the fact. For the benefit of any skulking predators, they display nonchalance in the face of pain. Maybe they'll have a casual graze, as though their fitness is so assured that they've got all the time in the world to leg it into the bush. It's a survival mechanism.

Chloe was employing much the same strategy when she arrived at the Queensland Ballet on work experience. The sixteen-year-old had woken up in her Brisbane hotel that morning feeling dizzy and fatigued, with a pounding headache. She ran her hands down her aching shins and noticed her thighs were covered in mysterious bruises. Knocking back Ibuprofen had little effect. Nevertheless, she vowed to force herself through the motions in class later, even though she could barely stop her head from lolling. Learning to conceal pain, fatigue and worry is as much part of a ballerina's training as stretching hamstrings and dressing blisters, and years of her family's sacrifices were riding on this one chance to make a good impression.

If Chloe was anything like her peers, she might have been out partying the night before. But Chloe lived vicariously through her friends' mysterious forays into hedonism and sex, because her own "rule-following brain," as she puts it, was entirely devoted to dance. It's a common paradox that dedicated young athletes are at once older than their years and hopelessly naive.

Every morning she began her regime with Pilates, then headed to dance school, fitting all the theory assignments and preparation for auditions, competitions and assessments around her exhaustive training schedule. She'd feel resentful when other girls were laissez-faire, blowing into morning class with smudged makeup and buns parked askew. So to have to admit to the Queensland Ballet teacher that day that she couldn't continue with the class was distressing, particularly when the teacher might assume that Chloe just couldn't keep up.

That evening, back in Newcastle—where Chloe was enrolled in the National College of Dance—the vomiting started. In the Emergency department, her jaw clenched up and the right side of her face became paralyzed. With a big performance of *Swan Lake*, alongside artists from the Australian Ballet, just five days away, Chloe did not yet know—nor would she accept for a long time— how ill she really was.

The late, legendary choreographer and dancer Martha Graham once said, "A dancer dies twice. Once when they stop dancing—and this first death is the more painful." It's an aphorism that applies to all athletes who are set on a path of greatness from their early teens, but who can expect to retire in what most of us would consider to be our prime, suddenly cut from their moorings of security, community and identity.

In Chloe's case, this first death was literally excruciating. She was suffering acute kidney failure due to a rare form of undiagnosed lupus. The news came just months after she had been accepted to the prestigious Washington Ballet School in the United States. The body that she had driven like a mule had turned against her: she needed blood plasma transfusions via a permacath—a port in her chest—and suffered sky-high blood pressure and seizures. She had to wonder if it was some kind of dancer's karma.

By the time Chloe and I speak, the multiple times she nearly died are fourteen years in the past, though she will live with lupus for the rest of her life. She's remembering the betrayal she felt by the body she had always controlled so precisely. An athlete became as helpless as an infant. She would watch the monitor by her bed as tubes were guided into her body, which no longer felt like *her* body. Today her relationship with her body is complex—it can't always do what she would like it to, but to a large extent it has healed itself. Just as she must always take medication, her mental relationship with her body will also require maintenance.

Chloe still looks like an off-duty dancer, sitting erect in activewear, with her hair pulled back neatly. "I've worked really hard over the years to accept my body for what it is, and my views have changed so much from when I was a dancer," she says. "I would look at myself in the mirror and just break down. It was like, *What is this body?* It was nothing to me."

When she was still hospital-bound and the reality of her situation sank in, Chloe cycled through the five stages of grief: denial, anger, bargaining, depression, acceptance. Acceptance was understandably slow to come. She describes a meeting with a social worker in the hospital, who tried to impress upon Chloe that there was more to life than dance. Chloe was furious. "I thought, *I* am *dancing. That's who I am as a person. I know nothing else. Nothing else is going to satisfy me as much,*" she says. "I tried to see a psychologist because I was really down, but when I spoke to her I was just like: *You can see what's wrong. I'm in a bed.*"

Being sick also ushered in guilt. Whether it's the time and money that a family has spent on their child, or the reliance a team has on their star player, athletes are burdened with expectations. When they're injured, they become an investment that failed to deliver.

When she was finally able to convalesce from home, Chloe took all the photos of her happy and healthy self that were around the house and stashed them in a drawer. In secret, she tried to dance—just a few simple moves—but her weakened body couldn't cope. As she lost her balance, a howl ripped from within. It was the realization that she had lost everything.

As devastating as all this was, Chloe was always going to have her dreams dashed at some point. A dancer's career is short, typically ending at around thirty-five years old. Upon retirement, a segue into choreography is common. Chloe tried this for a while. But she was also young enough to switch careers.

These days, Chloe is an actor, and better known than she ever would have been through dance. She first wound up on a set as a dancer in the television series *Dance Academy*. Initially she found the downtime between her scenes tedious, but then she became obsessed with studying the actors, to the point that she'd find a discreet place on set to tuck herself away and watch. She realized that here was a whole new craft to be discovered, and the idea of learning something new ignited a fire. So she started reading books on acting, attending classes and dissecting what she saw on screen. Eventually, she auditioned for an indie film and got the role, giving her the confidence to try out for more professional productions. Now she's most recognizable for her role of the devoutly religious Hayley in the Australian drama series *Doctor Doctor*, but has also had recurring roles in dramas such as *Reef Doctors*, appeared in the film *Backtrack* (2015) opposite Adrien Brody and Sam Neill, and starred in many stage productions.

"Sometimes I feel like I was meant to take that path, particularly when I first changed over and everything flowed very naturally and slipped into line," she says. But, of course, it took a willingness to explore and let go of her self-image as Chloe-the-dancer.

Chloe found the same guidance in directors as she'd found in dance teachers. She thrived on feedback and corrections, as well as the extraordinary feeling of trust that comes from that kind of dynamic. Crucially, acting also provided the pressure valve that dancing in character once did. As Chloe the myopically minded dancer, she had learned to suppress her emotions and focus on discipline, so the creative outlet of becoming someone else was vital.

"You can feel things on stage and there are no repercussions for it," she says. "Particularly when I was a teenager, I'd bottle things up. So even if it was just a simple choreography, I'd always be able to attach something or release some sort of emotion that was built up inside me, to make it appealing to watch."

The pandemic lockdown felt familiar to Chloe. As the film

and television industry seized up, and all her schedules and routines were replaced by uncertainty, she found herself thinking back to those hospital days. "It was devastating," she admits. "I thrive on routine and having things to work toward, this work ethic and this structure. I recently called Mum in tears, saying, 'What am I doing with my life?' I'm used to being in this bubble of working from eight to six, or whatever it is. It's really hard to just come out of that, because you feel lost. It took me a long time to realize that I am Chloe the person, not Chloe the dancer or Chloe the actor, and that I need to have all of these other things in my life that are going to fulfill me, but I struggle with that now. Because when I'm not working, I'm antsy."

Anyone who has experienced disease or injury will have the hard-earned wisdom that it's pointless trying to forecast your way out of it with a timeline. A timeline relies on the optimistic assumption that recovery is linear, and that is rarely the case; nor is life in general a linear course of self-improvement. So Chloe's advice is to not focus on grand plans that could fall through, or that might at times seem hopelessly unattainable, and instead to create small goals. "Accomplish those small things and then you'll build up to the bigger stuff," she says.

Back when she was barely out of the hospital, she decided to enter herself into the Sydney Eisteddfod, which was six months down the track. It was a performance level that she had surpassed, but she recognized that it was the kind of goal she needed to set in order to get herself fit. And when the day came, it felt like one of her most profound achievements.

While it's tempting to consider oneself a visionary—or at least a vision-boarder—fantastical dreams and five-year plans simply don't allow for the curveballs of life. As any slick personal trainer will tell you, goals should be SMART: specific, measurable, attainable, realistic and timely. *The New York Times* best seller *Atomic Habits* (2018) by James Clear is devoted to the benefits of tiny behaviors that lead to remarkable results: if a person gets 1 percent better at their pursuit each day, then in a year they're 37.78 percent better, he points out. The newly sober person who wants to run a marathon, for example, could aim to walk-run a 5K within a month and build up from there, rather than immediately splurge on the most expensive gear and book a spot in the most gnarly-sounding race. (True, my friend Kate did become a marathon runner after she legged it to the liquor store before it closed one day and found herself so taken with sprinting that she kept going well past the store and into the night. But take it from me, she's an outlier.)

There's also the fact that too-lofty goals can be fuel for procrastination. Writing in *Forbes*, Lewis Howes—a handball athlete and host of *The School of Greatness* podcast—explained this well. "Belief is like a muscle; unless it's developed it remains weak, small and basically useless," he summarized. "So when we set large goals, we are requiring ourselves to also have an equally large belief system to support it."

Reinvention requires self-belief, so it's important not to undermine that with impossible expectations. When fate intervenes, or resolve fails, those goals become impossible to achieve and set us back in confidence. "This of course leads to guilt, which then shifts to the feeling that it's a 'sign' of some sort—that it's 'not the right time' or 'I'll start again next Monday,'" Howes wrote. "Unfortunately, this kind of thinking can quickly turn a passionate and motivated person into a disillusioned goal-setter who finds him- or herself setting the same goals year after year, but only producing more disappointment."

TO PUT IT crassly, sports psychology is psychology on steroids. There's a swathe of business books that examine the crossover between athlete qualities and leadership skills, with titles such as *How Champions Think*, *Life as Sport* and *Win at Losing*. Less mercenarily, the BBC Radio 4 podcast *Don't Tell Me the Score* interviews athletes with the recognition that every aspect of their pursuit—learning resilience, cheating, pressure, setting goals, visualization, discomfort—is a heightened take on everyday life, and so has much to teach us mere mortals.

Until her late twenties, sports psychologist Jo Mitchell was an athlete competing in orienteering, and her identity was so tied up with the sport that she found herself in limbo when she quit. She left Australia for London, worked hard, partied hard and felt quite lost for a number of years.

Then she met Dr. Deidre Anderson, who has helped elite Australian athletes such as sprinter Cathy Freeman and swimmer Ian Thorpe navigate retirement, and who set up the Australian Institute of Sport's Athletic Career and Education Program, focused on transitioning athletes out of sports and into a new phase of life. Dr. Anderson gave Jo a set of values cards and asked her to look through them and explain which really mattered to her. "As I went through, I realized that something was missing, big time," says Jo. "It took me a few more months of researching and thinking about what my strengths were to work out that I actually needed an identity that was mine. So for me, that was coming back to Australia and enrolling in psychology."

Now she's Dr. Jo Mitchell, a clinical and coaching psychologist who specializes in athlete-transition counseling, which often means retirement. I visit her Melbourne business, The Mind Room, and we settle on a couple of sofas to talk about how Jo helps individuals broaden their self-identity. To demonstrate using herself, Jo says she would be falling into the same trap she did when she was an athlete if she were to simply fuse her identity to her new career as a psychologist. So she now considers herself to have many facets: psychologist, former athlete, businesswoman, aunt, and so on. Increasingly, I see athletes list multiple labels on their social media bios, suggesting sports psychologists globally are cutting through with this wisdom.

Jo asks if I've heard of the Blue Zone studies, by filmmaker and National Geographic fellow Dan Buettner, which examine communities that have the lowest rate of middle-age mortality or the highest concentration of centenarians. One is the islands of Okinawa in Japan, where there isn't even a word for "retirement." There *is* the word *ikigai*, which translates as a purposeful "why I wake up in the morning." This aligns with a longitudinal Canadian study which found that people who could articulate their sense of purpose had a 15 percent lower risk of dying. Ideally, an individual will feel a sense of purpose without it becoming their identity.

The findings of the Blue Zone studies also tie into Martha Graham's theory of a dancer dying twice. The researchers found that there are two years of a person's life in which they have a higher risk of mortality: one is the year of their birth and the second is the year of retirement.

After some years away from orienteering, Jo realized that she was heeding its call once more. But if she was ever to reengage with her sport without it overriding her sense of self, she would need to integrate herself back into running for enjoyment's sake. So, early on in training, she learned to get rid of her watch and anything else that reminded her of how she did things in the past, back when she was fixated on the outcome. Otherwise she'd beat herself up over how poor her speed and performance were.

Jo asks me what drives my work output. I answer that journalists tend to be overthinkers who are always striving to make sense of the world around them. Similarly, if there's any kind of situation that's beyond my control in my personal life, I have to immediately establish a goal in some other area of my life, such as in work or fitness. It's a distraction technique.

"Right," she says. "If I can control my environment then I don't feel so ... *something*."

Highly driven people in any profession will often not only try to control their environment but also flog themselves with critical self-talk. Like a jockey with a whip, they're relentless: *You've got to be the best ... You can do better than that ... You really fucked that up.* Perfectionism can easily flip over into burnout. As Jo says, "The problem with whipping yourself into performance is it will maybe get you through to your thirties, but then the system crumbles. You can't sustain that, because that kind of motivation, where you activate the fear network, is only intended for short bursts of effort."

For athletes, that kind of ruminative mindset is ripe for a

descent into problematic drug use. When training and competing abruptly stops, a person still has momentum, as surely as if they were to step from a moving treadmill. For me, having worked in the music industry for decades, an athlete's retirement from sports reminds of the danger period a musician can go through when they come off a long tour and find themselves drifting aimlessly, without routine, which can lead to anxiety and depression. Whether you're an athlete or a musician, you've likely been fixating on yourself for years, and have been used to other people structuring your day and taking care of the admin.

On the voyage from hero to zero, drugs often become the life raft. In the BBC One documentary *Life After Football* (2005), British soccer player Paul Gascoigne admitted that retirement had "ripped his heart out"—and it similarly left his liver in tatters. Countless players and fighters have hit the headlines for drunken bar brawls and street fights; there's a whole book, *Retired: What Happens to Footballers When the Game's Up* (2016), that digs deep into this problem. Its author, Alan Gernon, discovered that almost half of professional soccer players face bankruptcy within five years of retirement, a third will be divorced in less than a year and many will struggle with mental health, addiction and the law. When you add potential brain injuries and chronic traumatic encephalopathy, which might impair mood and cognitive function, retirement can be a tumultuous rather than restorative time.

In Jo's opinion, highly driven people shouldn't beat themselves up if they think their lives are going off script. "You don't have to change anything," Jo advises of behavior that deviates from how we think we *should* be. "It's making a conscious choice that's important. Live your life as you want, but just do it consciously, rather than just repeating the same pattern without knowing why. We're constantly evolving, and we don't need to stop being curious about ourselves and our own experience, or decide 'this is now me.'"

Ultimately, Jo thinks sports are cathartic. People keep at it because they feel better, they enjoy the accolades and the feeling of being valued, and the sense of mastery is rewarding. "But it's important to work out what the function of this practice is for you, she says. 'How does it serve you? *Does* it serve you? If it's a need for approval from people because of a previous miserable life, then you'll continue to need other people to make you feel okay about who you are and how you're living.'

The biggest shift occurring in sports psychology is helping people understand the idea of self-compassion and acceptance. "It's not that you kill the drive," she says. "It would be incredibly boring if people didn't strive. You just temper this over-flagellation."

In fact, what Jo loves most about her work is that much of it is just normalizing the human experience to her clients. "People come in and confess they have really bizarre ideas about how they should feel and what they should be thinking," she says. "You know what? That's all okay. We just need to find some ways that you can go with it."

THIS WASN'T THE book I was supposed to be writing. I was all teed up to coauthor one with a psychologist I greatly admire, Dr. Matthew Berry, about what he calls "twenty-first-century syndrome"—people using dopaminergic "supernormal stimuli" such as social media, porn and junk food as a method of distraction from emotional discomfort.

I was coming off the back of writing an addiction memoir that had necessitated an entourage of distraction techniques. Lighting a cigarette dispersed that keening grief in the chest as efficiently as wafting around a bunch of burning sage. Launching Instagram displaced old memories with a few swipes. Jamming in my earphones helped me briskly walk off that antsy feeling about what the press cycle might bring. The vortex of a porn site was a relief to fall into when trying to translate boring scientific papers. So I have to admit, when Matthew first proposed that we write that book together, I was puzzled when he talked about distraction like it wasn't a great thing. *Got something against productive people, Matthew?* I joked, drumming my fingers against the arm of a comfortable chair he'd set out opposite his.

Both chairs were angled ever so slightly away from each other, which was probably some psychologist voodoo. And fitting, too, because my diametrically opposed view to his was that distraction was a clever coping mechanism. When anxiety has you pacing the room like a tiger in a zoo, it can be efficiently extinguished by reaching for your phone or doing a round of push-ups. Where's the harm?

"Ah," Matthew said, probably lacing his fingers. "The problem is that distraction has become the number-one avoidance technique when it comes to difficult emotions, but our brains aren't evolved enough to handle such stimulation."

At this, I thought guiltily of my habit of visiting the gym three times a day, to blindly whale at a bag and upload the video to Instagram while the thing was still swinging.

Within a few months of us working on the book, I asked Matthew if he could hold on a sec—I just had to bash out this *other* book. I'd had an idea kicking around the back of my mind about profiling the all-or-nothingers, the void-chasers, the death-wishers, the hell-for-leatherers, the up-the-ante-ers. And, okay, the distractors. I didn't want to pathologize them, either; I wanted to celebrate them. These people who don't know when to stop, they're *my* people. Some flog their reward pathways like dopamine jockeys; some careen toward injury because of an unwillingness to slow their pace; some goad themselves on to ever-greater heights or more depraved depths; some explore new frontiers of physical pain as a form of self-flagellation; some have knitted their identity so tightly to their pursuit that they risk tumbling into an abyss if it's taken away.

I've often heard musicians fret that their songs keep coming true—that the verses are magical portents of doom that somehow hold the power to forge the songwriter's destiny. I don't know about that, but I find my own projects tend to be a chicken-and-egg scenario. Which came first: the angst or the idea? They seem formed in the same cell. If I quiz the interviewees a little too ghoulishly about the inevitable identity crisis brought on by injury, retirement or public downfall, it's because I can relate. I've had three identity crises in my lifetime, which seems a bit excessive, but they all marked transition periods.

The first came at puberty, when I felt I was suddenly an amoeba in need of features. The golden era of complex playground adventures and throwing tennis balls at the heads of aesthetically pleasing boys had ended by high school, and so I would study my female classmates, trying to figure out which attributes I admired in each and whether I could make them fit. I urgently needed a role. The problem was solved when I latched onto drugs: I would be the tragic antiheroine straight from a pulp-fiction book cover.

The second crisis was when I quit drinking in my thirties. Not long after that, I was rejected from a dating website because I failed the psychometric assessment. Around five key questions were phrased in different ways to make up 248, and my answers were inconsistent because I had no idea who I was anymore.

The third was when I published that addiction memoir. Having closed the book with a slap on my extended misspent youth, I felt in limbo, falling into the trap of endless scrolling, gaming and hate-reading books with titles such as *Find Your Why*. Writing this book has ushered in a new stage. Who will I be when I finish? How do I avoid identity crisis number four? Will I go back to slinging increasingly far-fetched ideas ("monkey tennis?") at my agent, like the proverbial mud at the wall? Worry about that later.

It's Matthew's view that we're living in an era in which there is more stress around identity than in previous times, because we can construct our identities on social media platforms that are specifically designed for artifice—and he thinks people who would have historically had less freedom may now experience more stress. Take women, for example. In centuries past, women had very few options around constructing their identity, simply because there were limited roles open to them in society. Those who naturally fit those roles had very low stress about identity. Those who didn't appreciate being defined as, say, a housewife, had a lot of stress. A woman could either be authentic and rejected by society, or inauthentic, attempting to conform.

"It's a double-edged sword," Matthew says. "We've now got the freedom to construct our own identities, which is a wonderful thing, but it's how we do it. Do we construct our identity based on things within our control, or outside of it? An identity that's based on factors beyond your control is going to be stressful, such as identities based on others' opinions of you. Narcissists actually have low stress because their identity is based on self and the idea that everyone else is basically an idiot. Donald Trump doesn't worry about his self-esteem."

Just as Dr. Deidre Anderson gave Jo Mitchell values cards to look over, so Matthew does values work with clients who lack a solid sense of self, sometimes to the extent that they have no idea what their values are. It's deeply important stuff, because when our actions aren't aligned with our values and beliefs, we feel cognitive dissonance—emotional discomfort—and that can lead to self-destructive behavior.

If there's no hitting pause to look inward, many people who come to a crisis or crossroads will reinvent themselves in a way that's just another opportunity to do the same old thing. The reformed drunk who goes to AA meetings increasingly to shark on the newcomers, replacing booze with sex. The entrepreneur whose new risky venture goes bankrupt like the last. That's because the things we feel we perhaps *shouldn't* be doing anymore have served us in some way in the past, and that's hard to give up. Maybe our ploys have distracted us from necessary but painful self-examination, or have shielded our vulnerabilities by inflating our ego.

I've noticed that if someone is forced to quit one extreme profession, they will likely have the urge to leap straight into another with the same momentum. There's a Venn diagram of extreme pursuits I've observed while researching this book—former wrestlers exploiting their alter egos in adult films; defeated MMA fighters reborn in hammier wrestling roles; retired porn stars putting on wrestling leotards. Psychologically speaking, it's as though slowing the record from forty-five to thirty-three revolutions per minute would be to admit weakness. In neuroscientific terms, it's an example of "cross-sensitization"—when the brain's reward system has become so revved up by one drug or activity that it is hypersensitive to other high-octane stimuli.

Porn is a particularly hard hotel to leave. That's partly because the individual has been living as an alter ego, like many athletes, musicians, actors and comedians, and partly because they have been living in a fringe environment, with its own rules and moral codes. Once they leave, they no longer fit in anywhere.

Some performers, such as Candida Royalle, Stormy Daniels and Tera Patrick, hovered around the industry after throwing in the wet wipes, becoming directors and producers. Shelley Lubben, Bree Olson and born-again Christian Crissy Moran did the same thing—of sorts—only they launched crusades *against* the industry.

Caroline Pickering, who meets me one afternoon in a pub, describes her strange new life as a solo parent in a well-heeled suburb. When she quit porn for a serious relationship, her lifestyle changed dramatically. She flipped from being Monica Mayhem—a pneumatic blonde who had starred in more than four hundred films, often for top production companies, and strutted the red carpet at porn awards in Los Angeles—to plain old Caroline. Now, the only hint of a life beyond Pilates and lattes is the faded flame tattoo peeking out of her cardigan sleeve.

"I try and keep a low profile, keep it low-key," she tells me.

These days, Caroline leads the kind of clandestine existence more familiar to those in witness protection, seeking to avoid recognition and the likelihood of titles such as *Milf-O-Maniacs 2*, *Country Club Cougars* and *Dude, That's My Mom!!!* doing the rounds in her son's classroom (even in her twenties, which is middle-aged for a porn star, Monica was MILF material). "The mums at the school gates … nobody knows," she says. "I go there in my office gear with my hair tied back and my makeup natural. It feels like I'm living a double life and I can't relate to anyone. I don't really make friends easily because we've got nothing in common—only the kids, the weather. I feel fully lost. It's really hard, going from everything that I had to being normal." She laughs, though her eyes are glistening. Even so, I can tell her guard is still up, out of common sense—and habit.

On the surface, it may seem that little about a porn star's life is relatable, but Caroline's problem, in essence, was that she had created a persona, and a mythology around that persona, that couldn't be sustained indefinitely. Our constructions of identity, particularly the way we portray ourselves to others, are often just as complex. "I'm trying to find my place and who I am. It's a real struggle. It's helped that I've had a kid because he keeps me down to earth."

In a way, a history of multiple identities—including short-lived stints in an all-girl metal band and on reality television—has served her well for the present. "My partner said to me recently, 'You just adapt to any change, don't you?'" she says.

For a brief spell before she got into porn, she worked in banking, in foreign-exchange settlements. Now she's returned to that field and earns good money. But finance lacks the level of thrill-seeking that her brain is wired to expect. And as a former romantic partner—the one for whom she left porn—made her shut down her Monica Mayhem website and cut off her friends, her old life hasn't so much been laid peacefully to rest as abruptly snatched away.

"Maybe I should work in a brothel," she says.

I *think* she's joking.

The only pivot from porn I've seen that seemed to work exceptionally well was that of Jennie Ketcham. Jennie willfully took all the tough stuff she'd been trying to blot out in her life (as the musician Peaches once put it, to "Fuck the Pain Away") and turned it on its head. In her career as Penny Flame, Jennie made more than two hundred films and won nine awards. As she explains in her memoir, *I Am Jennie* (2014), which is a fascinating study of losing and finding self: "Jennie had no financial future—no current existence, even; thus, it would not be financially beneficial to be Jennie instead of Penny. Jennie could be stalked, captured, and hurt, all very easily, whereas Penny was not a real person and could disappear, run away, or smile and fuck it off." When she moved into porn in her teens, her psyche became neatly cleaved. Somewhere inside, there was a child raised by drug-afflicted parents and hungry for attention, but that had been all but buried by a bulletproof new persona.

In 2009, she accepted an invitation to appear on the VH1 show *Sex Rehab with Dr. Drew* to tackle her sex addiction—although not before performing in one last adult film, a spoof called *Celebrity Pornhab with Dr. Screw*. Her true motive in accepting the place in televised rehab was to further bolster her alter ego. "Being that I fucked for a living, I figured it was the perfect opportunity to get national attention," she wrote.

As it turned out, the arsenal of dildos she'd packed (knowing full well that a nurse would be going through her luggage on camera when she checked in) was not as shocking as she'd hoped. "I had expected to have the most confiscated cocks of all the patients," she wrote. "I couldn't believe what I was hearing. 'You weren't the worst,' she said. 'Don't worry, Jennifer.'"

During therapy—both in *Sex Rehab* and then in the related series *Sober House*—Jennie came to realize that "Penny Flame" was effectively a wall she had built, out of fear of intimacy. A week after leaving the rehab, she started the blog *Becoming Jennie,* to document her struggle to leave behind her porn persona. Her first post garnered more than ten thousand hits in a few days. "Up until that moment, I had been convinced that the people who existed on the other end of the internet only wanted to see me get fucked," she wrote.

This was gratifying, but it left a major problem: if she wasn't a porn star, who was she? For a start, it would be hard getting a regular job, so Jennie set up a donation button on her blog with the message that any funds received would help her stay out of porn by covering her living expenses. She sold off her porn merchandise and anything that connected her to Penny Flame.

Few in the industry believed Jennie was genuine in her mission. They thought Dr. Drew had brainwashed her, and they were variously keen to suck her back in or keep her as far away as possible, as though by changing career direction she'd become a leper and her newfound dissatisfaction might be a contaminant. So could she hope to be treated any better by the "outside world"?

"If I fail now," she wrote, "then every woman in the business who has ever wanted to leave will believe it's impossible. I became convinced the hopes of every unhappy porn girl rested on my shoulders."

Male porn stars experience their own kinds of problems when they try to leave "porn purgatory," as Tyler Knight calls the industry. In his nihilistic memoir *Burn My Shadow* (2016), the retired performer reveals the serious heart problems he developed from taking 300 milligrams of Viagra a day (he was originally prescribed 50 milligrams). As a colleague told him, "We're damaged goods, bro." Thankfully, once he quit the industry he recovered well enough to become a runner. An ultrarunner, of course. But it's women who can expect to experience the greatest stigma. A woman leaving porn is truly a fugitive. By choosing such a transgressive career, she has broken a social code, and so lowers her social currency further if she tries to depart that world. Even if she's used a pseudonym for her work, a link between her real name and her persona is likely searchable when she applies for a bank loan and a job, and if she does get a new job, her safety could be compromised if coworkers discover her identity. So far as I know, "arse on the line" is not a search term on Pornhub, but every woman who winds up on the site has put hers on it.

Jennie recognized that she had a wealth of lived experience that was relatable to a wider audience than that for porn. She toured talk shows such as *Oprah*, *The Tyra Banks Show* and *The*

View, and wrote for *The Huffington Post*, offering her insights on sex addiction (a predilection that predated her adult-film career), on the messages that erratic parenting sends to vulnerable young girls and on how to maintain on-set safety for adult stars.

If that sounds as though she was still forced to hover around the outskirts of the industry, within a few more pivots, Jennie did completely leave. Jennie completed a masters in social work and now works as a psychotherapist and a mindfulness practitioner in Seattle, specializing in anxiety—her latest study is around the use of mobile phones to distract from uncomfortable feelings. The role of a mindfulness practitioner could not be further from the life of the coke-tootin' porn star described in her memoir, but her experience of both extremes gives her a deeper understanding of the concept.

It's this kind of purpose and sense of connection that Matthew Berry tries to forge with his clients. "I work to the philosophy that human beings will grow up to be healthy and functioning unless something blocks that process," he says. "So they were forming an identity but it got interrupted. If you can free them of that blockage, they will go back to forming their authentic identity. To do that, they need intimate experience, they need to be able to share their thoughts, feelings and needs with someone who meaningfully validates that and goes, 'Hey, that's cool. That's who you are.'"

THERE'S ONE PERSON we met earlier to whom I want to return: Camilla Fogagnolo. She's the strongman competitor and former Olympic powerlifter who, in Chapter Five, mentioned a study on super-elite athletes, which found that all had experienced child-hood adversity, and she thought that relatable—what doesn't kill you makes you stronger and all that. But when Camilla was nine-teen, her story took an unexpected twist.

No athlete wants to receive an unexpected phone call from the Australian Sports Anti-Doping Authority (ASADA). In civilian terms, it's the equivalent of a heavy door knock from the police, or being served papers while getting out of your car.

In 2005, Camilla was outside a hardware store in Hobart, Tas-mania, when she got the call and trudged back to her ride, having failed to persuade the store owner to contribute a wheelbarrow to a raffle she was holding to fund her trip to the Common-wealth Games trials in Melbourne. Eight weeks earlier, she had been drug-tested at a national athletics championship in Bris-bane. She'd told the doping control officers what she was taking: a birth control pill, various vitamins and a weight-loss supple-ment called synephrine from a company called Fortius. She'd already cross-checked the ingredients list by calling ASADA. But now, in this new phone call, she was informed that a prohib-ited substance, benzylpiperazine, was in that supplement, despite not being listed as an ingredient. It's a stimulant often used for weight loss that was at one point found in some energy drinks. "It was like being punched in the gut," she says. "I got in the car, crying, and drove straight to my coach."

Camilla sought legal advice and was told not to comment while an investigation was underway. Many of her athletic peers took her silence to be a form of admission. The evidence seemed to back her story: the managing director of Fortius admit-ted in a letter to the solicitor of Australian weight lifter Jenna

Myers—who tested positive at the same time as Camilla—that "we believe a batch was contaminated with BZP." But ultimately, Camilla had signed an ASADA agreement that stipulated an athlete is entirely responsible for any prohibited substance found in their system, and ignorance is not a get-out clause.

In 2020, ASADA was integrated into Sports Integrity Australia. The home page of the website is chilling—half "Sports are *fun!*" and half *Nineteen Eighty-Four*. Under bright pictures of dynamic young folk in action, there's a hotline listed in a prominent point size. On another page there's the Integrity Blog, with posts such as "Supplements: A Cautionary Tale," in which promising young athletes recount being busted by ASADA and having their lives ruined:

> "It will always be hanging over my head," says Cassie of her sanction.
>
> Cassie says she found it difficult to combine her professional and athletic careers so she took a supplement she thought was safe to use in sports.
>
> She was wrong.

ASADA imposed a two-year sanction on Camilla. When it was made public, she was shocked by how many friends she lost. "Mainly people were saying that I was stupid for having taken something and not knowing. It used to make me so angry because I thought, *Well, what was I meant to do?* I couldn't afford to have everything tested—I was a penniless student."

It's hard to prove innocence in doping cases, and "cheat" is one of the loudest words in the English language, drowning out nuanced explanations. There was also gossip that Camilla had been caught taking steroids. "I had years and years of abuse from people because I was the dirty, steroid-taking weight lifter," she says. The Tasmanian papers had much to say, too. "There was a big increase of interest in Australian weight lifting in that period, and every time they did an article they'd use a caption along the lines of 'disgraced local weight lifter' and then a picture of me and maybe my coach, looking forlorn."

Being shamed can reignite every previous incident of shame we've experienced into one out-of-control dumpster fire. It's such a powerfully unbearable emotion because it's part of the body's emotional warning system. In hunter-gatherer times, shame served the purpose of binding us to our community. If we did something to earn it, we might be cast out and left to die.

Camilla dropped out of her university. "There was zero point continuing because there's no point trying to get a job at a private school as a health and physical education teacher with a very visual and highly exposed drug ban," she says. "It's like trying to get a job as a childcarer with a history of pedophilia. It's not going to happen." Her recruitment processes to join the Australian Federal Police and then the Tasmanian Police were similarly cut short, which she believes is because her ban was made so public in the media.

In 2014, Camilla made a comeback to the sport. She competed on and off until 2018, representing Australia at the 2015 World Weightlifting Championships in Texas, and ranking highest in the country in her weight class, but she became disenchanted with the sport. Then along came strongman, which became codified as a sport in the late 1970s, and in which competitors lift

Atlas stones and logs, carry refrigerators, flip tires, pull trucks and hoist circus-style dumbbells. It's more of a rough-and-ready, egalitarian sport than most, and a spectacle—in the vein of caber tossing or competitive woodchopping, guaranteed to draw oohs and ahhs. Camilla reckons it's also more relatable to the general public than weight lifting, "because nobody knows what three reds on a bar weighs, but everybody knows that a fridge is heavy."

Camilla entered her first strongman competition just a few months after quitting weight lifting. Her big brother Pris was taking part, and as usual with him, she felt tempted to tag along. She was a natural talent. In June 2019, she won in her division of the Static Monsters World Championships, and a few weeks later at the 2019 Australian Strongman Alliance Nationals she won in her division, also breaking the national female record for lifting natural stones.

The last time I saw her was in Yapeen, a wild corner of country Victoria where the strongman equipment company Stand or Submit is based. In January 2021, it hosted the Compound Carnage/Chaos strongman festival, amid a rugged terrain of wrecked cars and rusty white goods. The festival had a Hawaiian theme, at odds with the Mötley Crüe and KISS blaring through the speakers. A curious smell wafted through the air—a combination of ammonia from the smelling salts used for alertness and the overenthusiastic shakings of talc, used for improved grip, making everyone in the vicinity cough.

Camilla had needed to lose 14.5 pounds to compete in her preferred weight category. She shifted the last few the night before, sweating in her car with the heater on full blast, chewing gum in order to muster enough spit to fill a mug. There was no sauna in town, which would have been her preferred method of losing liquid.

She competed in her events and then, on day two, took the event with a 660-pound silver-dollar deadlift (so-called because old-time strongmen would fill barrels with dollars and invite the audience to lift and win). Not satisfied with that, she added more plates and secured the world record of 826 pounds—that's 5.7 times her body weight—making it the heaviest silver-dollar deadlift performed by any woman on the planet.

Camilla has burned some bridges associated with her athletics career in the year since I last interviewed her. The first clue was a social media post in which she sets fire to a team T-shirt and makes an impassioned speech about being "fucked over" and needing a "re-sleeving." When I ask for an update, she tells me, "The lack of people willing to put their foot down for something that was right, I just couldn't deal with it. I hate weakness in people."

The politics of the conflicts—with a gym and some promoters of strongman—aren't relevant here, but her new resolute stance is. You might remember Camilla describing being taught as a child that ego is nothing, and she was nothing, with the result that she always shouldered the weight of others' expectations—those of her father, her coaches, fellow athletes and the media. She had to wonder if her stoicism worked to her detriment at times. For most of her life she'd accepted the status of "human squeeze toy." Well, not anymore—and she's not about to reignite that dumpster fire of shame at others' command.

"I used to be more careful about what I said publicly because I might damage my professional reputation," she says, "but this year I've decided that I don't care anymore."

Sports stars are not supposed to be outspoken. We prefer them to be humble role models, or contrite for falling off their pedestals—completely out of step with Camilla's unapologetic approach. Reality programs such as *SAS Australia* (and its UK counterpart *SAS: Who Dares Wins*), *I'm A Celebrity* ... and *Reputation Rehab* recruit celebrities, among them a smattering of sports stars, who are often appearing as part of a positive PR campaign after some kind of tabloid fall from grace. They're there to be liked and to seem apologetic, to throw themselves at the mercy of the court of public opinion. They weep. They confess. They're real. They talk about family and family values. They also generate more headlines. See those surrounding swimmer Shayna Jack, who—like Camilla—was accused of doping: "Disgraced swimmer joins Seven's new show," "Swimmer Shayna Jack reveals her living nightmare during interrogation" and "SAS Australia: Shayna Jack TV breakdown over doping scandal."

No matter how much Shayna atones, she is never going to escape the negative association; the road to redemption is in fact a dead end. Seeking approval is pointless because the likelihood is we will never be let off the hook—there's just too much soap opera satisfaction in seeing someone prostrate themselves. As recently as 2019, a newspaper canceled a photoshoot with Camilla after learning about her ASADA ban thirteen years earlier.

If the road you're on leads nowhere, it's time to plough a new path.

"I've questioned myself so many times, especially this year. I've always tried to be positive and helpful. I try not to be a cunt," she tells me. At this, her boyfriend, Carl—also a strong-man athlete—laughs affectionately. "But I'm treated like one a lot! There's a common denominator here: me. So, is it me? Is it the way I behave or is there something I do?"

Ultimately, Camilla came to the conclusion that she knew her own worth. External approval was unnecessary. "What can they take away from me?" she asks me. "I'm good at strong-man, I've achieved more than many other females in the field in Australia. If you don't want me, that's fine—I'll find some-where else."

This new resolute attitude has brought with it a sense of catharsis and liberation, tying in with Camilla's motto that she's been using for the past few years: "In a world of unicorns, be a fucking draft horse."

AS THE OLD saying goes, "Be careful what you wish for—it may come true." Achieving your goals and reaching the peak of your field doesn't exactly sound like a problem, but as two-time Olympic gold medalist Kayla Harrison explains it, it can bring about quite the existential crisis. Thankfully, the Ancient Greek philosophers have a solution, as usual, and it applies to every kind of full-tilting, goal-stalking high achiever.

Kayla's journey to gold was so traumatic, it's unsurpris-ing that it was so important to her. As a teenager, she was the United States's bright young hope in judo, acing at national and international tournaments. Then she took her coach, Daniel Doyle—with whom she would often travel alone—to court for sexually abusing her. Judo chat rooms rippled with speculation.

There was much discussion as to whether Kayla was lying for attention. Compulsively, she checked the internet to see what was being said. She did that for years, even after Daniel eventually pleaded guilty. And for even more years, well into her success, she would look around a room at a judo event and wonder who there had been one of her faceless critics. Daniel may have gotten years without parole, but Kayla was being ostracized.

Having been stripped of confidence by Daniel's various methods of control, and shamed by many in her community, Kayla was so depressed that she could barely leave her bed. When she did make it onto the mat, she often dissociated or had PTSD flashbacks. Then, one of her new coaches, "Big Jim" Pedro, gave her a life-changing pep talk. He persuaded her that her experience did not define her. She needed expert help, and she would have to tackle this directly, like any other fight in her career. But she could prevail. It was a language she understood.

"The next day I got out of bed and I brushed my hair," she tells me, "then the day after that I got out of bed and I brushed my hair and my teeth, then I went to training. Some days I would cry the whole practice, but I was there, and then things started to happen. I medaled at a tournament, and then I won a tournament, and success started to breed success, not only inside, and not only in my athletic career, but also as a person."

Before, she'd had natural talent. Now she had an extra dimension of grit and determination. Her main coach, Big Jim's son Jimmy, told the media, "Mentally, Kayla will not break. She's already fought the toughest battle of her life, so walking onto a judo mat is nothing for her."

Kayla says, "My story could have been so different; it could have ended really badly. Some days I wake up and I still can't believe it … the little ripple effects that continued to happen in my life after the abuse, it completely changed my life but it also has meant that I am literally unbreakable. I have such a strong sense of self, and such a strong inner confidence that will never be shaken again. That kind of self-confidence is something people search for their whole lives."

You would think that being awarded Olympic gold in judo, twice, would be the ultimate in having the last word, but after her second gold medal, Kayla slumped into what she calls post-Olympic depression. It's a classic case of where-to-from-here when you're at the top, and her story becomes even more interesting when considering how she tackled this new setback.

Goals provide us with motivation, particularly if we trumpet them. But once we achieve them, we can feel empty and without purpose. Kieran Setiya, a professor of philosophy at the Massachusetts Institute of Technology and the author of *Midlife: A Philosophical Guide* (2017), has identified the paradox faced by type-A high achievers: by pursuing projects to success, they extinguish the things that give meaning to their existence, in a self-destructive cycle of wanting. Disappointment is built into any behavior that's goal-related: dopamine is released in a flood every time a reward is anticipated, its evolutionary purpose being to motivate us toward goals necessary for survival, but the high wears off shortly after the deal is sealed. Ultra-runner Charlie Engle confessed that the most exciting part of a drug binge was the acquisition and corresponding anticipation of taking the drug, not the high itself. And researchers have found that gamblers get a bigger rush of dopamine from a near miss than from a win. Winning and scoring is, in other words, a comparative letdown after the thrill of the chase. To paraphrase oft-quoted essayist Ralph Waldo Emerson, "Life is a journey, not a destination."

Kayla recalls, "The night that I won, they put me in a car, we went to get me drug tested, you do the press conferences, and then you go to NBC, and they run you through the circuit of every talk show. Then you go to the Team USA house, and you celebrate with your family and friends, and teammates and coaches, and everyone is there."

Back in her room, she couldn't sleep. It wasn't from excitement; Kayla was having a panic attack. "Like, oh my god, what now? My significant other at the time was like, 'Kayla, just breathe, it's okay, just enjoy this moment.' I was like, 'Oh, I don't know if I can.'"

Kayla stayed in Rio's Olympic Village until the closing ceremonies, to make sure she really soaked up the experience. When she flew home to the States, her schedule was still busy at first. There were the parties, the shows, the events, the speaking engagements. Then it all petered out. I picture her like Wile E. Coyote in the *Road Runner* cartoons—legs still pedaling frantically, but all out of cliff.

"Literally my entire life I had an end point, a shiny gold medal that I was trying to attain," she says. "When you reach that and you're at the highest of highs, you made your dreams come true, you made history, then all of a sudden it's done. I had a major identity crisis for a bit there, like who am I if I'm not Kayla Harrison, the judoka? What am I gonna be now? You go from being someone who has an alarm clock set every morning to not getting out of bed, because there's no reason to. On days that I didn't have an event to do, I just stayed in my pajamas and watched TV all day. I didn't work out, I didn't go to the dojo, I didn't want to do anything. I felt very untethered."

This is reminiscent of something that another former judoka, Ronda Rousey, wrote in her memoir *My Fight/Your Fight* (2015), about investing everything in her goal to the point of literally having nothing left:

> I will never be scared of anyone. But one thing I am scared of is retirement … When I'm finally done fighting, when I walk away from MMA and I don't get that rush anymore, how am I going to deal with it? … I'm scared of ending up in the same mess I was in after the 2008 Olympics.
>
> The day after I won my medal, I was sitting in my room in the athlete village. It was late morning and I was just sitting on the bed, when my heart started beating fast out of nowhere. I couldn't catch my breath.
>
> I am a homeless Olympic medalist, I thought to myself.

So how do we keep ourselves motivated with goals without losing our sense of purpose and identity once we reach them? Professor Setiya suggests we have both "telic" activities (taken from the Greek word *telos*, meaning "goal"), which have an end point, and "atelic" activities, which are ongoing. An example might be swapping aiming for a gold medal by a certain age (telic) to training for the sheer enjoyment of mastery (atelic), which can be enjoyed in the present, and might offer growth in a way more oriented to well-being. Singing, gardening, going for hikes, learning a language, playing a sport purely for enjoyment, as Dr. Jo Mitchell learned to do with orienteering—they're all atelic activities, provided you don't build in some kind of mission statement.

If we're not mindful, though, sooner rather than later we will probably start sneaking goals into an atelic activity. It was not a huge surprise that when Kayla took up Muay Thai to try out striking and discovered a newfound passion, her training started to become goal-oriented. At first, doing something new was liberating. It didn't matter that she'd effectively gone from black belt in one sport to white belt in another; having to bend her mind and body around the moves was all she needed to stay fascinated. Now, thanks to that Muay Thai training, Kayla has achieved eight wins and zero losses as an MMA fighter, for some of the world's biggest promotions. Whoops.

"That high of winning is like no high on earth," she admits. "I'm still obsessed with getting better. I overtrain, I put my body to the test every single day, I struggle with all those things for sure. I'm always asking myself, 'Am I happy? Am I doing the right things? What's going to bring me real peace?'"

It's not that telic activities are harmful. Ten years ago, I stopped teetering on the brink of depression by engaging in a highly distracting turbo-telic "mission," in which I had to try something new every day for a year, from riding a horse to blowing up a wheeled trash can. It improved my mood the second I began blogging about it, thanks to the newfound sense of purpose.

Maybe telic activities motivate us out of a hole, and atelic activities could be considered mood maintenance.

Kayla has learned to be more balanced. Her Twitter bio makes clear that her identity is multifaceted: she is an activist and a student as well as an athlete. She keeps in mind that taking part in a pursuit for the sheer enjoyment is as critical to her well-being as competing is to her sense of ambition. That's a message she wants to impart via her Fearless Foundation, which aims to enrich the lives of young sexual abuse survivors through education and sports. "I don't care if it's painting or knitting or tennis or archery, I truly believe that everyone—but especially survivors—needs to have an activity that they can do where they just get to be themselves for a while," she says. "That kind of mastery and that kind of being present only in the now, not thinking about the past, not thinking about the future, is so good for your mental health."

When imagining the reader of this book, I picture someone who laughs in the face of "everything in moderation." So I know as well as you that you'd sooner make two columns in a notebook—telic / atelic—and start trying to direct all the action than go with the flow. Are those prone to extremes just destined to go harder than everyone else until they burn out?

Often, yes. But there *are* some simple takeaways to reinvent oneself into a more flexible rendition, better able to swerve around catastrophe and disappointment.

Chloe Bayliss recognized that she needed an outlet for her emotions, since she wasn't naturally adept at expressing them. When that outlet could no longer be dance, she transitioned to acting, which allowed her the same. Whatever you've been doing, even if that's hoovering up lines of drugs, identify what it is about that activity which has a positive effect on your life and then find one strand of it in something else. Jennie Ketcham, for example, took a deep dive into the psychology of her sex addiction and used that insight to forge a new career, just as those who have experienced problematic drug use often later train as peer workers, clinicians and counselors. Experiencing burnout from endless judo tournaments, and being matched in fights over and over with the same people, Kayla segued into a sport she had to learn from scratch. Literally and metaphorically, she went from black belt to white belt, and in so doing had a newfound sense of delight.

IN CASE IT wasn't obvious, the title of this book, *Everything Harder Than Everyone Else*, has a double meaning. Some people are destined to make their lives more difficult in the quest to prove themselves, and I've identified, empathized and sometimes winced in recognition when talking to those I met while writing it. So it shouldn't be surprising that their words of caution in this chapter would become a personal prophesy.

The same week that I receive the final proofs of this book, I have my first amateur fight, under the grand chandeliers of the Melbourne Pavilion. I've been working up to this moment for two years, but curiously, I'm disengaged from the screaming of the crowd, which is by now quite revved up after twenty bouts of boxing, seven of kickboxing and an unknown quantity of beer. The deeply creepy Benny Mardones song "Into the Night" has been assigned to me as I walk to the ring: "She's just sixteen years old …," and above that I hear a lone cheer from a friend in the peanut gallery.

As soon as the bell sounds, my opponent and I go at it hammer, tongs and kitchen sink. At one point in the third round, there's a boisterous crowd response when I'm punched to the canvas. This sort of humiliation had been my worst fear, but the joyous baying only registers abstractly. There's a job to do, and my sole focus is on bouncing back up for an eight count—and then making her pay. So if that was the biggest shame-job I could dream up, the fear has been declawed.

Immediately after the fight I'm on an almighty high, despite getting the silver medal. There are photos, hugs and congratulations, then a sprint for last orders. I crash an hour later, halfway through my cocktail and dinner ... and the comedown persists for a week. It's not because I didn't win, or because of the bruises and the headache. It's because I did the thing I set out to do, and now it is done. I've fallen into the telic trap of losing purpose and identity by completing not just the fight, but also the book that I had come to embody. That's what you call a home goal.

I could carry on with the fighting, but now that all this intense focus has reached its zenith, my interest has flicked off like a switch. I take a week off training, having not spent more than two consecutive days away from my gloves in the past two years. It feels weird and wrong. Half-heartedly, I sign up for a mandala-drawing workshop and other lovely atelic activities.

Professor Setiya admits that an atelic lifestyle is hard. He told the listeners of the podcast *Philosophy Bites*: "Have I tried? Yes, I've tried to reorient myself to atelic activities, to think [that] whether I finish this paper is not the point; it's just that I'm doing philosophy. Unfortunately, just trying or saying that to yourself, at least in my case, does not seem to get you all the way to the reorientation of value that I'm recommending. I'm still trying and I'll keep trying, but it hasn't worked yet."

I turn to a closed group of athletes on Facebook. Did anyone else abruptly change sports upon reaching a goal? Some say yes, but many more advise me to cool my jets. This malaise is normal. This sport is a rollercoaster.

A week after the fight, I head to the gym, to ponder the issue while in motion. I think about Dr. Jo Mitchell, and her recommendation that we continue to be curious about our own evolution of character, rather than deciding, *This is me.* And the words of Dr. Matthew Berry, who cautions us not to construct an identity reliant on external validation. It would be foolhardy to ignore his advice *twice.*

After a shy sizing up of the space by shadowboxing a few rounds, I launch myself at the punching bag. Over and over again, I take ridiculous run-ups: flying knees, spinning hook kicks, Superman punches; all the things I'm usually told not to do, because when training for a fight it's wiser to hammer the kinks out of the basics. After ninety minutes I feel the familiar brace of chemicals tearing through me like a cool change. Today is Good Friday, and thankfully there's nobody here to see what a goofy time I'm having, grinning to the grandiose soundtrack in my headphones.

When I pack up my bag, I bundle in the heavy skipping rope that I didn't get around to using. Maybe next time I'll start with three rounds of that. And then focus on building up the arms, just in case I need to strengthen my guard against an opponent in the future; can't eat another punch like that last one. There's still a notebook in the bag's front pocket in which I can lodge my reps and sets. Renegade rows. Skullcrushers. Pull-downs. These faithful friends that keep me in line.

I'm tuning back into the relief brought by structure, and into the pleasure of purpose, both of which mitigate those intense highs and lows of triumph and disappointment with a steadying ballast. Taking up a sport has offered me an unforeseen magnification of the human experience in all its complexities.

Is my choice of Muay Thai an extension of my youthful self-harm, indicative of some longstanding death wish? Every impact and concussion could be physically reinforcing a psychological message that's deeply ingrained.

But pressure-testing also feels fortifying and character-building, and that paradox has been explored by almost everyone I interviewed for this book.

Over the days, if I keep coming back, this gale-force mood will intensify into something verging on mania, until there's a necessary crash and the cycle begins again.

Like a dog chasing its own tail, it may not be rational, but it never gets dull.

ACKNOWLEDGMENTS

TO THE LEGENDS of this book: it was a joy to be revved up to your speed, if only for a short while.

To the people who listened and read, counseled and sparred—Thom Conn, Stephanie Convery, Brigid Delaney (thanks for talking me out of being waterboarded, very silly), Richie Hardcore, Hamzah Hassan, Michael Hogan, Leah Johnson, Eilish Kidd, Lee Kofman, Joanne La, Cassie Lane, Nick Mann, Don Millar, Jim Moran, Kat Murphy, Kortney Olson, Somsurat Rangkla, Peter Reynolds, Julie Rudner, Rung Samanthong, Ajay Sharma, Georgia Verry, Wyndham Wallace, Rachel Winterton and Kru-Dip Yuanjit—thank you so much for challenging me, and if there's any fallout, it's on you.

To the Black Inc. dream team of Julia Carlomagno, Chris Feik, Kate Nash and Erin Sandiford: thanks for always being in my corner and never allowing me to mix my metaphors. And to my agent, Jane Novak, for listening patiently to every whack-job idea before zeroing in on this one.

Parts of my interviews have also run elsewhere: Charlie Engle, Alex Mann and Kortney Olson in *The Guardian*; Karen Adigos in *ABC News*; Camilla Fogagnolo in *The Age*.

ACKNOWLEDGMENTS

In places, some autobiographical details have been changed to protect an individual's privacy.